P9-DTE-256

Writing
a Book
that makes a
Difference

Philip Gerard

STORY PRESS
Cincinnati, OH
www.writersdigest.com

Writing a Book That Makes a Difference. Copyright © 2000 by Philip Gerard.
Manufactured in the United States of America. All rights reserved. No part of this
book may be reproduced in any form or by any electronic or mechanical means
including information storage and retrieval systems without permission in writing
from the publisher, except by a reviewer, who may quote brief passages in a
review. Published by Story Press, an imprint of F&W Publications, Inc., 1507
Dana Avenue, Cincinnati, Ohio 45207. (800) 289-0963. First edition.

Other fine Story Press books are available from your local bookstore or direct
from the publisher.

04   03   02   01   00   5   4   3   2   1

Library of Congress Cataloging-in-Publication Data

Gerard, Philip.
    Writing a book that makes a difference / by Philip Gerard.
        p.   cm.
    Includes index.
    ISBN 1-884910-44-0 (alk. paper)
        1. Fiction—Authorship. 2. Authorship. I. Title.

    PN3355.G37   2000
    808.3—dc21   99-086355
                                                                      CIP

Designed by Clare Finney

for Carl Stach (1952-1990)
who tasted glory.

Acknowledgments

In preparing a book of this scope, I relied on the wisdom, good will, and the good writing sense of many people—beginning with several gifted and passionate writing teachers who from the start challenged me to write about the public world: the late Tom Molyneux at the University of Delaware; Bob Houston and Dick Shelton at the University of Arizona; and at the Bread Loaf Writers' Conference Ron Hansen, Tim O'Brien, and the late John Gardner.

A compadre and gifted colleague during those many fruitful seasons at Bread Loaf was Carl Stach, who spoke eloquently of the need for writers to attempt ambitious projects of public importance. At the time of his death in an airplane crash, he was working on a book about his father's experiences in the Pacific War, the fate of the Marshall Islands as atomic testing grounds afterward, and the link between the two.

In addition, Jan DeBlieu, Valerie Boyd, and Dorothy Lazard talked eloquently about their books and writing in general and patiently answered many questions.

Stanley Colbert, Nancy Colbert, and Peter Gethers offered valuable and candid insight into the world of editing and publishing.

Bob Reiss helped shape many of the ideas during our long late-night discussions about writing.

Dean JoAnn Seiple of the College of Arts and Sciences at the University of North Carolina at Wilmington provided summer support during a crucial stage of writing, and Philip Furia provided a wealth of practical and moral support from start to finish.

My students, both at UNCW and in the Goucher College summer

residency M.F.A. program, helped me question my assumptions and often inspired me with their own daring work.

Sharon High graciously allowed me to discuss her work-in-progress.

My agent, Jim Trupin, helped to make the book a reality.

My wife, Kathleen Johnson, gave constant sound advice and support.

Finally but perhaps most significantly, Jack Heffron helped to conceive and shape this book, and if the book has any lasting merit, a large share of the credit belongs in his deft editorial hands.

Thanks to all.

P.G.
October 1999

Contents

"Every true apprentice writer has, however he may try to keep it secret even from himself, only one major goal: glory."

—John Gardner, *The Art of Fiction*

PART I: Subject and Theme

1

What's the Big Idea?

Every writer has a book he *needs* to write—the one that has been keeping him up nights, invading his dreams, teasing him with scraps of scene, dialogue, fact, invention, idea, image, memory. The book that in some way speaks profoundly to the core of his beliefs, the emotional and spiritual and intellectual center of his life. The book that will take the best that is in him and every bit of craft he can muster.

The Big Book.

It may be rooted in personal experience—Frank McCourt's *Angela's Ashes* was inspired by a terrifying childhood that haunted him into middle age. It may be inspired by an encounter with a public phenomenon—John Steinbeck's *The Grapes of Wrath* grew out of his immersion in the world of the migrant worker in California, climaxing as he witnessed whole families starving to death during the great floods of 1938 in Visalia. Both, in very different ways, write about injustice. Both books won the Pulitzer prize.

The Big Book is so close to our heart that its very importance flusters us, makes us doubt our own ability to write it as well as it deserves to be written. The event to be chronicled is large, the ideas complex and controversial, the issues public, the themes so universal they make our head spin. We feel ourselves standing on the verge of something significant, yet reluctant to take on a project so overwhelming.

We've been thinking about it for months, years perhaps, the last thing before we fall asleep at night and the first thing when we wake up. We daydream about it when we're supposed to be doing other things. We've lived with it, the great distracting shadow that looms over our other projects. We may have notes, jottings, sketches, even an abortive beginning, tucked away in our drawer. We just can't seem to get it done. We back off, divert our effort into other stories, other books, other activities outside of writing altogether.

We keep running up to the high bar, afraid to leap.

We know it will be *big* in every sense—demanding great resources from us, a large imagination, a big soul. Huge blocks of time. The mental and emotional stamina to see it through to the finish. It's no exercise. A lot is at stake: If we fail, we fail big. It matters that we succeed.

We put it off. We'll get to it, we tell ourselves. *Some day.*

It is common—and a healthy sign—for the writer to approach a great subject with humility, uncertainty, doubt. He wants to get it right, and he's smart enough not to underestimate the challenge.

But a writing project begins not just in doubt but also *faith*—that if your passion is genuine, if you have mastered the elements of your craft, in the act of writing you will learn the rest of what you need to know in order to do justice to your subject.

As Steinbeck writes in *Journal of a Novel*, "A good writer always works at the impossible."

McCourt spent many years sorting out the narrative of his memoir, and Steinbeck took half a decade in evolving his novel from newspaper reportage to an aborted text-and-photo documentary to a great novel. For both McCourt, a high school writing teacher, and Steinbeck, a seasoned literary veteran, the challenge was the same echoed by beginners and experienced writers alike: "I want to write about a subject that is really important, but everything I try sounds hokey and clichéd."

As soon as you recognize in yourself an ambition to write a story with great themes, unless you're Homer, you also experience the frustration of having ambition that outstrips your craft—especially if you're crossing genres. You're an experienced newspaper reporter, but you're sure this big thing wants to be a novel. You're a novelist, and this big thing will demand investigative skills. You're a personal essayist, and this big thing is historical and sometimes quite impersonal.

But *ambition*, properly understood, is a good thing: It has nothing to do with your own ego and everything to do with aspiring toward an enduring truth—a durable narrative that will enlighten and delight, a representation of life that is also larger than life. Ambition for the story can help your craft rise to the occasion. The writer learns what he or she needs to learn in order to do justice to such a story.

At this crucial stage, when the book begins to pull on the imagination so strongly it will not be denied, the developing writer falters: You want to write about some issue or idea that's very important to you, but you don't know how to do it. Early attempts have failed from self-consciousness, timidity, didacticism, lack of focus, diffidence, lack of research and authority, lack of a compelling voice, lack of craft, or just plain inexperience. You're passionate about the subject—but for these reasons and others, the emotional connection that you feel for the material has not made it onto the page and therefore into the heart and mind of the reader.

This book is about how you can make that connection.

The more experienced writer often has the same doubts to overcome, old habits to revise, fresh strategies to master, a new attitude to forge. This book is about helping that writer take a deep breath and at last begin writing the book that has hooked you and won't let go.

This book has a simple message: Once you have recognized your life's work, get on with it.

A Calling, Courage, and Faith

Valerie Boyd describes in almost mystical terms how she embarked on her biography of the writer Zora Neale Hurston: "Primarily, I have to say that I feel it's a calling, of sorts, that it's destiny, unavoidable. If I didn't think very strongly from a spiritual perspective that this was the work I was supposed to be doing, I would have been frightened off by it—because it was huge, and sometimes it just seems unwieldy, particularly as a first book."

Hurston, who published celebrated novels including *Their Eyes Were Watching God*, collaborated with Langston Hughes and was a lively presence during the Harlem Renaissance, died poor, was buried without a gravestone, and emerged as a major literary figure only after her death. Up until Boyd wrote her book proposal, however, Hurston had inspired just one biography, though there were undoubtedly scholars waiting in the wings who would sooner or later write their books.

A journalist, editor, publisher, and freelance writer, Boyd had been captivated by Hurston's writings since college and had made annual pilgrimages to the Zora Neale Hurston Festival at Eatonville, Florida, beginning in 1989. "At the 1994 festival," she recalls, "Robert Hemenway, who had written the 1977 biography of Hurston, which I thought was an excellent book, stood up and crtitiqued his own book and pointed out everything he had missed and said, 'It's time for a new biography to be written, and it needs to be written by a black woman.' And I just felt a *knowing* that that was me, that I was the one who was supposed to do that."

But Boyd didn't rush home and immediately write her first chapter, or even the first lines of a book proposal: "I really didn't feel up to it at that point. I just thought, well, maybe in ten years I'll be able to do that. But I just didn't feel I was ready."

She had plenty of other projects on her desk, including a nationally circulated African-American health magazine she had just started, but the feeling stayed with her that somehow she was destined to write Hurston's life. In the summer of 1995, she received a phone call from a young agent, John McGregor, who was looking for someone to take on exactly such a project. He'd been referred to Boyd by someone he'd met at a party. Was Boyd interested?

"And that totally reopened that door for me," Boyd says, "because I had just put this idea on the back burner and said eventually I'll get to that. Maybe. If someone doesn't beat me to it."

This unanticipated echo of her epiphany at the Hurston festival was too much to resist: "It made me start thinking, yeah, maybe that really was a calling that I was feeling, maybe this really is part of my destiny."

Even then, Boyd felt reluctant to take on such a big book. She suggested other writers with more experience, but ultimately realized that none of them had the same deep spiritual connection with Hurston, the passion that would drive Boyd's research and writing: "So in the process of trying to think of someone who would be better to do this, I kept coming back to myself and saying, hey, I might be pretty good at this. And I knew that it was a leap, something that I had to grow into, and I feel that I'm still growing into it. It's not like, okay, in '94 I wasn't ready and in '95 I was. I'm still readying myself."

When a writer such as Boyd takes on a big book, she often has to rise to the material, to go beyond previous work. Boyd says, "It takes a certain amount of courage and faith of some sort that, okay, I'm not going to totally embarrass myself and write a goofy book, and faith too that maybe I will write a goofy book but I have an editor, I have friends who are writers, so at least maybe someone will tell me before it gets published."

Boyd was fortunate to work with McGregor, a young agent who was also stretching his abilities, taking a chance on a new writer with an important book. Boyd laughs when she recalls the exhilaration she felt when the proposal was taken by Scribner: "The book sold and did well, there was an auction and everything, so there was a big splash about us. But that was all very funny—going to New York and meeting with all those publishers and then—I had spent all my money to put together the proposal, and John was broke—so we had to go have lunch at the Wall Street Deli, that was all we could afford. We were like, 'We're going to take over this town!' with our little sandwiches at the Wall Street Deli."

Then, of course, reality set in, and with it the hard work of researching and writing a book that will certainly be scrutinized and criticized by scholars and reviewers. But of course the writer can't think about that. She needs to remain centered, focused on the driving passion at the core of the whole enterprise. Boyd says, "It's a huge project. It's scary sometimes. But I really do feel that I have a responsibility to Hurston to tell her story as a black Southern woman. I feel very close to her in some ways, and I really do feel a sense of responsibility to tell her story through my eyes, through my voice. And I think that sense of destiny is what keeps me on course, even when it gets big and scary, which is often."

Risks and Benefits

A common complaint of editors over the past decade has been that, while the level of writing in American letters is higher than ever, much of what is written *about* is trivial, private, or merely personal—the writer's own firsthand experience that matters mostly to the writer, because it happened to the writer, without a greater sense of connection to the world. Writers like Valerie Boyd have managed to combine private passions with public subjects in a way that makes for durable storytelling, for lasting art.

There are risks and benefits to writing about big universal subjects, and we'll address them more thoroughly at other appropriate moments later in the book. You don't avoid doing something important just because it is risky. But understanding the nature of the risk may enable you to turn it into an opportunity. The greater the risk, the greater the potential payoff. Here is an example of one risk and one benefit:

• **One risk:** Just as certain subjects compel the immediate attention of certain readers, they can be immediate turnoffs for others. A recent sensational example: Kathryn Harrison's *The Kiss*, the story of her love affair with her own father, repels for the same reason it fascinates. It's not the standard, awful tale of child abuse; on the contrary, Harrison makes it clear that she consented to the affair willingly as an adult. The tone of the narrative suggests approval. In other words, the *narrative stance* is that incest is okay. The reader's repugnance—if he or she feels such—comes from the unwillingness to be complicit in Harrison's incest, which the narrative excuses. Typically, the more disgusted we are by sexual child abuse, the more sympathy we feel toward the victim. But the subject cast in this light offers no true victim—just two people deliberately breaking one of the strongest cultural taboos in the world. But when all is said and done, Harrison's book was a best-seller—which means that a great many people, however troubled they were by the subject, found it irresistible.

• **One benefit:** Some *apparently* standard and hackneyed subjects, such as war, can be intriguing and complex enough below the surface to yield layers of unforeseen opportunities and ultimately challenge the writer to greater achievements of craft—as Tim O'Brien's breakthrough Vietnam novel, *Going After Cacciato*, a National Book Award winner.

The novel begins as a typical chase story: A soldier, Cacciato, deserts his unit, and a squad is sent to bring him back. But we're talking about deserting the *Vietnam* War, a war many argue was unjust and unnecessary, a war that polarized the nation and sent demonstrators into the streets of Middle America, so the chase becomes a morally charged action that asks hard questions about the nature of duty in a misbegotten war. Was Cacciato right to walk away from the war? Are the squad members doing the right thing or the wrong thing in attempting to bring him back?

Paul Berlin, the viewpoint character, also becomes the focal point for the book's ongoing argument about duty, and his conclusions resonate beyond even the squad to all theaters of American society. So reflective sections sound the deep waters of Berlin's—America's—conscience, even as the action becomes more and more surreal, the ultimate chase, across Asia, through the streets of Tehran, all the way to Paris, the pinnacle of Western art and civilization. The writer broke through the war-novel clichés into profound territory.

Defining Basic Terms

Originality—the writer's singular, arresting vision—begins with *accuracy*: telling the truth in precise physical, thematic, and psychological detail. Accuracy is built on a habit of being alert, observing the world around you attentively, so that you're writing the thing as you know it from your own observation and not merely borrowing a cliché from other books, television, or the movies. Then to tell about it you ransack the language—as O'Brien does—for a way to say what you know that exactly captures the sense of it. You don't just pull some tired expression off the shelf and toss it in: You work hard to find the precise word or phrase to make the thought real, to bring the experience to life.

In his hilarious send-up of *The Pathfinder* and *The Deerslayer* called "Fenimore Cooper's Literary Offenses," Mark Twain sets out a series of sensible rules for writers.

> There are nineteen rules governing literary art in the domain of romantic fiction—some say twenty-two. In *Deerslayer*

Cooper violated eighteen of them. These eighteen require:

1. That a tale shall accomplish something and arrive somewhere . . .

2. They require that the epsidoes of a tale shall be necessary parts of the tale, and shall help develop it. . . .

Twain continues to rail at Cooper for his lack of attention to accuracy of observation and precision of expression, ticking off the first eleven of the rules before mentioning a couple of "little ones."

In addition to these large rules there are some little ones. These require that the author shall

12. *Say* what he is proposing to say, not merely come near it.

13. Use the right word, not its second cousin.

So originality begins in accuracy and accuracy requires precise expression. In the interest of saying what I propose to say and not merely coming near it, and using the right word and not its second cousin, it's worth defining some basic terms, since they'll appear throughout this book and since we may be using definitions a little less cumbersome than those offered by standard literary criticism texts.

Aesthetic Distance: a deliberate emotional remove from the events of the story that can be closed or opened, resulting in the reader's paradoxical awareness, in the captivating throes of a gripping story, that he is reading a story, not experiencing real life.

Didacticism: the teaching element carried too far, so that the writing becomes lecturing or preachy.

Essay: from the French *essayer*, "to try"—an attempt at locating a larger truth through the connection of ideas and experiences, through rhetorical or narrative argument. Typically, the essay attempts to "prove" a thesis—not in the courtroom sense but in the sense of testing it against all the best contrary evidence.

Idea: an abstraction of thought that underlies an action/observation.

Narrative: a real or fictional event told as a story, based in concrete characters, actions, and details that move toward conclusion in a coherent, unified way, rather than as an abstract argument or exposition.

Narrative Stance: the technical point of view (first person or third person) combined with *psychic distance* (level of emotional identification with characters) and *tone* (narrator's attitude).

Nonfiction novel: a long, unified work of nonfiction that mimics fiction, raising both exciting possibilities and troubling ethical questions. Some consider the term an oxymoron, since traditionally the novel has been, by definition, fiction.

Novel: a long, unified work of prose. The novel we're concerned with has large ambitions—including a *great scope* and *effects of scale*: the cumulative weight of many characters, scenes, chapters, repetitions, and the time that has passed both in the novel and in reading the novel. Another definition: a great work of prose fiction that has something important wrong with it (see *The Adventures of Huckleberry Finn*). This definition is not as facetious as it sounds, and in fact cuts to the core of what we're talking about. The greater the ambition of the novel, the more likely that at some point it will overwhelm the author's ability to control it. This is a compliment to the author, not a criticism. E.M. Forster, one of the greatest novelists who ever wrote in the English language, at last stopped writing novels because, as he relates in the famous first Writers-at-Work interview in *The Paris Review*, he put his characters on a train expecting he could plot their return, but they went off and left him.

Persuasion of Continuity: Canadian literary critic Northrop Frye's term for "the direct experience of literature," for whatever it is that keeps the reader reading: ". . . the power that keeps us turning the pages of a novel and that holds us in our seats at the theatre."

Plot: a sequence of causally linked events in a story that result in an outcome that matters; typically these "events" are really actions—reflecting choices—taken by a protagonist after an initial triggering circumstance. For instance, in Steinbeck's *The Grapes of Wrath*, as a result of the Dustbowl Depression in Oklahoma, the Joads lose their farm and decide to trek west to the promised land of California. Along the way, each member of the family makes choices that have consequences—causing other choices and determining their fates, both as individuals and as a family.

Possession: (Frye) the reader's sense of what the story is *about*, the overarching themes of the work, held in memory after the plot has wound up and the *persuasion of continuity* loses urgency.

Profluence: "our sense, as we read, that we're getting somewhere" (John Gardner); the effect of any element, idea, or device that moves the story along. Related to Frye's *persuasion of continuity*, or whatever keeps the reader reading for the duration of the narrative (as distinguished from what Frye terms the "possession" of the work by the reader's memory: the larger impression or theme that remains in mind long after the urgency of finding out what happens next has passed).

Psychic distance: the emotional attachment we feel for a character—either as writer or reader.

Public subject: a subject linked directly to the community rather than just the individual. Like most definitions, this one exists on a continuum: At one end are clearly private concerns (e.g., an adopted child's search for her real parents); at the other are matters of ongoing community interest (e.g., the Kennedy assassinations). The subject of coming-of-age, for example, may be universal in theme but private: Coming of age during the Holocaust has an immediate connection to a public, historical circumstance; the Holocaust itself—the evil extremity of "civilized" human behavior—is clearly a subject in the public arena. You could argue that the most interesting subjects successfully link private experience with public importance, as Anne Frank's *The Diary of a Young Girl*.

Rectitude: humane moral principles implicit in the narrative stance of a story.

Resonance: like many literary terms, borrowed from music to describe the effect of one story element playing off another so that the reader experiences "harmonics" of meaning. When we first meet Tom Joad in *The Grapes of Wrath*, he has just been released from prison for killing a man in self-defense; late in the novel, he must again become a fugitive for beating to death a police thug while defending his mortally injured buddy, Casey. Thus an isolated, individual case of past injustice now reads as part of the class struggle against the oppressive forces of "law"—each incident plays off the other, making each mean more than either one alone.

Sentimentality: relying on predictable emotional responses, rather than a well-crafted story, to move the reader.

Story (see *narrative*): the arc of movement through time and space that unifies the actions of characters into meaning. *The Grapes of Wrath* is an old story: Someone goes on a journey, in this case seeking a better life elsewhere. It has a natural beginning (the Joads pack and leave), middle (they toil on the road for many hundreds of miles), and ending (the survivors make it to California and find—or don't find—a better life). Typically, a character whom we care about acts to gain what he or she desires, other characters and forces oppose the fulfillment of the desire, and the outcome produces important consequences—something is changed irrevocably.

Subject matter: the concrete, real-world stuff of the book (e.g., World War II, fire fighting, ballet dancing, the exploration of the Congo basin, acupuncture, gourmet cooking).

Subtext: the subject that underlies the apparent subject in a book, chapter, scene, or sequence of scenes. As screenwriter Robert McKee points out in *Story*, every scene contains *activity* and *action*. Take a scene from Abraham Verghese's *The Tennis Partner: A Doctor's Story of Friendship and Loss*. The *activity* addresses the apparent subject: Two doctors are playing a recreational game of tennis that suddenly turns cutthroat—that's what we watch in our mind's eye. They serve and return, take each other to the net and the baseline, strategize, maneuver, and miss. The *action* of the subtext is the testing of their friendship, carrying it to a deeper level of honesty: They're not being merely polite anymore but revealing their true natures and abilities. The theme (what the scene is thinking about beneath both activity and action) is that genuine enduring friendship is based on honesty, not just courtesy, and that many friendships cannot stand up to such risky candor.

Suspense: related to *profluence*; the anxiety experienced by the reader of a story awaiting the answer to an urgent narrative question. At a deeper level, Gardner claims that through suspense we share the characters' anxiety of choice and thereby participate vicariously in the drama. The question that causes suspense is not really, What will happen next? but, What will the character choose to do next? Other questions naturally follow, in ascending order of complexity:

- *Why* will the character choose that course of action?

- What are the *alternatives*?
- What *should* the character do next?
- What will others do to *stop* him or her?
- What will be the *consequences* of that action compared to the alternatives?
- What do *I* the reader want the character to do next? And is it the same as what the character ethically or reasonably *should* do?

Theme: what the piece is thinking about underneath the apparent subject: the large idea or ideas that govern the progress of a story. One recurrent major theme in Steinbeck's novel is the sacred importance of family to spiritual survival; a minor theme is the generosity of the poor toward each other, contrasted with the greed and self-interest of wealthy landowners.

Thesis: an important assertion that can be proven wrong.

Tone: the attitude of the author toward the story, as reflected in the diction and stance of the narrator.

Universal: touching some basic truth of human experience and therefore accessible to a large and diverse audience.

Creating Aesthetic Distance

In 1895, the first public movie theatre opened in Paris and featured a film by the Lumière brothers, *The Arrival of a Train at the Station* (*L'arrive d'un train en gare*). As the locomotive steamed head-on toward the camera, patrons ducked and screamed in terror.

They were experiencing an absence of *aesthetic distance.*

They were so caught up in the movie—the onrushing train—that they forgot they were watching a movie and not a real train. The audience's inability to distinguish fantasy from reality is understandable: They had no experience with the medium of film, which is, after all, based on an optical illusion called the *persistence of vision*. Watchers think they are viewing continuous action, but in fact they are seeing frames of projected images in between frames of blackness. The brain can't register the interruptions in the flickering images—they happen too fast—and it fools the eye into "seeing" the moving picture as reality.

While watching a movie, more than half the time viewers are watching utter darkness. Nothingness. An absence of image and light.

As writers, we work in another kind of illusion and we create another brand of persistence of vision in the imagination: We create an interior "movie" in the reader's head through words on the page. Even in nonfiction narratives, we create the fiction that we are delivering characters' continuous, whole experiences, when in fact we are pasting together collages of a very few selected scenes connected tenuously by summary and transitional exposition—narrative sleight of hand—and leaving out far more than we can ever include. Like all those frames of darkness.

You'd think that this absolute captivation would be desirable, but in fact it also works *against* a story, even one told on film. The reason is that captivation is an *emotional* response—basic, primitive, visceral, and in part physiological: Readers' pulses race, their palms grow clammy, they feel the rush of adrenaline from fear or excitement, their tear ducts are stimulated. It creates the first necessary virtue of a great story: *persuasion of continuity.* They read on, breathless.

We try so hard to pull the reader in, to connect him emotionally to our story, that we can easily forget the need for the second virtue of a great story: *aesthetic distance.* It's one of those contradictions that makes a story work. And what goes for fiction goes equally for nonfiction crafted with fictional technique. (More intellectualized essays implicitly create distance.)

Aesthetic and intellectual appreciation—the sense that we, as readers, *possess* the story as our own somehow—require that we are captivated by a story knowing all the while that it is exactly that: a story. A book, not a real experience. A movie, not an actual onrushing train.

Now, it might seem as if this is a trivial concern. After all, we can't help but know the difference between real life and the book in our hands. Usually the hard part for the author is making us forget we've got a book in our hands, to see through the words into the imaginative world beyond them. But in a good captivating book, we aren't just caught up in an experience that will become instantly forgettable once the lights come up. Aesthetic distance gives them staying power.

For long stretches, we may forget—the phone rings and jars us out of the novel we're engrossed in—but occasionally we pause, lift ourselves out of the book, ponder its ideas, appreciate its movement, its language or symmetry. We become cognizant of a story structure that makes sense out of the chaos of the world, giving us insight, stimulating thought, pleasing our sense of beauty.

Indeed, this may happen most powerfully upon completion—if the book remains alluringly memorable, so that it stays on our mind and we ponder all that we've read, and ultimately are tempted to reread— and we are rewarded with greater insight, made possible by cool distance. We step back and the story begins to *mean* something.

When we reread, for instance, we tend to read beyond plot, since we already know how things turn out, and open ourselves to other layers of a story and their effects: character, structure, imagery, irony, themes, and so on—all the subtle connections and patterns we didn't notice so acutely on first reading, especially if the book was a pulse-pounding page-turner.

Wordsworth's definition of poetry serves the prose writer, too: "Poetry is the spontaneous overflow of powerful feelings; it takes its origin from emotion recollected in tranquility." The strong emotion provides the passion for the *vivid and continuous dream* of story—for the persuasion of continuity that keeps us reading; the tranquility creates aesthetic distance, so that we *possess* a story in a more profound way after the plot has wound down.

One test of a book is whether it stands up to rereading. Many thrillers and mystery novels, for instance, completely captivating "reads," melt from our memories as soon as the plot is solved. Because the gripping plot, the persuasion of continuity, is not only complete but is all there is to the book. We're left with no ideas, no impressions that challenge or provoke us to thought, no intriguing patterns that tease us into comprehension on a higher level, no experience of beauty, no significant new understanding of ourselves or the world. In short, there's nothing to possess.

We read *The Grapes of Wrath*, on the other hand, utterly engrossed by the travails of the Joad family, and when we're finished feel we somehow *have* the book: We've understood the biblical metaphor of wandering in the wilderness toward the promised land, we've absorbed ideas about justice and poverty, and we've been spellbound by the awesome power of optimism, the incredible resiliency of the human spirit in the face of seemingly insurmountable adversity. We probably don't recall the many details of plot, the turns of action, the moments when we held our breath waiting to find out what happened next; we've awakened from the vivid, continuous dream. The book now lives in our imagination as a memory of patterns that pulse with meaning.

Practical Techniques

When a subject has you by the throat, when it arises from your deepest passions as a person and a writer, the heat of personal commitment can blur your aesthetic judgment, interfere with your craft. We want not just heat but light. Not just a thrilling ride, but also a sense that we've arrived somewhere important.

The writer requires a certain distance from his characters, his subject, his themes. Otherwise he will be so enthralled by the reality of his material that he will not be able to find the dramatic pattern, the artful arrangement of parts that will make the story succeed and endure.

So like Steinbeck, profoundly moved by the suffering of migrants in California—and outraged by the injustice of their plight—the writer must step back, figure out a way to handle such an emotionally "hot" subject, respecting both its compelling reality and its complexity.

Psychic distance is the emotional attachment we feel for a character—either as writer or reader—and it's an important component of aesthetic distance.

As a deadline journalist on assignment and later as a documentary reporter, Steinbeck was very much on the scene. The people were real—folks he'd met, talked with, shared meals with. The very act of turning those real people into fictional characters was one way of stepping back and creating psychic distance from the characters and aesthetic distance from the story: He could manipulate the fates of fictional characters to suit plot and theme—something he could never do in nonfiction to real people for whom he felt loyalty, friendship, and accountability. He could change their names, dress them in different clothes, combine several into one. Fictional characters are once re-moved from reality.

And in choosing a third-person narrator, Steinbeck removed him-self as eyewitness reporter from the story, avoiding the temptation to be the hero of his own epic and to editorialize or hold forth with his own private opinions and judgments. Third person is emotionally cooler than first person.

Even Steinbeck couldn't keep his passions totally under control: His masterpiece is occasionally marred by sentimental or politically preachy passages reflecting his own deeply felt beliefs. Early in the novel, a group of anonymous farmers—representative of the type of noble individualists who people the Great Plains in his book—ask that their taxes be postponed until a better crop comes in so they can keep their land: "Can't we just hang on? Maybe the next year will be a good year. God knows how much cotton next year. And with all the wars, God knows what price cotton'll bring. . . ."

Their pleading is reasonable and their voices genuine, but their time is up.

The owners' representatives answer them in a monolithic voice: "The bank—the monster has to have profits all the time. It can't wait. It'll die. No, taxes go on. When the monster stops growing, it dies. It can't stay one size."

Now, you and I know that nobody talks that way. No bank represen-tative would ever call his bank a "monster" and spout such portentous allegorical rhetoric. That's Steinbeck talking.

Clearly, Steinbeck feels a passionate camaraderie with the farmers and has no sympathy at all for the owners' reps, and the narrative takes on a lecturing tone: "These last would take no responsibility for the banks or the companies because they were men and slaves, while the banks were machines and masters all at the same time. Some of the owner men were proud to be slaves to such cold and powerful masters."

By casting the farmers as free-thinking heroes and the "owner men" as enslaved villains, Steinbeck weakens his drama. He has prejudged his characters—rather than explored them with compassion. Ideologi-cal polemic has overwhelmed drama. His class politics are showing.

And his passion foreshortens the aesthetic distance the reader experiences, turns the scene into visceral melodrama—largely because Steinbeck identifies too well with certain characters and not at all with others—that is, one element of aesthetic distance, his psychic distance from his characters, is not sufficient for a fair and complex representation of motives and actions that he personally finds reprehensible.

The writer needs appropriate psychic distance in order not to identify too strongly with a single character at the expense of other characters and the book as a whole—the claim of some critics against Truman Capote for his infatuation with Perry Smith, one of the real-life killers of *In Cold Blood*.

The reader needs the right psychic distance to feel engaged with the characters and also able to judge their actions in context.

John Gardner, in *The Art of Fiction*, argues forcefully against too much distance—going too far in interrupting the "vivid and continuous dream" of the novel: "In bad or unsatisfying fiction, this fictional dream is interrupted from time to time by some mistake or conscious ploy on the part of the artist. We are abruptly snapped out of the dream, forced to think of the writer or the writing. It is as if a playwright were to run on stage, interrupting his characters, to remind us that he has written all this."

All narrative, like all great art, comments implicitly upon how it is made. But Gardner saw an artistic dead end in *metafiction*, which deliberately reminds the reader over and over again that the story is an artificial construct, constantly calling attention to and parodying the elements of storytelling. In other words, the aesthetic distance is so great as to ruin the conventional sense of story. The reader feels no emotional involvement—only intellectual satisfaction. The signature example of metafiction is John Barth's short story "Lost in the Funhouse."

E.M. Forster puts it another way in *Aspects of the Novel*: "The novelist who betrays too much interest in his own method can never be more than interesting; he has given up the creation of character and summoned us to help analyse his own mind, and a heavy drop in the emotional thermometer results."

But enduring works of narrative seem to achieve a golden balance between immersing the reader wholly in the world of the story and making the reader aware at some level of its beauty and meaning—its art. The reader hovers just above full immersion, and that perfect space of distance, like the cushion of air beneath a hovercraft, keeps us airborne very close to the ground.

Even in the case of nonfiction—perhaps, for ethical reasons, especially in the case of nonfiction, in which people are real and the events actually happened—the reader must realize the story is nevertheless a construct of a writer who selected, sequenced, and lent his or her perspective and knowledge to the work. That is, it is not gospel, but one writer's version. To forget that is to pretend to absolute knowledge and complete truth, which of course is never possible.

In 1965, with great promotional hype and fanfare, Capote introduced what he called the "nonfiction novel," a true-life story of the heinous murder of the Clutter family in Holcomb, Kansas. It's a spellbinding book, a triumph of true storytelling. The story reads novelistically: The reader becomes utterly absorbed in the events, the paranoia of the little community, the private conversations of the Clutter children, the last thoughts of Herb and Bonnie Clutter on the day they died—wait a minute! How did Capote hear those conversations? Know those thoughts? How indeed did he know all sorts of other "facts" in the book? How did he record lengthy conversations without a tape recorder or even a notebook? How did he experience the minds of the killers, especially Perry Smith, in such fine detail?

Capote took some liberties usually claimed only by fiction writers—the very point he was trying to make in defining his project as a "nonfiction novel." He foreshortened aesthetic distance. In a famous interview with George Plimpton in *The New York Times Book Review*, Capote claims to have a photographic memory, capable of 95 percent perfect recall of extended conversations. He also had a long-standing personal friendship—some claim love affair—with Perry Smith, and the two exchanged many intimate letters. Though you wouldn't know it from the narrative, Capote was actually present at Smith's hanging, and the execution sickened him. In his will, Smith bequeathed him all his worldly possessions.

Capote was not just investigator, not even just witness, but finally a player in the drama, causing certain things to happen and others not to. By leaving himself out of the narrative completely, some critics have argued that Capote falsified the experience sufficiently to cast large doubts on the accuracy of his "nonfiction" book. One critic, Sol Yurick of *The Nation*, dismissed it as "done in the best tradition of newspaper sob sisterism wedded to Southern Gothic prose." But most critics—and readers—remain stunned by the shocking immediacy and power of the story, its realness. Ironically, by distancing himself from the narrative, Capote closed the aesthetic distance for the reader, creating the fiction of an infallible omniscient narrator, of a perfectly recorded episode of real-life crime and punishment.

This may have been precisely what he was trying to do. So it is not the technique alone that creates or closes aesthetic distance: Steinbeck took himself out of the story and created distance, while Capote took himself out and closed the distance. It's the technique in service of a particular story told from a particular stance.

An absence of aesthetic distance can lead the reader to take the story at face value, without critiquing its presentation or inquiring about its truth. As Gardner warns us, "Nothing in the world has greater power to enslave us than fiction." Unless it is convincing novelistic nonfiction.

Didacticism and Sentimentality

The writer needs distance for another reason: to avoid *didacticism* and *sentimentality*. Literature has always had a didactic function; that is, the best books teach us something about the world, about actual places and events, about the history of ideas, about ordinary life. Victor Hugo (*Les Misérables*) teaches us Napoleonic military history; Hemingway (*Islands in the Stream*) teaches us how to fish for marlin; J.F. Powers (*Morte d'Urban*) teaches us about the private quotidian life of a Catholic priest; Toni Morrison (*Beloved*) teaches us about slavery. In many works of nonfiction—for example, *The Fatal Shore*, Robert Hughes' engrossing account of the settling of Australia—the teaching element is paramount.

But a writer who identifies too closely with his material risks being preachy—taking this didactic function to an extreme. Nobody likes to be preached at, especially not sinners. True believers make dull dinner companions.

Writers with fiercely held political or religious convictions are tempted to slip into didacticism. This is not surprising—great writing often arises out of deep conviction. For example, Jack London was a famous champion of the poor, as he demonstrated most eloquently in *People of the Abyss*, an immersion account of London's East End slums. But even his characters sometimes spout canned socialist rhetoric. And Richard Wright was a powerful and articulate voice against racial oppression. But the long-winded diatribe spoken by Max, the socialist lawyer defending Bigger Thomas of the murder of a white girl, near the end of *Native Son*, mars the book.

How to be usefully didactic without being preachy?

One solution in fiction is to *let characters act like characters*—to say and do the things *those* characters would plausibly say and do. Avoid the temptation to make them the author's mouthpiece. Even Steinbeck, one of the greatest American writers of the century, doesn't always take this advice. His character Casey the preacher seems to function as the spokesman for many of Steinbeck's own principles. But at least when Casey—or any *character*—is speaking in fiction, we hear him within the greater context of other characters, action, and narration; his is not the only voice. We don't have to believe a word the characters say. Indeed, we may passionately believe the opposite. They may function to goad us into examining and defending our own principles—as does Amon, the charming, articulate, and ruthless death camp commandant in *Schindler's List*.

In fact, one successful technique for arguing ideas within a novel is to have various characters present different facets in their actions and words—though rarely directly—leaving the final choice up to the reader. The characters act plausibly within their roles and aren't necessarily "flat" or predictable characters. But mostly they wind up representing one way, more than others, of dealing with the issue at hand.

Michael Shaara's *The Killer Angels* succeeds precisely because he turns the historical commanders—including Robert E. Lee and James Longstreet on the Confederate side; John Buford, George Meade, and

Joshua Chamberlain on the Union side—into complex human figures agonizing over their choices, which carry the consequences of life or death for thousands of men. But when all is said and done, Lee is the voice of fatalism: We are in God's hands. Longstreet is the voice of caution and restraint: Dig in and make them attack us on ground of our choosing. Buford knows one truth: Hold the high ground. Meade's solution is corporate: Let the organization function and things will come out all right; Chamberlain's is audacity, personal initiative, resourcefulness: Try the one bold tactic the enemy doesn't expect. Their philosophies are tested within the action of the novel: The Battle of Gettysburg ensues and we learn which approach—or combination— carries the day.

This technique works in certain kinds of nonfiction. It has long been a staple of newspaper journalism: Get a quote from a principal on each side of a controversy, report the facts as they are known and can be confirmed by at least two sources, and let the reader be the judge of what is true. The writer does not necessarily have to believe— or agree with—any of those quoted.

The key is always to include your reader in the process by which you arrived at your position. Instead of demanding that the reader experience anger or love or indignation or outrage over injustice simply because you say so, create for the reader the same experience that led you to your reaction.

In satire, characters are likely to be flat: The Horse in *Animal Farm* is merely an earnest drudge, the Pig a scheming opportunist, and so on, for satire is one brand of a novel of ideas. In a novel of ideas, characters may be deliberately invented to embody a philosophical position—hedonist, rationalist, romantic. We read such a novel as we follow an argument, listening to dialogues and speeches that don't really advance plot so much as they wrestle with a proposition, as in Umberto Eco's *The Island of the Day Before*, about the quest to discover the secret of longitude, as a navigational principle but more importantly as a divine calculus for understanding the nature of time, space, eternity, and finally the nature of God. Such novels appeal to the intellect. The reader makes a bargain not to care too much about *story* so long as the argument remains intellectually fascinating.

The writer who is too close to his material also risks sentimentality—relying on predictable emotional responses, rather than a well-crafted story, to carry his effect. In Gardner's terms, "the attempt to get some effect without providing due cause." Such a writer can "push the reader's buttons" the way nineteenth-century popular melodrama did, evoking pure heroes, black-hearted villains, and virginal victims—along with cuddly puppies and kittens, sweet grandmothers, Christmas Eve homecomings, crippled orphans, and whores with hearts of gold—in order to provoke stock, superficial reactions. The characters are flat and exaggerated, and the reader has only one choice of reaction in reading them.

Sentimentality can infect nonfiction as easily as a novel, especially in autobiographical writing, if the writer has close emotional ties of love or hate to the real "characters" (little psychic distance). The writer may be drawing on his or her own emotional response, not fairly presenting complex people. Gardner again: "That is, in great fiction, we are moved by characters and events, not by the emotion of the person telling the story." The writer may be too close to the material to be able to present it artistically.

In the opening pages of his thrilling true-life adventure on Mount Everest, *Into Thin Air*, writer Jon Krakauer wrestles with the choice of whether to tell this harrowing tale while he is still painfully close to the events.

> The Everest climb had rocked my life to its core, and it became desperately important for me to record the events in complete detail, unconstrained by a limited number of column-inches. This book is the fruit of that compulsion. Several editors and authors I respect counseled me not to write the book as quickly as I did. They urged me to wait two or three years and put some distance between me and the expedition in order to gain some crucial perspective. Their advice was sound, but in the end I ignored it—mostly because what happened on the mountain was gnawing my guts out. I thought that writing the book might purge Everest from my life. It hasn't, of course.

Moreover, I agree that readers are often poorly served when an author writes as an act of catharsis, as I have done here. But I hoped something would be gained by spilling my soul in the calamity's immediate aftermath, in the roil and torment of the moment. I wanted my account to have a raw, ruthless sort of honesty that seemed in danger of leaching away with the passage of time and the dissipation of anguish.

Krakauer is at least aware of the risk of writing "in the roil and torment of the moment," and he succeeds admirably—largely, I think, because he has sound habits as a journalist, developed over years of practice. He observes, he listens, and he never thrusts himself into the forefront of the narrative. His craft is there to serve him when he needs it. And had he "spilled his soul" about merely private household events, we might only have looked away in embarrassment. The majesty of Everest and the life-and-death stakes of the story upstage any confessional faults. The writer is too busy chronicling events and other people's actions to become preoccupied with himself.

Lastly, Krakauer brings to his telling one of the writer's indispensable virtues: humility.

Theme Fits Subject

In a good book, the real-world external *subject* is intrinsically ballasted by deeper, universal concerns, the ideas underlying the vision of the book: *themes*. What the book is thinking about.

In Don DeLillo's novel *Libra*, for instance, his subject matter is the assassination of President John F. Kennedy. DeLillo's themes derive naturally from his subject.

- The "conspiracy theory" as a governing metaphor for nearly everything in public life, from presidential elections to big business.
- How a novelistic "plot"—analogous to a conspirator's "plot"—is constructed and operates on the reader's imagination.

Nicholas Branch, a retired senior analyst with the Central Intelligence Agency (CIA), is charged with getting to the bottom of the JFK assassination—writing the definitive history of the event. Fifteen years into his task, he realizes he is actually farther behind than on the day he started. So many pages of new reports, so many new books and videos and films, so many more court cases and transcripts arrive every day that he despairs of ever being able to account for those "Six point nine seconds of heat and light" in Dallas that changed history.

Worse, each document contradicts the last, an endless whorl of cover-ups, plots, and counterplots, false trails and fake IDs. Lee Harvey Oswald is a real man; he's also a character created by the CIA. He's a villain, a patsy, a nut, a patriot, an abusive husband, a loving son. He's in two or even three places at one time—according to reliable evidence. Inside a plot to kill Fidel Castro hatches a bizarre plot to *pretend* to kill the president in order to ignite anti-Castro fervor, within which another plot is hatched to actually kill the president. Not all the characters understand which plot they are serving.

It's a hall of mirrors. Everybody seems to be conspiring against something, and Branch has to create the illusion of a coherent story amid the paradoxes—just like the author of any complex novel.

DeLillo's two large, overarching themes resonate purposefully off nearly every aspect of our contemporary life. A private story, say, about a shy boy coming of age on a farm in Depression-era Georgia would be too delicate to carry such thematic weight, and the theme would falter doubly because the Great Depression was not an era of conspiracy theories.

Theme must fit subject.

The Writer's Authority

And that brings us to the question of doubt: As a writer, from what do I claim the authority to address a large public subject? Who am I to write about the Civil Rights Movement, the Rwandan genocide, the experience of AIDS victims, "Okies" on Highway 66, the Fall of Communism, the Great Age of Exploration, a world war? I wasn't there, I didn't experience it, so what gives me the right to tell about it?

Even if I'm writing about my childhood, what gives me the right to be the spokesman for a lifetime shared with brothers and sisters, parents, relatives, teachers, and friends, in which I, not they, will be the protagonist, or at least the viewpoint character?

My answer is simple: The working writer earns the authority by writing well and honestly.

That is, you respect the subject—that's the first thing. Everything else derives from that essential respect. You begin with this proposition: Whatever I think I know, I must question and prove. I must not kid myself. You begin not in the arrogance of sure knowledge but in the humility of doubt.

Then you delve into the subject, investing yourself emotionally, intellectually, aesthetically—and probably also financially. You research it any way you have to in order to know—really *know*—its truth. You are resourceful and obsessive in this quest, not passive or lazy. You don't wait for the world to come to you; you go out into it. You are prepared at every stage to be surprised, to be wrong, to change your mind. You take the frustration, the hard work, the sleepless nights, the anxiety of responsibility. You pay your dues: You do the hard research, you wrestle with the difficult contradictions, you revise over and over, you use every bit of craft you know and then learn some more in order to express the subject in an accurate way that does justice to it, both for you and for others. You don't for a moment underestimate the importance of the undertaking: Somewhere, someone you've never met will be exalted, shamed, enlightened, shocked, overjoyed, vindicated, frightened, amused, confused, disheartened, surprised, angered, or given courage by your words.

It matters that you find the right words. The quality of your struggle to find those words, to make the best use of your God-given talent in service of a subject, earns you the right to be its author.

And what of the objection that writers shouldn't presume to cross certain boundaries? That men shouldn't write about women's experiences, whites shouldn't write about blacks'? Only Native Americans should address Native American subjects, and so on?

The most eloquent answer to that insidious notion comes from a 1993 *Associated Writing Programs Chronicle* interview with Charles Johnson, author of *Middle Passage*, which he characterizes as a combination slave narrative, philosophical novel, sea story, and send-up of the nineteenth-century novel: "Actually that would limit everyone to writing autobiography," Johnson says emphatically. "I take a real strong position against that in *Being and Race: Black Writing Since 1970*. You cannot make that argument and convince me unless we have far stronger evidence than we have, because throughout time great writers have always been able to transpose themselves imaginatively into not just the racial other, but the sexual other and also into other historical periods.

"What this argument says is that, in effect, you can't imagine what it's like to be in the nineteenth century. You close off all historical curiosity." He goes on: "Ultimately that argument forces us not only to autobiography, it forces us to solipsism, the self knowing only its own operations."

He concludes by addressing the moral imperative for a writer to cross those lines: "Everything we're talking about with integration in terms of America—certainly with black people—hinges on some ability to understand across racial lines. But that other argument is racially bound. That's scary. Ultimately, that is racist. That's Nazism. That's fascism. Yes, it disturbs me greatly. . . . I think that's censorship and really tying the writer to a lie. It might be one that is politically correct or something, but I just don't think it's allowing the writer to speak the truth of what he or she sees."

When I wrote *Cape Fear Rising*, a novel that is accurately based on an actual racial massacre carried out in the city where I live by white supremacists in 1898—a subject I felt strongly that I could not ignore—a very few vocal blacks felt that I had usurped *their* story, that as a white writer I had no right to the story. Many whites—especially those who are descended from the perpetrators of the massacre—felt I had no right because I was an outsider, a newcomer, a Yankee, with no family tradition of the events. My answer: It is *our* story. I'm a writer. My job is to tell the stories that define our community, whether that community is Wilmington, North Carolina, or America, or the world.

I believe in the writer as a witness to evil, as a reporter of injustice, as a chronicler of human compassion, even on occasion of greatness, as one whose skills illuminate the Truth with a capital *T*, without irony.

27

I believe it is the job of the writer to put into words what is worst—and also what is best—about us. To light up our possibilities, discover the finest lives to which we can aspire, and to inspire our readers to greatness of soul and heart.

Many of us have come of age under the received wisdom that the writer is somehow a marginal creature, always on the outside of the culture looking in, an adversary to tradition—disaffected, alienated, unconnected to society. And in truth, at certain times, the writer may be all those things. But I believe that, especially in America, where we enjoy unprecedented freedom of expression and the technological and economic means to find that expression, the writer stands squarely in the middle of the public forum, central to every deliberation and debate in our national and local community.

Like Tacitus who satirized Roman self-importance, Dickens who painted vivid scenes of exploitative child labor practices, Harriet Beecher Stowe who created the first popular humanized American Negro slave characters, Stephen Crane who captured the interior face of war, Frances FitzGerald who gave us a sane and candid history of the Vietnam War, James Baldwin and Richard Wright who dueled privately and wrote publicly about the meaning of the African-American experience, and hundreds of other writers, I aspire to write about public subjects that matter, great themes reflected in private struggles informed by provocative ideas.

Every writer, even the tentative novice, is part of the great legacy of narrators in history, who help create and sustain a culture's ideas of itself and what it values. If you haven't tackled certain important subjects and themes because they intimidate you, it's time to realize that writing about small, private moments prepares the writer only to continue to write about more small, private moments—which can be fine and honorable work as witnessed by Proust's *Remembrance of Things Past*, Montaigne's essays, or Raymond Carver's short stories. Sometimes small subjects can surprise us with their power and resonance: Frank McCourt gives us an "ordinary" childhood in *Angela's Ashes*, but he conjures up a universal coming of age in a hard, circumscribed world—a big subject.

Think of yourself, as E.M. Forster suggests in *Aspects of the Novel*, sitting in the reading room of the British Museum, where your peers are not other aspiring or apprentice writers, or even all contemporary writers, but all the great writers who live or have ever lived— Shakespeare, Dickens, Virginia Woolf, Thomas Wolfe, Truman Capote, Edith Wharton, John McPhee, Annie Dillard, Toni Morrison, Henry James, E.B. White, de Maupassant, Hawthorne, Melville, Poe, James Baldwin, Zola, Balzac, Tolstoy, Jane Austen, Rousseau, Flannery O'Connor, even Homer.

The only way to learn how to tackle big subjects and themes is to try. Your subject: the world, in all its thematic brilliance.

Exercises

1. In fifty words or less, answer the following question: What is the most important thing that ever happened to you, and why? Don't assume it is the obvious memory; it may turn out to be a small, quiet moment buried deep in your childhood: a word from a teacher, a scene you witnessed from a train window, a Christmas present you yearned for but *didn't* find under the tree. Don't be glib. Peel off the layers of the experience to the fourth or fifth sublayer below its obvious meaning.

2. If you had the power to instantaneously change one thing in the world that didn't affect you personally (forget adding millions to your bank account), what would it be? Why would you change it? What's the most eloquent argument *against* changing it? What makes you believe the change would be for the better? What would be the effect on a specific community of strangers? What would be some possible unintended consequences?

The answers should give you some clue about your preoccupations as a writer—the things you care about most deeply. This awareness is the first step toward writing the book you need to write.

2

Choosing a Worthy Subject

The famous editor Max Perkins once counseled James Jones, then in the throes of writing *From Here to Eternity*, "One can write about nothing unless it is, in some sense, out of one's life—that is, out of oneself."

You can't fake interest in a subject.

In his letter to Jones, Perkins advised keeping a journal of a very specific kind—a loose-leaf binder with stiff pages on which the writer scrawled notes about experiences, one item to a page, each page identified with a rubric or key word: "The key word might, for instance, be some topic like, say, 'Fear.' Then, just let the cards accumulate for quite a period, and then group them together under the key words. I think if a writer did that for ten years, all those memories would come back to him, as you say, and he would have an immense fund to draw upon."

Perkins hits on an important truth here: Large themes derive from private passions. And from time to time a writer does well to inventory his passions, to remind himself of the pattern of his previous work, the preoccupations that dominate his writing over and over again, even when he is unaware that he has such preoccupations.

Peter Gethers, Vice President Editor-at-Large for Random House, followed a similar logic when he created the Library of Contemporary Thought, a monthly series of short trade paperbacks addressing a variety of subjects, from Susan Isaacs on the image of women in the media to President Jimmy Carter on the values of aging.

"I don't read magazines anymore because they're not writing to me, not writing about the issues I care about," Gethers explains. "I know all these smart writers, a lot smarter than me, and I would love to hear their opinions on these issues. I thought, why aren't all these smart writers whom I admire available on issues I care about?"

So he launched the series, "borrowing" writers he admired from their regular publishers for one book: "In a way it's pamphlet publishing in the American tradition of Tom Paine." The concept was simple: "I realized I could get smart, interesting people who don't have a format to write about their passions and I could give that to them."

He commissioned paleontologist Stephen J. Gould to write about reconciling religion and science (*Rock of Ages: Science and Religion in the Fullness of Life*) and comedian Harry Shearer to explain Americans' love/hate affair with President Bill Clinton (*It's the Stupidity, Stupid: Why (Some) People Hate Clinton and Why the Rest of Us Have to Watch*). From *Miami Herald* columnist and mystery writer Carl Hiaasen came *Team Rodent: How Disney Devours the World*; from best-selling novelist Anna Quindlen, *How Reading Changed My Life*; and from journalist Pete Hamill, a critique of his profession in *News Is a Verb: Journalism at the End of the Twentieth Century.*

Gethers observes that these days, lots of important public issues wind up on *Oprah* or *Geraldo* or other TV shows: "I don't think there are any great issues that aren't out there for discussion. The question is, how are they being presented?" Because the written word is more thoughtful and controlled, writers can do what a transient medium can't do: create a simulacrum of imaginative thought. Gethers says, "You can't have substantive thought on TV. You can only *provoke* substantive thought."

The only rule for the library selections is that each writer must write from a personal passion for the subject—and not necessarily the one for which he or she is best known. Robert Hughes, the cultural critic, writes about fishing.

Somehow the personal connection to the public story can capture it far better than a generic, long-range view. Both the personal connection of the writer drawing on the deep experience of his or her own life and, through individual characters—real or imagined—a personal impact on the reader.

We think of *War and Peace* as a big sprawling book about the nature of war, but in fact it's a very intimate portrait of several families whose fortunes intertwine; and through the triumph, heartbreak, bravery, and cowardice of a few key individuals in those families, we come to understand war as a social phenomenon, a disastrous extension of drawing-room politics and class self-interest.

It is only in Part Ninth, after hundreds of pages of following these characters' lives, that Tolstoy allows himself to draw any abstract truth from the action of the novel: "On the twenty-fourth of June, the forces of Western Europe crossed the Russian frontier, and war began: In other words, an event took place opposed to human reason and human nature. Millions of men committed against one another a countless number of crimes, deceptions, treacheries, robberies, forgeries, issues of false money, depredations, incendiary fires, and murders, such as the annals of all the courts in the world could not equal in the aggregate of centuries; and yet which, at that period, the perpetrators did not even regard as crimes."

The language is spare and straightforward, a catalogue of evidence, a parsing of the great paradox of free will versus destiny that is the ultimate subject of the novel—indeed, the ultimate subject of history: Can the individual affect history, or is history itself in the grip of fate? But it draws its force from all the preceding pages of individual suffering, heroism, and loss.

Likewise, *The Grapes of Wrath* takes on the whole capitalistic American enterprise in the context of a pivotal historical era, but Steinbeck evokes the era and the economic system by creating the saga of a single American family on the road toward its misbegotten American dream. Not millions of people, but a handful. In fact, it was not until he could envision the story as a personal human struggle, not a social phenomenon, that he was able to write it convincingly. In the end, it's not the social phenomenon that remains in our imagination's eye; it's the vision of Rose of Sharon, lying in the barn as the flood waters rise all around it and Ma looks on, suckling a starving man at her shriveled breast.

Truth and Consequences

So what makes a worthy subject? And bear in mind the question applies two ways: What is worth your trouble to write about, and what is worth the reader's time to read about?

Another way of asking the question: What makes a story *matter*?

The answer, usually, is *consequences.* What is at stake.

An event, whether in real life or in fiction, is like a stone dropped into a pond. The waves of disturbance ripple outward. A pebble makes a tiny splash and the small ripples recede quickly, barely noticeable. A boulder throws up a plume of water and the waves swamp small boats, break like surf against the banks.

Getting stood up for the junior prom is a pebble. You'll get over it, and probably soon. One day it will make a nostalgic dinner joke, if you remember the incident at all. Meanwhile, nobody else is much affected—your friends have a good time without you, your parents go on with their lives, the president continues meeting his cabinet, the pope leaves for Africa, the GNP rises and interest rates fall . . .

The Holocaust is a gigantic boulder. Personal lives are shattered. Millions die. Generations will go unborn. Whole societies, whole nations are nearly wiped out, will never be the same again. Everything we thought we knew about human nature and civilization must be reexamined. History has taken a sharp and dangerous turn, and it will require decades, half a century or more, to pick up the pieces, and things can never be the same. The waves race turbulently into the future, rocking everything in their path.

Between prom night and the Holocaust lies a continuum of consequences, ranging from the trivial to the momentous. A worthy subject lies closer to the latter than the former.

Biographers understand this rule. The biography is, after all, the study of an exemplary life, the life that has achieved something in the public arena, caused and suffered great consequences. The biography of a private individual who lives a predictable and not very exciting life is usually of interest only to family members—those in the inner ripple.

Memoirists who fail to understand this commit the sin of narcissism—excessive self-absorption, the mistaken notion that they are the center of the universe and everything they do or think matters implicitly just because it matters to them.

In "Me, Myself, and I," *Vanity Fair* critic James Wolcott complains of confessional writing: "Never have so many shared so much with so many." Citing example after example of "crisis memoir"—personal accounts of surviving cancer, abuse, incest, alcoholism, and madness—he goes on: "Creative (fiction) writing and creative nonfiction are coming together, I fear, to form a big, earnest blob of me-first sensibility. Both share the same premise—that writing is primarily self-expression, not a voyaging out but a foraging in."

Wolcott makes the useful point that some masterful writing has indeed turned on the author's personal tribulations—F. Scott Fitzgerald's famous account of his own psychological unraveling, "The Crack-Up," for example. And Wolcott admits, "I eat literary memoirs like candy, if there's a crunchy Mary McCarthy anecdote inside."

But near the end of his withering attack on this new trend of memoir, he can hardly control his disdain: "The new confessionals are tonally different from what's come before—needier, greedier, the worst of them evincing a flayed, righteous, yet willowy sense of grievance that's like *Mein Kampf* on spiritual retreat, while others piddle away into pointless passive-aggressive chat."

Discounting the shrill hyperbole and the nasty tone, Wolcott makes an important point: The best memoirists turn their memoirs on the people and events around them, interpreting them in a way that brings to bear their special insight, their accumulated knowledge and experience, their unique way of looking at the world. In fact, in a vicarious way, the reader becomes the memoirist, the *I* narrator of the book, experiencing universal emotions, not simply reliving private anecdotes. The experience is not raw diary but shaped into cohesion and coherence. The best memoirs are about the memoirist only indirectly and implicitly, as a reflection of the subject at hand.

Making the Personal Connection Matter

The writer owes the reader a large experience—one that will increase his imaginative grasp. One way to deliver this is to recognize the obvious: Subject matter *matters*.

It starts by mattering to the writer, naturally, but it goes much farther, as the writer steps back from his material and ponders its consequences—for the real people or characters inside the story, for the reader, for the world at large. The writer is asking *why* it matters.

Steinbeck was haunted by the faces of the Okies he met starving amid the bounty of California. Suffering always matters in a general way, because it touches our humanity. But the suffering Steinbeck witnessed mattered urgently for at least three more pressing reasons:

1. He knew the people firsthand—they were no longer abstract statistics. Like it or not, their haggard faces were now and forever after part of his memory. He, not some other writer, was the witness. With the act of witnessing injustice comes the obligation to tell the truth about it. To be silent is to acquiesce, which is to lie.

2. In a nation so rich in natural and man-made resources, the suffering seemed unnecessary—and therefore morally and politically unacceptable. Steinbeck's own relative wealth in the midst of national depression added the urgency of personal guilt, or at least a discomfiture with his own affluence. And if honest, hardworking people could suddenly find themselves homeless and starving, having lost everything except their humanity, it could happen to anyone.

3. And, at least in Steinbeck's view, the suffering was the consequence of deliberate decisions taken by those who had the power to stop the suffering but for selfish reasons chose not to—the bankers, the company growers, and certain politicians. In other words, if he could tell the truth about such suffering, perhaps he could help to change it.

He first envisioned a documentary project—returning for months of journalistic research in the field, interviewing, watching, listening—struggling for years to find a medium large and deep enough to do justice to his vision of an American refugee class, and at last, once he was able to focus not on the immense public phenomenon but on a few representative characters caught up in the great public phenomenon, wrote *The Grapes of Wrath*.

This was the book he felt he must write—well and truthfully.

His passion for the subject was fierce: "I want to put a tag of shame on the greedy bastards who are responsible. . . ." His problem was acquiring enough distance to gain perspective so he could create a lasting work, rather than merely a shrill editorial diatribe that would fade with the headlines.

Some connections are straightforward: Tim O'Brien served as an infantry sergeant in the Vietnam War. He humped through the bush on combat patrol, lay in ambush in the jungle dark, stumbled into nightmare firefights, collected the dead and the maimed as a matter of routine, and he was changed forever by what he had witnessed. No wonder he writes with such authenticity in *Going After Cacciato* and other Vietnam stories.

In "How to Tell a True War Story," as in others, O'Brien communicates not only his own fear but also his passionate ambivalence: "The truths are contradictory. It can be argued, for instance, that war is grotesque. But in truth war is also beauty. For all its horrors, you can't help but gape at the awful majesty of combat. . . . It's astonishing. It fills the eye. It commands you. You hate it, yes, but your eyes do not. Like a killer forest fire, like cancer under a microscope, any battle or bombing raid or artillery barrage has the aesthetic purity of absolute moral indifference—a powerful, implacable beauty—and a true war story will tell the truth about this, though the truth is ugly."

And sometimes the connections are not obvious at all.

How does an Australian of Irish descent, Thomas Keneally, become obsessed with the Holocaust—which happened a hemisphere away, on another continent, in another generation, to people with whom he had no direct connection?

In his Author's Note to *Schindler's List*, Keneally tells how he accidentally stumbled across the subject: "In 1980 I visited a luggage store in Beverly Hills, California, and inquired the prices of briefcases. The store belonged to Leopold Pfefferberg, a Schindler survivor. It was beneath Pfefferberg's shelves of imported Italian leather goods that I first heard of Oskar Schindler, the German *bon vivant*, speculator, charmer, and sign of contradiction, and of his salvage of a cross section of a condemned race during those years now known by the generic name Holocaust."

But Keneally's fascination with Schindler is not so far-fetched; in fact, it's quite personal, once we move beyond thinking of the generic Holocaust as the subject. Keneally's subject is not the Holocaust as an event, but rather the curious action of a single man *on the wrong side* of the fight—a German businessman who gets rich from the Final Solution. A strange choice for a hero.

Schindler joins a long parade of Keneally characters from other novels—qualified heroes who are privileged insiders making an ambivalent and somewhat altruistic connection to outsiders—such as Frank McCloud, the white manager of an Australian aboriginal dance troupe in *Flying Hero Class* who acts to thwart the hijacking of their airliner.

And Schindler also resonates with Keneally's long-standing passion for history, especially those moments of history shaped by the will of an ordinary individual. In *Gossip From the Forest*, Matthias Erzberger, a minor politician "of country stock, big-boned to his friends, obese to enemies," is charged with negotiating the armistice to end World War I—securing as favorable terms as possible for Germany before revolution sweeps the nation. A monumental challenge for an ordinary man, one that will eventually kill him.

Schindler's List is not an important novel merely because it treats a significant event in history; rather it's important because it forever refutes the Nuremberg defense, cited again and again by those accused of the most heinous atrocities: *I was only following orders.* If Schindler, a German businessman, could act to save Jews, then it was at least possible for others far more powerful to act with moral courage. He single-handedly refutes an entire nation's claim of helplessness in the face of Nazi coercion. It's a powerful truth—one of the most important ones a writer can address. It reinstates personal accountability as an absolute virtue. It takes away all excuses for collaborating with evil.

Clearly, other themes make the novel large in scope and meaning—the documentary of specific atrocities not least among them. The point is that Keneally went much farther than simply borrowing the drama of a great event. In later chapters, we'll explore just how he and other writers create a thematic understanding of a public event.

Recognizing Your Themes

So in Keneally's case, the genesis of his personal connection to the Schindler material is subtle but not so very complex: A chance encounter leads to knowledge. The knowledge gets a grip on the imagination. The writer's lifelong passions converge on the subject at hand, coloring the encounter. Pretty soon a big book wants to be written.

A bit of introspection may be called for—even if the connection seems fairly obvious: Is my interest in writing about the breakdown of the American family (the writer asks) masking my truer interest in writing about my feelings of estrangement from my own family? Just because the connection seems obvious in hindsight doesn't mean it was obvious before.

One element of this introspection is *recognizing subjects and themes you care about but did not realize you cared about* until you sorted out memories, came to terms with personal experiences, and cast those subjects and themes in terms that resonated with your passion.

Sometimes we're fascinated with a subject, keep coming back to it, mulling it over, feeling it is somehow crucial to write about, yet we are blind to our own personal connection to it. And without knowing that, we flail around, never quite getting a handle on it. Sometimes our passions come to us disguised as something else.

When I first heard about the historical event that formed the foundation for my novel *Cape Fear Rising*, it seemed a classic case of racist violence: A small cadre of rich white men manipulated a lot of poor white men with guns into attacking the black community.

I have always recognized the injustice of racism, but it has not been my particular passion as a writer. But as I investigated the chain of events that led to November 10, 1898, when a thousand armed white men took to the streets of Wilmington, North Carolina, and murdered an untold number of blacks, I discovered that the flash point for the whole ugly business was *The Daily Record*, which billed itself as the first "Afro-American" daily newspaper in the country. The editor, Alex Manly, was banished from the city under a death sentence and his newspaper office was burned to the ground—*because of an editorial he had written*.

Now I was circling closer to my passions. I've always been passionate about freedom of expression—a writer usually is. In particular, I'm passionate about writing: the sublime mystery of how the right words in the right order excite our emotions and rouse us to thought and action. Without that passion, I wouldn't be writing this book.

In an important way, the events of 1898 were played out first in written and then spoken words—in narrative: newspaper stories, white supremacist campaign speeches, political resolutions (including The White Declaration of Independence), sermons from the pulpits of white and black churches.

In the midst of the violence, the white vigilantes hauled the mayor and the board of aldermen into city hall at gunpoint and made them resign. It is widely believed to be the only coup d'etat in American history.

At last I had penetrated to the core of the incident—and to the core of my passion. Sure, it was a story about racism, and about freedom of expression. But it was more than that: It was a story about the failure of democracy. About that moment when the social contract breaks down, all bets are off, and a progressive community with good schools, telephones, an opera house, and a well-educated citizenry turns into Kosovo.

That's why the events fascinated me so, and my passion lay in uncovering the *why* of such a civic failure: What were the motivations of the principal players? What were the conditions that made the city ripe for violent revolution? Was it inevitable, or could determined men and women of conscience have stopped it?

The novel was not about a Southern city in 1898. It was about every city in the world in 1998 and beyond.

Refining *Topic* Into *Subject*

Remember that a general topic is not necessarily a subject. A *topic* is a broad area of inquiry: "war" or "sports" or "immigration." A *subject* is refined, narrow, cast as a particular case: "The Civil War," "Negro League Baseball," "Irish servants in Boston."

Even these are a bit too broad to handle. The writer has to keep narrowing, defining, refining, until he recognizes his deeper subject, the underlying theme that the piece will bring to light. Eventually, they yield fascinating books about women who disguised themselves as men in order to enlist in the Union army; about Satchel Paige and all the other players who thought they, not Jackie Robinson, were going to break the color barrier in the white major leagues, and their bitter disillusionment; about single, young Irish women who got their first taste of the upper class while working as live-in maids and elevated the social ambitions of thousands of their immigrant countrymen.

Note that it is just as hard to write about positive themes—heroism, patriotism, love—as it is about negative ones, and for some of the same reasons: the temptation to lapse into clichéd ways of talking about the subject; the pull of emotions that may distort reasoned analysis and argument; our strong biases based on anecdotal but dramatically personal experience. In other words:

- Sentimentality.
- Lack of aesthetic or psychic distance.
- Didacticism.

Reclaiming "Issue Themes" From the Freshman Comp Swamp

The five-paragraph "theme" we all remember from high school and college freshman English can trivialize important subjects forever: abortion, addiction, AIDS, cancer, child abuse, the death penalty, gun control, the Holocaust, homosexuality, nuclear war, patriotism, racism, religious faith, to name a few. In this usage, *theme* means a kind of formulaic essay: three paragraphs of development sandwiched between an introductory paragraph and a concluding paragraph.

If you ever learned the formula, forget it; you've outgrown it now.

Such a short, formulaic "theme" doesn't offer the space or scope to really get to the bottom of an important, complex subject. It skims along the surface, rehearsing trite arguments, offering clichéd examples, reducing the beautiful complexity of the subject to an either/or proposition.

And complexity *is* beautiful. Inside any truly complex system resides a harmony of elements, whether you're talking about a coral reef or the three branches of the federal government. A big subject is a galaxy of parts—facts, ideas, arguments. It has its own history, its own cast of characters, its own dramatic logic, sometimes even a definite plot.

Think about "gun control"—another nebulously named subject that encompasses many contradictions. It begins in English common law hundreds of years ago *as its opposite*: Each yeoman is required to be ready to defend his country and to have at hand the proper weapon—a long bow. Across the Atlantic, in the British colonies, guns become a necessary tool of survival on the frontier. Then come Concord and Lexington—a British expedition into the Massachusetts countryside to confiscate weapons stockpiled by minutemen against British regulations. Out of that startling turnabout—from the requirement that an armed citizenry be ready to defend the country to a punitive expedition against those same British citizens—comes the later amgbiguous rhetoric of the Second Amendment to the Constitution: Are firearms meant to be kept solely in the hands of a "well-regulated Militia"?

The issue is couched in a long and complicated history—of wartime regulations, peacetime laws, gangster-era bans on machine guns, presidential assassinations and high school mass murders, left- and right-wing politics. It has a rhetorical dimension: that troublesome amendment. There's also a political dimension: all those campaign dollars that flow from the National Rifle Association. And of course at bottom lie two thorny philosophical issues—the best kind:

1. The balancing of individual freedom and the rights of the community, including public safety.

2. The right and responsiblility of a citizen to resist tyrannical government by force of arms—as the minutemen did during the Revolution—versus the rightful government's need to maintain control over its citizens.

And most of us will experience the gun control issue personally, as well: We hunt or abhor hunting; we belonged to rifle clubs in school or didn't; we or our loved ones have been the victims of a gun crime or not; we trust the police and government to protect us or we don't. Or we used to hunt but don't any longer; we were victims of a crime and have considered carrying a gun but don't; we trust the government some but not all of the time.

And we haven't even defined the terms yet: Is gun control the banning of machine guns, or background checks for gun buyers, or outlawing all guns, or simply mandatory registration of all firearms? Or some combination?

And beyond the practical effect of gun control laws or their lack, how do they reflect our national identity—how do they define America? All aspects of the gun control debate are tied in fascinating ways to our national myths of self-reliant frontiersmen, minutemen, and cowboys sticking up for themselves and their own against bad men and tyrants.

The writer delights in discovering the harmony within the complexity, the order in the chaos, the method in the seeming madness.

But so many subjects have been worried to death by politicians, columnists, and TV talking heads that it's easy to throw up your hands, convinced that it's impossible to write about those topics without wallowing in clichés and boring your reader silly. But that's not true. These are the issues that drive legislation, incite public violence, and affect our daily lives and the lives of our neighbors. The thing is, you just can't expect to cover any of them with any authority or originality in a short formulaic essay.

A book is a different matter entirely: The shape of the book can derive in large part from the subject. You're not locked into a forumla. You have to invent the form that will best serve the subject. In later chapters we'll disucss in detail the kinds of forms successful books take. As you begin your engagement with your subject, it's enough to realize that you need to do some hard, smart thinking about that subject before you're even ready to cast it as a book. Only then can you take advantage of the flexibility and scope offered by the long form.

Often the subjects themselves are a kind of blurred shorthand—we commonly refer, for example, to "the issue of AIDS," as if the contours of the debate are obvious and irrefutable. But AIDS is a *disease*, not an *issue*. It becomes an issue only when reasonable people begin to disagree about how to treat it, about whether testing should be mandatory or voluntary, about whether records of testing should be public or private, about how we should spend public research dollars, or about how various political agendas are being served.

So first, last, and always, *be precise.* You the writer have to define the issue, describe it, teach us why it matters, create a definite and promising subject.

What facet of AIDS compels your interest? The way research dollars are spent—or not spent? The privacy versus public health issue at the heart of the testing controversy? The horrific nature of the disease itself, and the personal stories of the victims?

It's easy to say, "All of it," and in a sense that will always be true: A writer usually is dazzled and excited by the complexity of a subject, and the very complexity offers a satisfying challenge. After all, why take on the cut-and-dried, the straightforward, the obvious? We love to fall into a tangle of contradiction and conflict, to sort out the multifarious connections, to wrestle with a cascade of meanings.

But what is the single thing out of the hundred things that snagged your interest in this subject? How do you enter the subject—what is your "doorway" into AIDS?

Figure out why the subject first claimed your passion—and articulate it for yourself as precisely as you can.

Some subjects, such as affirmative action, are so specific to a time and culture, particular manifestations four or five layers removed from their universal human truth, that they probably will not endure with any lasting impact for their own sake.

Affirmative action is a policy, not a universal truth. It must be enlarged, shown to be a particular case of a more general and important truth—one answer to the question of how a nation promotes equality and fairness for all its citizens under the law. The writer must peel back the layers and decide, at bottom, what the affirmative action debate is all about. Is it a discussion of racism, of states' rights and Federalism, of equal opportunity, of reverse discrimination? Is it purely an American problem, an artifact of our history of slavery? Does it even work? And if it works, but you disagree with the principle, does that justify the policy? And if it doesn't work, but you agree with the principle, does that justify the policy?

What is the subject, *exactly*? And what theme does it echo?

And precision doesn't stop there—it's just beginning. Go slow. Do you have any opinions, preconceptions, assumptions? What do you *think* you know about the subject? Put that all on the table so you can inoculate your writing against fulfilling your own prejudices. To take on a subject honestly, you must be willing to cast all your preconceptions into doubt: You might be right, but then again, you may be forced to change your mind, to reconsider, to amend your worldview. If you're not willing to do this, if you're writing to "prove" what you're already sure of, then what's the point?

Always remember the object of the exercise, as they say in military circles: to learn. To gain fascinating and original insight and to share that with readers. To do so serves your own imagination and intellectual growth, your reader, and the larger culture.

In addition to recognizing your own preconceptions, go further:

• Define your terms. Just what do *you* mean by "gun control"? Don't run ideas or terms together glibly. Sort them out. This takes patience, like untangling a stubborn knot. But each thread leads off in its own direction. *Accuracy, for the writer, means being able and willing to define your terms exactly, and your position with precision*, and goes a long way toward writing a book that defeats the cliché.

• Don't generalize. Of course you can—and usually must—cite general principles, but life is full of exceptions and special cases. Test your principles with specific examples. Do they hold up? When you cast all welfare recipients as lazy bums, or when you claim that all gun owners are violent fanatics, or even that education is always beneficial, you close down inquiry. Almost no generalization is ever true all of the time. Note "almost."

• Avoid hyperbole, especially in making comparisons. When you equate all consensual marital relations with rape, for example, as do some feminists, you destroy the ability to make significant distinctions. And writing is about *nuance*—subtle but crucial gradations, differences in degree that ultimately shade into differences in kind.

Exaggeration blurs nuance and tends to shut down reasonable discussion.

• Don't assume your reader agrees with a word you are saying. In fact, assume the opposite: that the reader will bring a healthy skepticism to your book. Why should he believe you? Convince him.

Doubt Ignites a Passion to Know

Dorothy Lazard, formerly a librarian at the University of California at Berkeley, found herself squarely in the middle of the affirmative action debate. Proposition 209, passed by California voters in 1996, mandated an end to affirmative action. As the Berkeley campus came to grips with how to comply with the new law, she witnessed an emotional upheaval among colleagues, professors, administrators, and students.

It occurred to her: *This is the end of affirmative action.*

Not just at Berkeley—but all over California and eventually the nation. The signs were all there: the court decisions accumulating, the political pendulum swinging inexorably to the right. What did it mean? Whether you were for or against affirmative action, one thing was undeniable: This was a major change in how a democratic government defined its responsibility toward a significant population of its citizens.

The affirmative action debate was not an abstract policy quarrel but a very real turning point in the public life of a great nation. Lazard's interest began with a personal connection—in her working life, interacting with students of diverse backgrounds, she simply could not avoid the issue—and drove her to examine the larger meanings of everything she witnessed.

This was a big subject—too big for any form but a book. Just to explain what policy was being changed would take many pages. As she began researching her book—interviewing, collecting data, observing the changes around campus, attending meetings, digging into the archives—Lazard spent a good deal of time searching her own soul: "I kept asking myself how I felt about all this, what I believed in. I don't know why this was so important to me, but it was."

She wanted to be sure not to lose sight of her own principles; she also felt an obligation to announce her biases clearly to the reader: She was an employee of the institution, a professional with certain standards and expectations, and as an African-American, a beneficiary of the policy.

What she discovered was a troubling ambivalence: For every virtue of affirmative action, she found an important flaw. People did the right things for the wrong reasons, and vice versa. The situation was complex, fraught with emotion, and fluid. In one case, affirmative action seemed to provide justice and fairness; in another case, it seemed to cause a travesty of those very ideals. Sometimes it emboldened minority students to speak out, and sometimes ethnic and racial differences effectively closed down discussion.

And something else became clear: The debate was often driven by misinformation, myth, ignorance of the process, and political agendas. It was sometimes hard to get two people to even agree on what affirmative action was, or was supposed to be. All Lazard could do was keep digging, keep asking questions, keep observing carefully, and try to sort it all out into a coherent story.

And realize this: Dorothy Lazard is not a rich writer with a team of researchers doing all the tedious legwork and feeding her juicy information. Nor is she backed by a wealthy publisher footing the bill for her travel, photocopying, phone calls, and time. In fact, she has never written a book before. She began the book as an M.F.A. student at the Goucher College summer residency program in Creative Nonfiction. There's no guarantee she will ever publish her book. The odds are against it—though I'd bet on her. But when she found her subject, she could not turn away from it.

So an important book may begin in doubt, uncertainty, a sense of being overwhelmed by the sheer volume and complexity of information. But such doubt itself can ignite a kind of passion—it can become a driving curiosity, a fierce desire to know the truth, and knowing it, to tell it.

The Fallacy of Dichotomies

One challenge in writing about issues is that we tend to reflexively cast them as dichotomies—an adversarial, all-or-nothing "for and against"—which is an intellectually naive and artistically boring framework.

James Fallows, in his book *Breaking the News*, traces this pattern in the media: the tendency to cover every subject as a political battle with a winner and loser, so that the progress of the battle itself, not the substance of what it is being fought over, becomes the sole preoccupation.

This in effect is the problem Gethers alluded to about how important subjects are talked about on TV. The producer finds the most radical position on polar sides of an issue and lets them loose at one another. This method arguably results in compelling entertainment—tempers flare, people shout and punch—but it creates a lot of heat and not much light.

Four ways to reclaim such subjects:

1. Cast the subject not as a dichotomy (either/or, yes/no, winner/loser) but as *a complex and fascinating paradox* of conflicting facts, claims, and moral positions. There are not two sides to every story—there are probably five or a dozen or more. Allow the reader to participate in the *suspense* of the paradox, sharing the author's anxiety of choice, recognizing that in real life, choices are rarely completely clear and even doing the right thing can bring about unfortunate and unforeseen consequences.

In Philip Roth's *American Pastoral*, "Swede" Levov moves his family out of decaying Newark, New Jersey, into a tony suburb. He wants them to be safe and financially secure, and that's no longer possible in riot-ravaged Newark. But the very safeness of the lifestyle is the catalyst that turns his daughter Merry into a terrorist.

And doing the wrong thing, or the right thing for the wrong reasons, may bring about genuine good in the world—recall Keneally's *Schindler's List*, in which Oskar Schindler, exploiting Jewish slave labor during the war for profit, ultimately saves hundreds of lives.

2. *Personalize the issue*, squarely anchoring it in some real person's life. Remember that in narrative, a well-drawn fictional character can be just as real as a flesh-and-blood person, and that even real people have to be invented as characters. Your best chance at being original

is to be *concrete* rather than abstract and *specific* rather than general. Defining a large issue as an issue in a particular person's life, taking care to fill in the circumstances and details, will persuade the reader to match his or her abstract position with the real-life implications of that position.

Joyce Johnson's riveting book *What Lisa Knew* tells the story of the killing of a six-year-old child, Lisa Steinberg. The book addresses spousal abuse, battered woman syndrome, child abuse that leads to manslaughter, justice, the rights of children, and society's moral and legal accountability for protecting its children, but it is *people*, not issues, that we remember most vividly. Their faces and attitudes are stamped on the reader's imagination—and with them, of course, all the difficult issues they raise. Joel Steinberg and Hedda Nussbaum, Lisa's surrogate parents, are living villains, their actions dramatic and vivid. The child is so real she could be your own.

Here's how Johnson describes Steinberg, later convicted of first-degree manslaughter: "Before the morning of November 2, 1987, it is probable that if you happened to observe Joel Steinberg as he passed you on the street, you would have accepted him as the man he purported to be. A lawyer, therefore a relatively solid citizen—though he wore his black hair too long for the 1980s and his expensive suit may have needed pressing and his dark eyes may have glittered a bit too restlessly behind the thick lenses of his glasses and his loud nasal voice, carried back to you in a fragment of conversation, may have jarred you for a moment."

The too-long hair styled "from the wilder days of the 1970s," the wrinkled expensive suit, the dark restless eyes, the loud nasal voice create—out of apparently neutral details—a manic, potentially menacing figure.

Johnson turns that description even more sinister in the next paragraph: "At St. Vincent's though, the long hair became suspect, the black mustache criminal, the eyes guilty. According to Nancy Dodenhoff, a nurse on duty in the emergency room when Lisa was brought in, the eyes of Steinberg were 'glazed. His visual field kept darting back and forth.' She observed that he was nervous. 'He was wringing his hands. It was not concern for the child.'"

And the victim: "At the age of six, Lisa Steinberg weighed forty-three pounds. She was a little thinner than most other first-graders. She had big hazel eyes and red hair." So far, quite objective and matter-of-fact, the stuff of careful observation and reportage. Then the writer reminds us why we're reading about a cute little girl: "If she had ever grown up, people would have called her an Irish beauty."

"If she had ever grown up." A simple, devastating subjunctive. A condition contrary to fact.

The crux of what defines Lisa: a girl who never got the chance to grow up.

The description now takes an ugly turn: "The fine shoulder-length hair hadn't been shampooed for a long time; it was terribly tangled and matted. It hid a large red bruise on the right temple that would be discovered in the emergency room of the hospital, along with two other fresh bruises on her jaw and the back of her head."

It's hard to read such sentences, hard to entertain such a vivid picture of obscenity, the violation of a child's body. But if the writer wants readers to understand the *issue*, she must compel them to look at what they would rather turn away from: a little girl who has been beaten to death.

A good book is about the struggles of vividly drawn individuals, not issues. Through their travail, we comprehend the issues profoundly.

3. Use *indirection*. In writing about the behavior of Little League parents, for instance—immersing your reader convincingly in the world of summer twilight games, expensive uniforms, the drive to win, and one father's ambition for his ten-year-old son to one day earn a multimillion dollar salary in the major leagues—you may be addressing, with some irony, one aspect of "family values," a hackneyed catchall term flung about so carelessly by all parties in the last election. Or you may be addressing the genesis of male violence in our culture.

A good piece of writing fans out in many directions, discovering many truths. Some of those truths will constitute your thematic main line; others will be subsidiary. And your purported subject, Little League parents, keeps your reader firmly anchored in an entertaining and perhaps disturbing reality that he can see, hear, touch, taste, and smell—rather than the abstract op-ed forum of the talking head.

The subject then becomes more than itself—it becomes a live window into our world, an excuse for reflecting on the most significant matters of the human experience.

4. Dramatize the issue. Not in the sense of falsely hyping it with exaggerated staging, but in the sense of creating a dynamic story, a sequence of actions that moves forward toward consequence, holding us enthralled in the suspense of the scene.

Abraham Verghese's *The Tennis Partner* begins with a scene we all recognize from TV hospital shows: "He had started rounds at five-thirty in the morning, working his way from one room to the next, writing progress notes as he went. He was at the bedside of his last patient when his beeper went off."

So far, standard fare. The doctor is being paged. Then the story takes a leap into mystery, what screenwriter Robert McKee calls opening a "gap" between expectation and reality: "When he saw the number displayed, his throat constricted. A crimson flush spread up his neck, to his cheeks. The elderly woman with Crohn's disease and a short-bowel syndrome, who quite liked the blond, boyish doctor, looked up at him with concern. A minute ago he had been listening to her heart; now she could almost swear she heard his."

A routine page, something that must happen dozens of times a day, and this young doctor is coming unglued! What's going on here? Whose number is on the pager? What's happening on the other end of the phone to cause such visceral panic? The reader can't help but wonder—and turn the page to find out.

The drama continues: The young doctor stalls, scrawling case notes with a trembling hand, not answering the page from the pay phone nearby. Instead he takes the elevator five floors, walks down a corridor, and presents himself at Dr. Lou Binder's office. " 'What have you done?' Lou asked, softly."

The mystery deepens: Who is the young doctor? What *has* he done? Who is Lou?

The story careens along. Within the hour, still wearing surgical scrubs, the young doctor is put on a plane. At the Atlanta airport, he is collected by four other doctors. Only when he arrives at the Talbott-Marsh clinic do we finally realize that we have just witnessed an intervention: The young doctor is an addict. That's the issue.

But we're not thinking about the issue per se. We're not thinking about clinical words such as *intervention* and *substance abuse*. We're hooked on the drama of this young doctor's life, the mysterious phone call, the sudden flight without a change of clothes, the phalanx of surgeons who meet his plane, the fact that he is in deep trouble and has only one way out.

Verghese could have opened at the clinic and cited statistics about how doctors are especially vulnerable to substance abuse and outlined the program of recovery, but we would just be reading words. Now that he has led us dramatically inside the world of the recovering cocaine addict, we are curious to learn the context for his situation, all the back story of the young doctor's life and the facts about his condition, the clinic, the scope of the problem nationally.

Good drama always carries an emotional charge, and the charge comes from the struggle of an individual squaring off against antagonists out in the world and within himself. Not *villains*. That would be too easy. Your character struggles against competing values, contradictory visions, indifferently hostile natural forces, bureaucracy, personal flaws, indecision, characters who are convinced they are acting for the good even as they seek to destroy your protagonist. And sometimes against genuine evil.

As the Greeks understood, the more powerful the antagonist, the greater the test of character. In pushing character to the limit, amid all the complexity of life, you arrive at story. When the story has great consequences for the community—a city, a nation, the world—you've transcended the private moment. Now your story radiates outward—big, public, and universal.

Exercises

1. Keep a "Max Perkins" diary—one experience to a page, each page titled with an abstract rubric, such as "fear" or "injustice." After

a couple of weeks, sort them by rubric. Then try to link the experiences under one of the rubrics in a story or essay.

2. Choose a current public controversy that is typically cast as a dichotomy (Tax money should/should not be spent as school vouchers, to be redeemed at the school of the parents' choice) and recast it as a *paradox*—an issue with many facets, some of them contradictory. Then personalize the issue.

3

Subject and Point of View

In the foreword to *The Perfect Storm,* his best-selling account of the loss of the swordfishing boat *Andrea Gail* with all hands, Sebastian Junger acknowledges the special challenge of his subject: "Re-creating the last days of six men who disappeared at sea presented some obvious problems for me. On the one hand, I wanted to write a completely factual book that would stand on its own as a piece of journalism. On the other hand, I didn't want the narrative to asphyxiate under a mass of technical detail and conjecture."

He wanted to tell a gripping story, not write a dry, endlessly qualified, informational piece.

But he had a big problem.

Six men had disappeared in a monster storm hundreds of miles out in the dark Atlantic off Nova Scotia, leaving no record, no witnesses, no bodies, and no wreckage—though an Emergency Position Indicating Radio Beacon (EPIRB) and some fuel drums from the deck of the *Andrea Gail* were later recovered. In all likelihood, these were physical evidence that the boat had sunk, but strictly speaking, they were not hard proof of even that essential fact.

The last radio message from the *Andrea Gail* was received before the storm hit her: "She's comin' on, boys, and she's comin' on strong." Junger, then, had little to go on: He could reasonably assume the boat had sunk—the Coast Guard presumed her lost—but he could not say *where, when,* or in exactly *what manner* the *Andrea Gail* had gone down.

Had she rolled, pitchpoled, broken up in the fury of the gigantic breaking seas? Had she been swamped by a rogue wave?

How long had the men survived in the storm? Had they all died at once, or had some lived longer than others? Did they abandon ship first—drowning or freezing in the icy water—or go down quickly inside the boat?

Had her captain, Billy Tyne, played a heroic part in keeping the doomed vessel afloat as long as possible, or had he panicked, made mistakes that cost his crew their lives? Other vessels survived the storm. Could the *Andrea Gail* have survived it?

What did the men say and do in the last hours of their lives? Had they acted with courage or cowardice, or merely waited for the end, resigned to their fate? What, finally, were they made of?

These may seem like gruesome questions that seek lurid answers, but the power of any story lives in its details, the hard accurate image of specific action occurring at a certain precise moment. That's what sticks in the memory and will redeem a lonely death from obscurity.

How do you describe an event so the reader can see it vividly—when you didn't see it at all, and nobody who saw it lived to tell about it?

Junger writes that he toyed with the idea of fictionalizing minor parts of the story to give it a realistic, human flavor, but rejected that tactic because it "risked diminishing the value of whatever facts I *was* able to determine."

Then he makes an astonishing claim: "In short, I've written as complete account as possible of something that can never be fully known."

Not only can the event never be fully known, it can never be known at all, in the journalistic sense: No single detail of the sinking left any trace, let alone can it be verified. The pure actuality of the sinking of the *Andrea Gail* and the deaths of six men forms a hole at the center of the book. The account of that final voyage becomes, after a certain early point, an exercise in imagination and extrapolation.

So in one sense, Junger's promise to the reader is an elaborate ruse. If you think through his claim, it cannot stand up. Junger admits, in an interview with Ellen Barry in *The Boston Phoenix*, "I didn't even think I could finish it, because the story, journalistically, looked so impossible: a nonfiction book about a boat that disappears."

On the other hand—the one that matters—Junger has written a thrilling book, and I bet he got it mostly right (more on what he may not have gotten right in chapter ten). His story *feels* true. He makes clear his contract with the reader—these are the limits of what I know and how I know it—and the reader is then free to question any part of the story.

Since he couldn't verify the actual event at the center of the story, he verified as much as he could on the periphery of the event: three weather systems converging on radar and weatherfax; the accounts of Coast Guard officers attempting rescues during the storm; reports from other vessels that survived; background on each of the crewmen through interviews with the loved ones they left behind; the general routine of the commercial fishing community in Gloucester; the shipboard routine of a swordfishing boat; the history of the *Andrea Gail*, including a controversial refit that may have made her top-heavy and prone to capsize; personal observations of people and places; library research on wave motion, meteorology, and technical aspects of ship construction.

He contends, rightly, I think: "If I didn't know exactly what happened aboard the doomed boat, for example, I would interview people who had been through similar situations, and survived. Their experiences, I felt, would provide a fairly good description of what the six men of the *Andrea Gail* had gone through, and said, and perhaps even felt."

The key word: *perhaps.* He was doing all he could to get close to an event that would always remain an essential mystery, and the lesson is clear: Just because you can't prove every detail of a story doesn't mean you should not tell it.

Junger is only making an extreme version of the same claim all story writers make—*I'm going to attempt the impossible: to tell you the absolute truth based on my limited knowledge in an imperfect way.*

This is true whether your story is fiction or nonfiction. Ask yourself the following questions:

- What is my contract with the reader—that is, how much absolute knowledge am I claiming? What do I know, and how do I know it? What don't I know, can never know? How will I write about what I can't know?

- How much of my story depends on the interior lives of the characters—and how much on outside observation of events?
- How will I get inside my characters so that I can present their interior lives? If it's fiction, how can I imagine my way into that deep corner of human experience? If nonfiction, how can I draw parallels, inferences, analogies from what facts I do know?
- What is my relationship to this material? Why do I care? How will that passion help the work? How might it interfere with my ability to present it accurately, truthfully?

The kind of truth you tell will depend on your *narrative stance* toward the subject—especially if the subject is as elusive as Junger's—which begins with *point of view.*

The Storyteller's Point of View

Point of view sets written stories apart from plays and movies, which have no narrator.

In movies, we watch and listen as men and women move about through time and space, as a drama unfolds, but only in the rare—and usually clumsy—case of voice-over narration do we encounter point of view. The camera goes wherever the action is, an impersonal, voyeuristic eye. In the theater, the scene plays out before our eyes without interpretation: bodies in motion, voices in dialogue. In neither case can we have access to the interior lives of characters, except as we learn about them, always imperfectly, through their words and actions.

The writer can of course adopt this *dramatic*, or *objective*, point of view, limiting the reader's experience to only what can be seen or heard—no thoughts, dreams, feelings, memories, or aspirations. Ernest Hemingway used it in some of his early stories, such as "Hills Like White Elephants," contriving a flat, reportorial style that radiates cynicism and loss: "They sat down at the table and the girl looked across at the hills on the dry side of the valley and the man looked at her and at the table." But precisely because it feels hollow at the core, it's a dry point of view that wears out fast, especially over the long haul of a book.

And why surrender the most exciting and provocative tool in the writer's toolbox?

In written stories, interior life is usually paramount, because that is where we make contact with the mystery of human personality. Point of view determines what knowledge the narrator, and therefore the reader, has access to, what interior lives the reader will know (even if, as in nonfiction, it is the interior life of the narrator), what scenes are witnessed by the narrator—collectively one aspect of narrative stance.

The other two aspects are *psychic distance* and *tone*—we'll get to them.

There are three most commonly used points of view:

• First person—the *I* narrator, with access only to the narrator's interior world and the exterior world only as perceived by that narrator.

• Third-person omniscient—the godlike "all-knowing" narrator, with access to the interior lives of all the principal and supporting characters and the whole universe of time and space.

• Third-person limited or assigned—the narrator with access to only one viewpoint character's thoughts and feelings, externally limited in scope to that character's world.

But in fact point of view is slipperier than such a technical catalogue indicates—more of a continuum than a series of discrete perspectives. The above list is a only a starting point for the maturing writer.

For one thing, point of view can change. In a novel, for example, the third-person assigned point of view might alternate among several characters, changing by chapter. Though less common, alternating first-person narrators can create an effective dialogue, as in Larry Brown's excellent debut novel, *Dirty Work*, in which two Vietnam vets trade their life stories in a VA hospital ward. (The risk here is that the reader will find one more captivating than the other and lose patience with the less interesting voice.)

The narrative can modulate psychic distance so that a very intimate third-person limited point of view might at times turn almost *objective* (*dramatic*), closing out the reader from intimate contact with the character's interior life, allowing access only to what the character does or says out loud.

> David worried that he might fail at some crucial moment of the interview, say exactly the wrong thing, forget to sit up straight, break into a heavy sweat. It was no use—he'd never get the job.
>
> He shuffled along the snowy avenue, hands stuffed into his overcoat pockets, a gray, hunched figure against the bright shop windows dressed with Christmas lights. A woman carrying a red shopping bag smiled and wished him a merry Christmas, and David answered so softly he might as well not have spoken at all.

It's almost as if the camera is moving in and out—close-up, long shot, medium shot, and so on, going for contrasting, complementary effects in different frames of the scene.

First-person narration varies widely in terms of reliability: Any first-person narrator is limited by his or her biases, judgment, experience, character, and the limits of perception and memory; a first-person narrator may lie knowingly or not; may massage the truth; may choose to leave out crucial information for all sorts of reasons, some innocent, some self-serving, manipulative, or even malevolent; may twist language, misquote, exaggerate, dissemble, trick; may be confused, mentally deficient, drugged, drunk, or clinically insane; may be absolutely sincere and honest one minute and flagrantly false the next.

The classic warning comes from Nick Carraway, the deceptively forthcoming narrator of F. Scott Fitzgerald's glittering tale of seduction and ruin, *The Great Gatsby*: "Every one suspects himself of at least one of the cardinal virtues, and this is mine: I am one of the few honest people that I have ever known."

Whenever the perceptive reader encounters such a claim, he checks his pockets and counts the silver.

Even a nonfiction first-person narrator, like Capote, who chooses to leave himself out of his classic *In Cold Blood*, creates a different story than the one that would include him. It's a complex business. Point of view is almost never absolutely consistent.

Writers workshops tend to become obsessive about point of view, citing "violations" as if the writer had run a red light or been caught speeding, as if a perfectly maintained point of view somehow carries its own aesthetic value. But it is only a piece of technique, part of the apparatus of storytelling—a means, not an end in itself.

Think about how meter works in formal poetry. The poet discovers the normative meter for the poem—iambic pentameter, let's say. Yet if he or she gives us line after line of perfect, unvarying iambic pentameter, the poem is likely to seem slick or singsong. Usually it is the subtle break with meter in a certain line that both reinforces the meter and creates a particular effect: humor, surprise, solemnity, drama, conflict, or some other kind of emphasis. The exception to the pattern both reminds us of the pattern and makes us notice that it is broken, and broken for good reason.

In practice, while the writer has to establish some governing point of view, his first obligation is to the story. The larger the book, the more likely that the point of view will have to shift somewhat to accommodate the story. The place where it shifts, the nature and necessity of the shift, will both reinforce the pattern and break it—again, for good reason. The ambitious story will spill over any neat vessel designed to hold it.

The narrative of *War and Peace* is omniscient when it chooses to be, limited when it tires of omniscience. At times a historian-narrator interjects a kind of essay on the state of Europe, or the effectiveness of General Kutuzof's strategy against Napoleon's invading army. There are times when Tolstoy deserts his serial viewpoint characters altogether for an excursion into the mind of Napoleon. And there are long passages in which Tolstoy himself seems to be narrating, interjecting personal opinion and family memoir.

Sure, these are technical violations, likely to get Tolstoy slapped with a ticket in a writers workshop, but the reader doesn't care. Remember, a novel—indeed, any story—is an elaborate delivery system for knowledge both trivial (details of a character's dress) and profound (the nature of war). Narrative succeeds because events are told in the right order to create the desired effect. We need to know one thing to comprehend the next thing, and so on, in a matrix of accumulated knowledge, always moving forward.

In *War and Peace,* the point of view shifts at the moment when the reader needs access to certain crucial information unavailable from any other perspective. The story moves along brilliantly, following the action, and the reader adjusts because the power of the scenes and the commanding intelligence behind the words compel his attention.

In fact, especially in a long book, the reader may welcome the change of pace.

Forster offers this very sensible observation: "A novelist can shift his viewpoint if it comes off, and it came off with Dickens and Tolstoy. Indeed this power to expand and contract perception (of which the shifting viewpoint is a symptom), this right to intermittent knowledge—I find it one of the great advantages of the novel-form, and it has a parallel in our perceptions of life. We are stupider at some times than others; we can enter into people's minds occasionally but not always, because our own minds get tired; and this intermittence lends in the long run variety and colour to the experiences we receive."

"If it comes off." That's the writer's absolute defense against any criticism. As soon as the reader is jarred into noticing the shift, he experiences a kind of vertigo, a narrative motion sickness. He can't get his bearings. As Flannery O'Connor was fond of pointing out, "You can do anything you can get away with, but nobody has ever gotten away with much."

Shifting implies a reliable, sure-handed point of view to shift *from*—not just a random mishmash of perspectives. With every shift in point of view comes risk: Will I confuse the reader? Will the story lose momentum? Will the reader's emotional involvement with the characters cool off?

Novice writers frequently are infatuated with technique—the dazzling pyrotechnics of multiple narrators and shifty authorial intrusion that can be great fun for the writer and hell on the reader, and can mask a thin story. *Simpler* is sometimes harder.

Create no more narrative apparatus than you need to tell the story—

no complicated point-of-view shifting for its own sake—but never cheat the story in order to preserve a perfect apparatus.

Ask yourself the following questions:

• What is the governing point of view in my book? Why? What advantages does it offer over other possible points of view in telling this story? Will it alternate according to some regular pattern, as in a novel with serial viewpoint characters?

• Whenever I shift point of view, what is the reason for doing so, the desired effect? What is the risk?

• Must I shift point of view to achieve this effect?

The Authorial Narrator

The ultimate omniscient narrator is God—also the ultimate first-person storyteller. In the early tradition of the English novel—of Fielding and Thackeray—the author typically adopted an authorial omniscience, in effect becoming the god of his own novel, a first-person yet omniscient narrator, entering the novel at will to speak directly and confidentially to the reader, while maintaining an all-knowing stance across time and distance, and into the minds and hearts of all the principal characters.

In "The Nature and Aim of Fiction," O'Connor writes, "Fielding, for example, was everywhere in his own work, calling the reader's attention to this point and that, directing him to give his special attention here or there, clarifying this and that incident for him so he couldn't possibly miss the point. The Victorian novelists did this, too. They were always coming in, explaining and psychologizing about their characters."

Forster has no patience with such direct authorial intervention: "It is dangerous, it generally leads to a drop in the temperature, to intellectual and emotional laxity, and worse still to facetiousness, and to a friendly invitation to see how the figures hook up behind. . . . It is like standing a man a drink so that he may not criticize your opinions. With all respect to Fielding and Thackeray it is devastating, it is bar-parlour chattiness, and nothing has been more harmful to the novels of the past."

With some exceptions—*A Man in Full*, for instance, or *The Bonfire of the Vanities*, in which Tom Wolfe is everywhere, commenting on clothes, architecture, social customs, and so on, an obvious ventriloquist lifting each typecast character to his knee by turns—you won't see this authorial point of view much anymore, at least in American novels.

But notice that in long nonfiction narratives, such as Krakauer's *Into Thin Air*, which like all nonfiction is limited to the first-person point of view, the author-narrator may become very much like Fielding's chummy raconteur: In a technical sense, he has no choice. Through experience and research, he has an almost complete knowledge of the story, including events that happened far away and at a different time; and he chooses to focus on the other people in the story, not himself, so that the narrative of events *feels* like an omniscient third-person narrative, until the author inserts himself personally into the narrative—sometimes startling the reader, who has forgotten all about him.

It's not an exact parallel, because the nonfiction author has no access to the interior lives of the other actors in the story—he only makes it *seem* as if he does. And the Fielding narrator is essentially a comic narrator. Because of the tragic content of so much popular nonfiction—personal calamity, public disaster, true crime, war, survival and recovery from trauma, and so on—the author-narrator is likely to be engaging the reader on a more earnest level, like Conrad's Marlow in *Heart of Darkness*, who recounts a sort of malevolent ghost story to his fellow captive passengers to while away the time till turn of tide. And the confidential tone may actually be a welcome relief from the sheer factual reportage—the unemotional, objective writing from the outside.

Me, Myself, and I

The first person—*I*-based—point of view can be extremely effective: It is intimate, psychologically seductive, and engenders the trust we reserve for an eyewitness. The memoirist—even the fictional one—is a reporter and interpreter, a unique lens to offer observation and insight through memory's encounter with the language of reflection. First person can also cast an overwhelming subject in a human scale, making it accessible to a reader. Thus it has become ubiquitous in books of all kinds—some would say overused.

But the appeal of an eyewitness narrator remains compelling.

The Cold War is a huge and abstract subject—and so are its attendant themes of nuclear terror mixed with bureaucratic absurdity. But the memoir of a CIA operative telling the story of the Cold War in terms of night flights to West Berlin, clandestine meetings with shadowy men using passwords, and then filing travel vouchers full of convenient fictions in order to be reimbursed for the trips without revealing where he went or what he actually did might capture the danger as well as the absurdity on a workaday scale we can comprehend—with the authority of one who lived it—much more effectively than an academic appraisal by a historian at Yale. We would have the *mind* of the spy, caught in absurdity, patriotism, contradiction, danger, and workaday craft.

The first drawback of first person, especially in a factual personal account, is the temptation to self-importance, to claiming significance for events merely because they happened to you, to slighting other people and events in order to focus on your personal feelings. To narcissism—see Wolcott's critique in "Me, Myself, and I," discussed in the previous chapter. The first-person narrator is already so much in the story that it takes a determined effort to keep him from upstaging the other characters and events.

The second is more subtle: the temptation to slip too far into the indulgent authorial intruder, à la Fielding.

Remember Forster:

- Don't abuse the reader's trust with instructions on how to read your book, standing him to a drink so he won't criticize your work.
- Don't editorialize, preach, psychologize, or explain beyond what is necessary to provide a reasonable context.
- Tell the story first. Allow the reader the pleasure to share the interpretation, the understanding, the discovery of truth.

The third temptation is toward *myopia*—a closing down of the aperture of the narrative lens. The more introspective the narrator, the greater the risk of putting on such blinders, suffocating the reader with a context so limited, so psychologically contained, often glued in place with the present tense, that the effect is a kind of claustrophobia.

This sort of first-person narrator is so focused, he or she does not observe the world, other people, or the greater sweep of events. In certain minimalist stories that pursue household truths or psychological insight, this myopic narrator may be effective.

But notice that in long works that have held up over time, the first-person narrator is more likely to be alert, focused outward, aware of the world, an energetic and accurate observer, full of knowledge and information, the crossroads character who becomes a matchmaker for other characters and in whom the others confide, who always manages to be in the most interesting place at exactly the moment when something exciting is happening there: Ishmael, Nick Carraway, Huckleberry Finn, Ralph Ellison's Invisible Man, Charles Johnson's Rutherford Calhoun in *Middle Passage*.

The novel is never ostensibly *about* such a narrator/character—like Nick Carraway, he may be hardly noticeable amid the action—yet of course in another way it is all about him. He brings a large vision to the story: the author's knowledge plus a willingness to stretch what he knows as far as the reader will believe it.

This is the classic novelistic narrator—the *comprehensive first person*. In a way, it comes full circle back to the authorial narrator with an important difference: It is driven by the requirements of the story, not the author's whimsy. The comprehensive first-person narrator's insights may seem almost omniscient, may even strain credulity, but credulity never quite breaks, and they remain the narrator's, not the author's.

The comprehensive first-person narrator may also at times be self-reflective. Again, narration exists along a continuum—at one end self-absorption, at the other a nearly effaced narrator looking outward. A narrator tends to be more one kind of narrator than another, and differences of degree are important.

The Factual Narrator

All nonfiction is essentially written in the first person, though the point of view can *seem* to be omniscient or limited. The author-narrator can be very much a part of the action, or he can slip off into the shadows, unnoticed, reporting as a disembodied voice from the sidelines.

The author is the real-life first-person narrator—either entirely self-reflective (myopic) or focused on the world (comprehensive) or at some point on the continuum between the two.

In her remarkable book *Wind: How the Flow of Air Has Shaped Life, Myth, and the Land,* Jan DeBlieu alternates between a very personal *I*-narrator recounting, say, her riding out a hurricane in her new home on Roanoke Island, North Carolina, and a more reportorial narrator, much as Krakauer does, although with more patterned regularity. The effect is a charming intimacy coupled with the satisfaction of learning fascinating and complex history, mythology, and science.

In the nonfiction novel, drama and story may overshadow an absolute sense of creating the truthful record of an event. But even in the nonfiction novel, the *apparent* third-person narrator of fact can only efface his or her own participation in the drama until the reader effectively forgets there is an intervening narrator (Capote's *In Cold Blood.*) It's not a true third-person narrator, though it *reads* like one.

That is, in such books, the reader is under the illusion that an objective, all-knowing narrator is telling the story—that the story is creating itself without any bias. But as we've seen, that's impossible: The narrator of a factual story is always a real individual with a point of view and a distinctive personality—the author. There's no way around it. In Capote's case, he—the author—was also a participant in the story. But the author can elect *not* to write about his own participation. He can pretend to be objective, an all-knowing presence. Even the simple tactic of not using *I* can make the reader forget that he is reading one person's account.

Think of this as the effaced narrator, similar to the one used in fiction. As Jerome Stern explains in *Making Shapely Fiction,* "*Effaced* narrators make the narration as invisible as possible so that the story seems to be simply telling itself." In other words, the reader notices the story, not the storyteller. You'll notice this is not far different from the reportorial stance journalists usually take in covering stories—or writing books about events of public interest in which they were not participants but detached, professional observers.

Of course, in nonfiction, there always is a storyteller, and because the story is factual, the nature and aims of that storyteller matter in determining the truthfulness of the story. A detached journalist probably belongs outside the story most of the time—his or her very detachment explains the agenda of the work, which is significant for reasons outside the life of the author. In Capote's case, though, we're getting the truth, but not the whole truth. What's left out—Capote's intimate involvement with the characters and events—may matter a great deal to how we interpret those events.

Fiction, by contrast, is after a different sort of truth. We expect characters and events to be manipulated or invented out of whole cloth, and the narrator is equally invented, an artistic construct.

In the fictional novel, the omniscient narrator allows the novelist large scope (Mailer's *The Naked and the Dead*), in which he is able to delve into the hearts, motives, and memories of a small cadre of soldier characters, testing the effect of combat on their personalities from the inside while moving between a lost patrol and headquarters, many miles apart. First-person narration would have skewed the novel toward a single personality, losing the ensemble nature of the work, as would third-person limited. Both would have limited the geography of the novel, which is essential to the irony: a place of danger (the patrol) juxtaposed against a place of safety (headquarters).

Fiction's greatest value is that it can pretend convincingly to know for sure what goes on in a character's soul, and one of the chief decisions a fiction writer makes is which characters' souls to explore and reveal.

But the nonfictional narrator can't know what goes on in the souls of his "characters"; he can only surmise based on actions, gestures, and speech.

The exception, as usual, is Tom Wolfe, who claims to be able to project himself into the mind of his subject, as he did in a *New York Herald-Tribune* piece on rock producer Phil Spector—"the first time

I actually went inside somebody else's mind," Wolfe reported in an interview in *The New Fiction: Interviews With Innovative American Writers*. Spector was seated on an airplane taxiing for takeoff when he suddenly jumped up and insisted the plane stop and let him off. Without interviewing him about the incident, Wolfe intuited what had been going through Spector's mind so convincingly that Spector himself later confirmed the accuracy of Wolfe's "projection."

But for nonfiction writers who lack Wolfe's uncanny intuition, narrative stance depends much more on the second and third elements: psychic distance and tone. And again, these are not necessarily all-or-nothing decisions. Psychic distance may be modulated, and tone may evolve.

In *What Lisa Knew*, Joyce Johnson at times speaks as a first-class investigative reporter—observant, alert to factual detail, and objective, as in this passage describing the arrest of Hedda Nussbaum, Joel Steinberg's live-in lover, whom he has abused horribly: "By 12:45, Hedda Nussbaum was standing in a viewing room at the Sixth Precinct in front of a video unit sent over from the D.A.'s office at the request of Detective Lackenmeyer. There was a stark white wall behind her. The first shots were closeups of her face, the color of the bruises leached out by the lights."

The narrator is almost a camera herself, recording the moment, picking up details such as the white wall and the lights that emphasize the washed-out quality of the scene.

Then she moves in just a little closer to her subject, describing her with the aid of apt metaphor and offering a nudge toward interpretation: "The impression is one of terrible pallor; the skin seems only a shade less gray than the hair. The nose with its bandages stripped away is pulverized and scabrous. The lips are thickened, distorted. It's as if a roller has passed over her face, flattening it. In Hedda Nussbaum's eyes, there is no agony, but something worse—a look of utter indifference."

By the end of the scene, the narrator is no longer effaced but emerges in plain view—as Nussbaum herself is revealed, part by part, in all her battered nakedness—talking directly to the reader: "The Hedda tape has an awful power—far beyond any still photos of Hedda

Nussbaum. The camera work is so absolutely frontal, so raw and devoid of the mitigations of art [read: aesthetic distance]. This is the whole truth about this woman, it tells you. How can you not trust it? This is all you need to know."

The brilliance of the scene—mirrored in countless other passages throughout the book—lies in the way knowledge is revealed to the reader. Not just the *content* knowledge—the progress of events, the crime and its aftermath—but also the knowledge of who the narrator is and where she stands. She reveals the subject first faithfully and accurately, and as we move closer in she begins to reveal herself, her attitude. By the time she does, we have the same evidence she does, and we are ready to accept—or at least entertain seriously—her interpretation, because we have had the chance to form our own.

This modulation of psychic distance that reveals attitude keeps the book from clopping along in a clinical monotone; it changes the pitch of the writing, keeps it from flattening out, quickens and slows the pace and then quickens it again, endows it with a human—and humane—intelligence.

Johnson's modulating narrative stance preserves the dignity of the murdered girl, the battered woman who may have had a part in her death, the writer herself, and the reader. One reads with compassion and deep respect for the terrible mystery of human violence, rather than for prurient stimulation. We can't be mere spectators to misery, viewing it from a safe remove.

Like it or not, the narrative stance draws us in as participants—and thereby makes us share responsibility.

Attitude and Tone

So along with point of view and psychic distance, the third, related, aspect of narrative stance is the *attitude* the author, through the narrator, expresses toward the material. This is reflected as tone in the writing. Word choice, selection, and arrangement of parts—especially juxtaposition—contribute to tone.

If writing has a morality, it is expressed in tone.

For example, in Bob Woodward and Scott Armstrong's book about the Supreme Court, *The Brethren*, there is a clear persistent tone of censure and disapproval for the pettiness, lack of intellectual rigor, and illiberality of most of the justices, especially Chief Justice Warren Burger, though the book is written "objectively"—that is, as a reporter would write, leaving out explicit opinion and backing up every quote with at least one source.

How is this possible? The devil, as usual, is in the details.

Soon after Burger assumes leadership of the court, for instance, he comes to believe that law clerks exercise too much power over the decisions of the Court. They accomplish this through an "underground inter-chamber communications system that Burger viewed as a rumor mill." Through their clerks, other justices know Burger's positions in advance and can outmaneuver him at Conference, where opinions are decided, and he determines to restore confidentiality through a memo to his own clerks prohibiting them from talking about confidential matters to the other justices' clerks.

Woodward and Armstrong report all this accurately—though notice their characterization of Burger's point of view: *underground* hints at paranoia, and *rumor mill* connotes a disparaging opinion of clerkly discussions on Burger's part.

After the clerks receive the memo, we're told, "So, Burger's clerks were permitted to talk only to each other."

But in fact the memo, as quoted by the authors, says no such thing—that's Woodward and Armstrong's construction of it. All Burger prohibited, technically, was discussion of his own opinions and confidential conversations within his own chambers—on the face of it, a reasonable position for the highest judge of the highest court in the land, whose charge is to set the tone for its decision making. It can be argued that it is an unproductive or wrong position, but such cannot be *assumed*. Yet it is, by the very absolute language—not of Burger's memo, but of the authors.

We read on about the clerks: "They *realized* that they had just been dealt out of much of the fun and meaning of their clerkship, head-on discussions about votes and positions. They *knew* that traditionally clerks communicated openly and freely with their peers *in order to better serve their Justices*." (italics mine)

Notice the verbs: *realized*, not *thought*; *knew*, not *believed*. The clerks' position is being offered—fair enough—but it is couched in verbs that indicate they are accurately interpreting reality, not forming an opinion that might be in error. The authors clearly agree with them—even to the extent of attributing to them, without comment, altruistic motives ("to better serve their Justices") when we have already learned earlier in the book that these same clerks are adversarial to Burger. In fact, by the authors' own account, the clerks *are* trying to undermine Burger.

Clearly the authors believe that one way of "serving" Burger is to help modify his "wrong" opinions through collusion with the other clerks.

Word choice—diction—plays a crucial role in coloring the facts, in manipulating the reader's impression of events.

Woodward and Armstrong are not unusual in forming a definite attitude about their subject—*nor are they wrong to do so.* The reader expects the author to have an attitude. Without it there is no narrative stance, no moral context in which to understand the story. In this case, the authors formed their attitude about the various justices during the course of exhaustive research that, as they report in their introduction, included transcripts of two hundred interviews as well as thousands of pages of internal court memoranda, diaries, letters, notes taken at conferences, case assignments, unpublished and published drafts of opinions—enough documentary evidence to fill eight file drawers.

The key point: They arrived at their attitude *after* doing their research. They did not approach their subject with prejudice. This open-minded approach allowed them the chance to discover their narrative stance—so that in the writing they could choose the language that accurately captured the *sense* of their research beyond the literal words of a given memo.

It allows them, with some confidence, to read between the lines.

In *What Lisa Knew*, Joel Steinberg, the convicted killer of six-year-old Lisa, emerges as a monster who regularly beat his wife and killed the child entrusted to his care, freebasing cocaine while she lay beaten senseless, dying on his living room floor. Johnson addresses the question of attitude directly: "To understand how a Steinberg could exist in our very midst requires us to look very deeply into ourselves and into our own experiences and histories as children and parents. It is much less unsettling to decide he is not like us at all.

"When we call a man a monster, we are saying that he exists somewhere beyond the pale of humanity, and that if we encountered him out there, we would be overwhelmed by his force. A monster is totally remorseless. It devours and lays waste according to its insatiable needs and does so without guilt. A monster has no history other than the history of its heinous acts. It simply is what it does. It is what it is. Therefore, we do not need to understand it."

"Nonetheless," she goes on—significantly—"the public did have a deep, inchoate understanding of Steinberg. . . ."

It would be too easy just to make him a monster, an anomaly. Johnson does not abdicate her responsibility to understand, however imperfectly, the monster. Like the public who are treated to one lurid tabloid headline after another, Johnson must struggle to terms with a human being capable of such an obscene crime. She cannot merely assume a tone of moral superiority. That would let her—and the reader—off the hook. But you don't write such a story to let the reader off the hook. She is trying to tell the truth, and to do so she must do her best to comprehend Steinberg, the monster—who he is, what motivates him, what made him.

And how much of him is in each of us.

The lesson: To judge, you must first understand, in a profound way. It is not enough to point out the villain: You must struggle toward insight, for your reader's sake.

Ask yourself the following questions:

• What is my attitude toward my subject, toward my characters? Is the attitude justified by honest, thorough, open-minded research? Or am I simply following my prejudices, leaping to conclusions?

• How much and at what point do I want my attitude to color the work? Remember, insisting the reader share your attitude—without convincing him through the details and events of the story first—can backfire, leading your reader to stubbornly resist your interpretation.

• In the language of my story, how does my attitude show through?

Am I unconsciously "loading" the story for or against a given character, toward a given conclusion? Again, is this fair and accurate, based on my large knowledge of the subject?

Attitude in Fiction

John Steinbeck left behind one of the most revealing records of how a novelist creates a big book. *Journal of a Novel,* a series of letters addressed to his longtime friend and editor Pascal (Pat) Covici, tracks his daily sessions writing *East of Eden,* perhaps the darkest and most troubling novel he ever wrote—more than ten years after *The Grapes of Wrath.*

In it, he sought to retell the story of Cain and Abel "against the background of the country I grew up in and along the river I know and do not love very much." The book was intended as a legacy to his two sons, Tom and John—in an early draft, there were sections addressed directly to them—and he wrote it like a man with a mission: "And so I will tell them one of the greatest, perhaps the greatest story of all—the story of good and evil, of strength and weakness, of love and hate, of beauty and ugliness. I shall try to demonstrate to them how these doubles are inseparable—how neither can exist without the other and how out of their groupings creativeness is born."

East of Eden tells the story of two brothers, Adam and Charles Trask, who become estranged over a dangerous woman, Cathy Ames. In the course of the story, Adam and Cathy marry, and she gives birth to twin sons, Cal and Aron—then deserts the family. The volatile, sometimes violent relationships between the two sets of brothers form the double core of the book. After a brief opening history of the settlement of the Salinas Valley, part one of the novel takes place in Connecticut, the other three parts in California. The fortunes of a second family, the Hamiltons, Steinbeck's own forebears, intertwine with the Trasks', adding a cast of secondary characters that often "star" in their own chapters.

Steinbeck obviously was aware of the challenge of such complexity—several generations of intermingled characters sprawling across a continent from the Civil War to the twentieth century, addressing biblical themes. And he knew his own temptations as a writer well enough to announce a very deliberate plan of style, directly appealing to his audience: "One can go off into fanciness if one writes to a huge nebulous group but I think it will be necessary to speak very straight and clearly and simply if I address my book to two little boys who will be men before they read my book."

Likewise, Steinbeck was conscious of tone before he ever wrote a word, beginning the project in great humility, a sense of wonderment almost, that carries over into the novel. "We now come to the book. It has been planned a long time. I planned it when I didn't know what it was about. I developed a language for it that I will never use. This seems such a waste of the few years a man has to write in. And still I do not think I could have written it before now," he confides early in the *Journal*.

He goes on: "This book will be the most difficult I have ever attempted. Whether I am good enough or gifted enough remains to be seen."

The author's voice—and his attitude—are evident in the novel in at least two ways. One is in the overtly authorial passages of history and family background, as in this passage about the settlement of the Salinas Valley: "Then the hard dry Spaniards came exploring through, greedy and realistic, and their greed was for gold or God. They collected souls as they collected jewels."

There's no pretense of objectivity in such passages: This is the judgment of a man who has pondered this material all his adult life.

Then, in dramatic sections in which his fictional characters take over, Steinbeck addresses the reader directly, as in the chapter introducing Cathy Ames: "I believe there are monsters born in the world to human parents. Some you can see, misshapen and horrible, with huge heads or tiny bodies; some are born with no arms, no legs, some with three arms, some with tails or mouths in odd places. . . . And just as there are physical monsters, can there not be mental or psychic monsters born?" Cathy Ames, he pronounces, was such a monster.

The crux of the book is an argument over the nature of free will, the moral choice with which each human being struggles. This is the big stuff of the book—the profound theme that makes this more than a novel about a couple of disaffected brothers. This great theme is why the book makes a difference. Steinbeck is using these brothers and their world to test the whole moral underpinning of the Judeo-Christian tradition.

In his deliberate way, Steinbeck is exempting Cathy Ames from the moral argument: She, the catalyst for much of the evil in the novel, has no choice. Evil simply exists *a priori*, a given premise for life on earth—as it does in the Old Testament—and the important thing is how the rest of us behave in a world that contains evil. In fact, without evil, we would have no chance to behave morally—for we would have no choice. And choice—free will—lies at the crux of Steinbeck's theme.

The reader can't help but notice a strong parallel between Steinbeck's novel and Tolstoy's *War and Peace*. Both have cast their characters into a complex moral universe in which a big argument is going on about whether fate or free will controls the forces of history. Both shift point of view in order to maintain contact with the interior lives crucial to a given passage. Both enter their novels in reflective moments to comment, ponder, and provide context—not in the comic "bar-parlour" manner of Fielding but in the weightier, more philosophical voice of a Conrad or a Melville.

You can argue that a more adept writer would have allowed his characters to play out the biblical drama without commentary. But Steinbeck, in writing to his sons, was harking back to an older tradition, the tradition of the Bible itself, which intersperses story with lesson.

He understands right from wrong, and that either is always a choice but hardly ever a clear choice, and he wants to pass on this knowledge to his sons. Steinbeck maintains a fairly intimate psychic distance, though at regular intervals he pulls back and offers the long view; and his technical point of view, while it shifts to follow the story, is ultimately encompassed by a first-person narrator, the author himself, recounting the story of his country and himself. A narrator essentially right out of the oral tradition—a storyteller to his sons doing what storytellers have done since the dawn of human time.

His comprehensive first-person narrator, which contains all the other narrators, has gone out of fashion, but in some ways it is the most natural and effective way to tell a novel.

His attitude derives from his hard-won beliefs, and it carries to the reader in the tone of the writing.

So the fiction writer brings an attitude toward made-up characters and scenes. Because we think of fiction as sheer invention, it's not always apparent even to the writer that in the fictional world the writer is expressing his deepest beliefs and doubts, his judgments, fears, preoccupations, and biases. His attitude is never really neutral.

Again, the reader would not want it to be. Presented with a fictional universe, the reader might need some centering, a moral compass. When that compass is missing, when we read, say, a tale of serial murder presented in a tone that glamorizes mayhem, revels in gore and violence, we may balk. We might not even understand what troubles us. It is the tone—an attitude that we have trouble integrating into our own set of values.

Even when you think you are being neutral, your fiction is projecting an attitude, even if it is an attitude by default. Pay attention to this. If the attitude, the tone, creates an effect different from the one you intended, change it.

The more troubling the material, the greater attention you must pay to tone: Every nuance will be magnified. The reader needs to know in every line that you, the author, are aware of the gravity of your material. If it is rough, so be it: The reader will face the unpleasant, the difficult, even the hideous, the monstrous, if he can be reassured he will be enlightened, not merely shocked by the experience.

Exercises

1. Watch a public figure deliver a speech in person or on TV. Being completely factual and objective (third person), briefly describe the public figure's dress and manner, first from the stance of an admirer, then from the stance of a detractor. Be concrete and specific, and do not use the word *I*.

2. Choose an important episode from your life and write it as narrated by (1) a third-person omniscient narrator and (2) a first-person narrator other than yourself.

3. Write a short scene about an abhorrent act so that the tone conveys your attitude about the act.

4. Write a short scene from a very self-absorbed first-person point of view; write the same scene using a comprehensive first-person narrator.

4

Research

If you're going after big ideas, universal themes, you have to know—really *know*—what you're writing about. The best books of this type—nonfiction and fiction—are firmly grounded in research. Research encompasses everything the writer does, accidentally or deliberately, randomly or systematically, to put him in direct touch with his subject.

While memory and reflection always play important roles in writing, research focuses the writer *outside* himself, beyond personal perspective, toward the facts of the world. In this way it opens up the subject. This tension between the personal voice and a larger context—social, historical, scientific, moral—drives the classic books in our literature.

Sometimes you've been researching a subject long before you realize you will write about it, or what form the writing will take. Some books you have been researching all your life. Sometimes your life experience has been your research.

Without Frank McCourt's deep familiarity with the specific, living detail of Depression-era Brooklyn and the slums of Limerick, Ireland, *Angela's Ashes* would not hold us so powerfully in the world where young Frank and his family endure so much suffering. Without the carefully researched background of how the banks and factory farms drove the Okies off their land, Steinbeck's *The Grapes of Wrath* would narrow its scope—our sense of large, impersonal forces pressing down on the Joad family would be diminished, and the novel would lose some of its epic power.

Tolstoy knows how armies maneuver in the field: He was an artillery officer with an insatiable curiosity, who spent his leave time exploring Napoleonic battlefields and interviewing soldiers. Dickens knows firsthand the secrets of inner-city London during the Industrial Revolution. Joyce Johnson knows the inside of a police interrogation room, a courtroom trial, a hospital emergency room. Jon Krakauer knows the history of every expedition that ever attempted to scale Mount Everest—he also knows what it feels like to suffer exhaustion, brain-numbing cold, and acute hypoxia six miles high on the windswept mountain with night coming on.

To write about big issues and themes—even in projects of a very personal nature—requires knowledge: specific facts, hard information, an accurate sense of history and context for your subject. Not just the stuff that dreams are made of—but the stuff of the world.

Even a memoir may require that you revisit places from your earlier life; interview old friends or family members; study photo albums, letters, and diaries; confirm or debunk family myths through courthouse or parish records. You want knowledge against which to test your personal intuition.

Some of that knowledge can be academic, gleaned from reading and analyzing data, listening to experts talk. But compelling books always leave us with the sense that the subject entered the writer body and soul—as visceral, instinctive, experiential knowledge.

While researching a piece about B-24 Liberator bomber crews in the South Pacific during World War II, I read detailed books about the aircraft, studied—through a magnifying glass—my father's photographs of his old bomber group, even built a model airplane to get an accurate sense of where the various crew members manned their stations on a bomb run. But it was not until I crawled inside an actual restored Liberator at an air show that I realized physically the most important "fact" of all: claustrophobia. The pilot's seat felt child-sized, hemming in my elbows, cramping my shoulders. The bombardier's "greenhouse"—the glass bubble at the nose of the plane—felt equally cramped, as well as nakedly exposed. Suited in electrically warned flight overalls and heavy fleece jackets, ten men had to wriggle into spaces so small that once they were installed at their stations they could hardly move. Inside, the plane seemed tiny, almost toylike.

Whatever was coming at them, they were stuck in place. They had to just sit there and take it.

And at that moment it dawned on me how very far away I would always be from understanding, in the most significant way, what those young bomber crews endured in combat. I could never know what it felt like to be flying through a flak bursts or a fighter attack, or feel the plane suddenly bounce with the release of the heavy bombs, or know the fear those young men lived with for months on end, or the nightmares that haunted them all their lives.

But the research wasn't a failure: In fact, one important function of research is to inspire you with a humility about your subject, reminding you that you can get only so close and no closer to perfect understanding, forcing your imagination therefore to work harder, forcing you to deeper research. Keeping you honest.

You must inspire the reader with the confidence that you know the fascinating inside story, that you're not just faking it. Not just that you can recite facts—but that you *feel* the truth of the subject, physically, emotionally, spiritually. That it has somehow entered you, changed you. It's not a superficial knowledge, the kind that wins trivia tests. It's something deeper, something about which you finally have come to a beginning of understanding. Even in a novel, your world has to be so convincingly grounded in the facts and feeling of the real world that the reader doesn't doubt it for an instant.

You're not a cocky expert. You're a captivated student of the subject—and your passion is contagious.

Research brings knowledge to your writing, where it mingles with personal experience, and intellectual and aesthetic judgment to create an authentic voice.

Research often can be a creative process—we don't always know what we're looking for until we find it. Start researching one subject, and you may discover in the course of your research a much more fascinating line of inquiry. The key is to be receptive to such insights, rather than so narrowly targeted that you miss them.

Good research can add knowledge, power, and authenticity to the writing, helping readers understand and more fully participate in the world the writer is creating.

Research Can Take You Beyond Cliché

Good research can take the writer beyond clichés, generalizations, oversimplifications—all the usual pitfalls in "issue" writing. It takes you beyond first impressions, conventional wisdom, easy assumptions you aren't even aware you are making.

Rule of thumb: If any subject seems simple, yielding neatly to your complete understanding, that's a strong signal that you don't know enough about it yet.

The case that inspired Johnson's *What Lisa Knew* was at first reported as a typical case of a violent, disturbed man (Joel Steinberg) beating his lover (Hedda Nussbaum) and fatally abusing Lisa, the child they had illegally "adopted." Many in the conventional press, including columnist Jimmy Breslin, assumed Nussbaum's victimhood at the outset and rushed to her defense. She seemed the prototypical "battered woman" we recognize from so many TV movies-of-the-week: emotionally beaten down, psychologically paralyzed, unable to act in self-defense, afraid for her life. Blameless.

The roles were all familiar. Reporters were certain they had seen this story all too often before.

But in Johnson's exhaustively researched account, Nussbaum emerges not as a victim but as a villain in her own right—a calculating, self-serving cocaine addict who is an equal partner with Steinberg in their sadomasochistic adventures and very likely the beating death of Lisa. Nussbaum's "battered woman" is more complicated than the familiar victim, and more troubling, defying stereotype.

Resisting what must have been a natural tendency, as a woman and mother, to empathize automatically with Nussbaum, Johnson delves into the deep background of the affair—going back years, beyond public statements and even trial testimony—interviewing neighbors, friends, co-workers, hospital staff, police officers; viewing the video-tape of Nussbaum's arrest and booking and of the Steinberg trial, attentive to all the nuance of body language and tone of voice; seeking answers from professionals in child abuse and mental health. Coaxing the horrible affair to reveal its deepest patterns.

She reads between the lines of the record: What doesn't Nussbaum do or say that an innocent victim would? What's not in the record that she could reasonably expect to find there? What's wrong with this picture? Piece by meticulous piece, she reconstructs the chronology of events, the context of the crime, until we can't help but share her conclusion—even as we realize that we've never heard this horrifying story before, anywhere, ever. It's one of a kind.

Johnson did not use her research to flesh out a preconceived outline of what the story was. She listened to the research—and what she heard were not just the novel details of a familiar, stereotypical story, but the arc of a very different story altogether.

Designing a Research Plan

Your genius will partly reside in being able to find what you need to find, before you ever write, and on a timetable that ensures you don't go broke doing it—making a research plan, including a timetable and a budget. It can be as simple as a scrawled list of primary sources that you must consult or as complicated as an annotated calendar that will dictate your life for the next two years. Brief or detailed, it can remind you of what you'll eventually need to learn to accomplish the project.

If you can't afford to do the essential research, if you don't have time to learn what you need to learn, the book will not happen.

The plan is a starting point, a working paper to be refined and revised as your project proceeds, but it can keep you on track. Because the nature of research is discovery, the plan will evolve. At times it will seem like no plan at all, just a muddling helter-skelter of jumbled cross-referencing and tracking down thin leads. Messy and full of digressions, blind alleys, wasted trips. It's a dynamic process. You can't ever be as methodical as you'd like—and probably that's a good thing.

For every dead end, there will be an unexpected discovery. It's almost never the thing you expected to find that enlivens the book. It's the accidental find, the surprising fact that ambushes you, the piece of evidence that changes your mind in some basic way. Research can become its own drama—full of recognitions and reversals, mystery begetting mystery.

Your research may take you into archives, onto the Internet, out into the field. You may need interviews, photographs, authentic artifacts. You may need to go someplace simply for the experience of being in that place. You may need to exercise your memory, mine your past, revisit old notebooks, reexplore the geography of your former life. You may need to master at least the basics of a new discipline—physics, child psychology, meteorology. There's no one right way; there's only the way that's right for your project.

Jan DeBlieu, author of *Wind: How the Flow of Air Has Shaped Life, Myth, and the Land*, understood the challenge of her subject—an obvious subject in one sense, but also a literally ethereal one. The very ubiquity of wind, the inexhaustible scope of the subject, made the prospect of researching and planning a book about it daunting. How do you get your arms around air?

She recalls, "The first thing I wanted to do was make absolutely certain that I could do the book, because it was something of a stretch for me. I mean, how the hell do you write a book about the wind? And can I really do this? All the questions that always confront an author, magnified a bit just because it was such a weird, unusual project. And the fact that I wanted to put a personal voice in it made it that much more difficult."

In other words, she started out by asking the most basic question of all: Can I do this book?

And to answer it, she first had to address its corollary: *How* can I do this book? As a practical matter, how can I capture this elusive subject? That's every writer's essential question, because all subjects worth writing about are elusive in some important way. And in figuring out an answer, she is really doing structural work, sketching a rough, preliminary blueprint of what such a book might look like—much as an architect might rough out a design before deciding whether a project is feasible, given a certain location, timeline, and budget. The blueprint will evolve and change, but at least the concept has begun to take definite shape as more than a daydream.

During this preliminary phase, DeBlieu did four very sensible things:

• Surveyed books in print to determine if anybody else had already appropriated her subject. She found one recent book that was purely scientific and objective in tone—a very different approach from the one she planned to take, which would integrate personal experience with science, mythology, and history.

• Visited the Library of Congress—not once, but three times—making notes about every reference to wind that she could find. From this archival foundation research emerged certain natural categories, and she began to design her book: a chapter on mythology, on animals who live in wind, on harnessing the wind for human use, on wind as a destructive force, and so on. The archives also suggested sources: who was doing cutting-edge research in physics, engineering, biology, and psychology on wind-related problems.

• Revisited an essay she had written years before about the wind—which encapsulated her passion for the subject—and revised it thoroughly as the opening chapter, the one that would set the tone of the book. Then she drafted all the sections about her personal experiences with the wind on the Outer Banks of North Carolina—writing she could do from memory, from notes she already had, from observations she could make close to home without an extravagant investment in travel.

• Put out the word: "I began telling people right from the get-go that I was writing a book about the wind and collecting their stories about wind. And that was really fun, and it helped shape the book. . . . For instance somebody told me about a rock in Alberta where people go to commit suicide when the poison winds called the chinook winds happened to be blowing. Somebody else told me about a researcher they knew in Florida who had proved through computer models that when Moses and the Israelites were fleeing Egypt, a strong east wind really could have parted the Red Sea." Each story led to potential interviews and further research, and her main challenge was deciding which of the hundreds of stories to pursue.

These four tactics are actually special cases of a general template that can be useful for any writer embarking on an ambitious project.

• Survey the books in print. Find out if anyone else has already written your book.

• Immerse yourself in the archives. It's not the glamorous part of research, but it can be the most economical and rewarding, especially as you are designing your research plan and refining your subject. The archives can provide a foundation for other facets of research: interviews, site visits, primary documents, and so on. They can also provide natural organizing principles.

• Inventory the work you have already done on the subject that might prove valuable to this project: notes, essays, published articles or stories, an old first draft in a drawer. Make new notes on relevant memories, personal experiences, any material close to home. These are your personal "archive."

• Cast your net farther afield. Put out the word to those who can help you find what you need. Using your archival foundation, track down the people mentioned in the archive—including other writers and researchers. Using the bibliographies of scientists, scholars, researchers, track down *their* sources—other books, papers, institutions, people. Each connection will lead to other connections.

One overarching principle: Organize your research. Create a filing system that makes sense to you, and sort your notes, photos, documents, and transcripts into the appropriate folders. Label audio- and videotapes and store them in a secure place. After a hectic outing, take a few minutes—or hours—to collate your notes, maybe even to rewrite them more legibly.

Don't just make notes—make notes on why you are making notes: How does this piece of information fit into my overall purpose? What was I thinking when I saved this newspaper clipping? You are not writing just for you—or for who you are now. You are writing for the you that will have to read and make sense of the material you've collected many months or even years from now. Don't be cryptic. Be systematic.

Terrific research is worthless if you can't find the piece of it you need, or having found it, can't make sense of it. Get in the habit of labeling, filing, making clear notes and redundant copies of crucial data—and keeping those copies separate from the originals, in a safe locale where you can get them. This habit will not only make it possible for you to write a better book; it may also guard you against legal challenges to the accuracy of what you eventually write.

Getting Started

Don't expect the research to unspool in a seamless, perfect line. Be prepared to muddle around awhile, browsing, even at times lost, trying to get your bearings. The only way to learn how to research your big book is to start researching it—and whenever possible to learn from your mistakes.

If you don't know where to start, start somewhere.

Think of your research experience as a kind of work-in-progress. You're not going to get it perfect in the first draft. You're going to make mistakes, waste valuable time in minor archives—time that could be better spent in major collections, only you don't know that yet. You're going to conduct a lousy interview, ask the wrong question, infer the wrong truth from a fact. You're going to overlook the obvious, get blindsided by new information, feel confused, dismayed, disappointed.

But it's okay. The indispensable virtue of a good researcher is persistence—a dogged determination to hunt down what you need to know wherever it lies hidden. If you persist, you will probably discover more than you ever dreamed possible—about *any* subject.

But you can't persist if you don't *start*. Break through the paralyzing inertia—an inertia we all experience at the beginning of a daunting project—and do the first thing: Go to the library or the Internet and find out some basic facts; call up a source and conduct a foundation interview, one that will help you get a handle on your project; visit a key site and walk the ground, making notes, taking pictures, even recording ambient sound. Do *something*.

Research, like writing, is a craft, and after reasonable preparation, the only way to learn how to do it well is to do it.

Like most writers, Valerie Boyd suffered from inertia, the resistance to start researching her biography of Zora Neale Hurston: "I didn't make the best use of my time at the beginning—because I was a little bit scared, you know? I just had to get over my initial paralysis—

ooh, I have a book deal, now I'm supposed to do this book—what to do! How do you begin! So I spent a lot of time spinning my wheels, making plans but not doing anything. And that was just that basic old human fear and having to muster up some courage and get started."

Out in the Field

DeBlieu, like Steinbeck and McCourt, set out to write about a subject close to her heart:

"One of the things that struck me as soon as I moved to the Outer Banks in 1985 was how the wind really would define everything about the feel of the day, whether it was sultry or pleasant, whether you could go out fishing, what have you. These islands are so lashed by the wind that it's really impossible to get away from it. I found that I had to accommodate myself, accustom myself, to living in wind, which I'd never really had to do before."

Her life-experience research included sailing a small boat in freshening winds and enduring a series of hurricanes in her adopted home on Roanoke Island. Reading the archives full of scientific data and historical information wasn't enough—it is her *experience* with the wind that imbues the book with such a thrilling immediacy. Chapter after chapter, the reader feels as if he is outdoors watching cumulonimbus clouds scroll across the sky, feeling a warm breeze on the cheek, swooping through the blue Atlantic sky, or watching the dark vortex of an approaching tornado. *Wind* is not a litany of facts but the story of a woman testing the facts of the natural world through her experience.

Once she had completed her initial phase of research, she was ready to write a proposal. With a publisher's advance, she planned research that would take her farther afield—to investigate each of the areas that had emerged from her archival research. Even then she was frugal, laying her groundwork through telephone interviews, using magazine assignments to finance some of the more expensive trips.

Among the many research experiences that helped shape *Wind*, DeBlieu did the following:

- Hiked into the canyons of the Arizona-Utah border to explore aeolian geology.
- Climbed inside a wind tunnel at Colorado State University.
- Stood on an observation tower at the Pea Island National Wildlife Refuge on Hatteras Island to spot migrating birds.
- Ascended to 1,500 feet in a hot air balloon near Albuquerque, New Mexico.
- Strapped herself under a hang glider, was towed to 2,000 feet, and glided to earth on the Outer Banks of North Carolina.

DeBlieu did not rely just on memory or random personal experiences. She actively sought out other experiences that would expand her knowledge—teach her about her subject in a deep, visceral way. So she wound up hanging under a nylon glider spiraling toward the earth, feeling the updrafts and air currents in every small movement of her body.

The logic of the research she did is obvious in retrospect—wind tunnels, sailboats, hang gliders, and so on. But in fact they were part of her imaginative vision that shaped the book. Other writers would have chosen other windows into the subject.

To bring to life a subject as ethereal as wind—which can't be seen—she needed to rely on what *can* be seen in the mind's eye: concrete images of wind affecting the world. Those tangible, arresting moments provide the bones of the book, on which DeBlieu hangs her wide-ranging discussion. The book is remarkably comprehensive: From those few well-chosen experiences with wind, she manages to touch on virtually all aspects of the wind in science, history, and culture, without seeming tiresome.

The stories of wind tunnels and hot air balloons make the subject real—as well as both dramatic and entertaining—in a way that dry exposition never could. And this combined virtue—compelling narrative full of important information—won her the John Burroughs Medal for an outstanding book of nature writing.

Again, this is a general principle. You can't write about abstractions. You need to incarnate those abstractions in interesting people, dramatic events, tangible experience. By participating in the experiences of living characters shaping events that matter, the reader also participates in the ideas that underpin the telling—the subtext of scenes, the themes of the larger story.

During the research phase, the clock is always ticking toward the moment when you will begin to write, but you can't rush. There are no shortcuts.

"In terms of getting the book done in a timely fashion—it never happens!" DeBlieu says, laughing. *Wind* took every bit of three years to research and write. "I had really hoped to do it in two years, but I think the creative process just requires some time. If I had turned the book in a year earlier, written it in a shorter amount of time, it would have suffered. It took the amount of time that it took."

And thorough research is likely to take more than time. The costs may be physical and emotional as well.

Alex Shoumatoff, in the course of researching *The World Is Burning: Murder in the Rain Forest*, visited the Amazon—not once but many times over the course of years—suffering parasites, risking injury and even death at the hands of the *pistoleiros*, not to mention from snakebite, malaria, and a host of other potentially fatal diseases. To get his story, he made a conscious choice to suffer extreme discomfort for extended periods.

The Internet, including the World Wide Web, with all its attendant databases and home pages and hotlinks, can serve a researcher well, but it can take you only so far. It's a great well of information, bogus as well as reliable, but it is no substitute for the real thing, for being there, for the thing itself. The great books seem to be earned, not always through physical danger, but through a deep experience with the subject.

And some courage to put yourself on the line.

Steadfast but Flexible

Boyd, in researching her biography of Hurston, faced some of the same challenges as DeBlieu, with the added pressure to be complete and definitive.

"I think an important thing for me in this whole process was flexibility," Boyd recalls. "I would have wanted to plan exactly what trips I wanted to take and just plan things very meticulously, but I realized pretty early on that that would have been a bit constraining, because there has to be flexibility. Steadfastness, but flexibility."

You focus on the goal, but you remain flexible about how to achieve that goal—recognizing that goals may change as you immerse yourself more deeply in your subject.

Like DeBlieu, Boyd sketched out a realistic general approach to her research while still developing her proposal. This included consulting the only other Hurston biography to date, written by Robert Hemenway. His bibliography gave her a good starting list of sources, including the major archives that hold Hurston's papers.

Boyd visited archives in nine states and the District of Columbia. One important early trip took her to the University of Kansas in Lawrence, where Hemenway is now Chancellor. She learned an important lesson: Other researchers are not necessarily the enemy. "I spent a week with him—he was very gracious about letting me look through his files." says Boyd. "And there were interviews that he conducted with people in 1977 who just aren't around anymore. Going through his files was just wonderful. And those interviews, actually, I can trust more in some ways than the interviews I'm doing now twenty years later, because people's memories have faded that much more."

So building on the work of another generous scholar, Boyd was able to get a head start on her primary research. She tackled the major archives first—a sensible way to begin building a foundation: "I hit those first to make sure I got them but also to get the biggest, the broadest picture of Hurston's life, to really get the broad strokes down and then fill in the fine details later. And the archives that I visited first are archives that contain mostly her papers, so that gave me a sense of chronology, a sense of the line of her life."

That detailed chronology became the backbone of her manuscript: "Again, I started with broad strokes. Year by year. She was born this year. Her brother was born this year. The family moved this year. Very broad strokes. This is when she went to college. And then I'm filling in those broad lines with really fine lines—you know, this letter she wrote on this particular day, 1929. February 4, this letter was written."

Whatever she chooses to include in the final book, however she moves backward and forward in the chronology of Hurston's life, she will have a firm grip on the events, a detailed reference. She will not be easily confused, and she will therefore have a good chance of being clear for the reader.

This kind of chronology is usually pretty tedious and boring to develop, but it can be an extremely useful and liberating tool. The more complex the events of your book, the more time it encompasses, the more useful the chronology is likely to prove. Once you have it straight, you've got the Bible: Here's what happened and in what order. It liberates you *not* to have to create a strict chronology in the work itself. You may choose to fragment the narrative, or to transpose the ending with the beginning, or to simply move around thematically rather than in chronological order. Once you have the chronology on your writing desk—and in your head—you'll never get lost, and you have a better chance of not losing the reader, no matter how you skew time. In some books, such as histories and biographies, you can even include a skeletal version of that chronology of major events as a reference for the reader. So your effort may pay off doubly.

Access and Archives

As any good investigative reporter will attest, exciting research often begins in a very unglamourous way: following a paper trail. Census records, court records, trial transcripts, birth and death certificates, government reports, scientific abstracts, letters, diaries, newspaper and magazine stories, handbills and circulars, minutes of meetings, corporate charters, annual corporate reports, budgets and auditors' statements, bylaws, legislative records, bills of sale, ledgers, invoices, check registers, tax records, property deeds, business directories, phone books, even private resumés—all are potentially useful mines of relevant information. The trick lies in connecting the dots, assembling seemingly unrelated facts into a pattern, a matrix of meaning.

I once read several months of corporate board minutes by a multinational corporation. In the first few installments, not much seemed to be going on—just the usual sales reports, budget projections, pro forma votes. But there was always one nagging voice at the table asking an apparently irrelevant or naive question that nobody could satisfactorily answer. As the months wore on, the minutes—and that one board member's stubborn questions—revealed a growing financial scandal within the company. By the time the dust settled, several company directors had been sacked and the one naive voice had been named CEO and president of the board. An entire drama acted out in the dry formula of board minutes.

But corporate board minutes, like many other documents, are not necessarily available to the public. So you have to make sure you have *access* to the ones you need. Sometimes, you can simply ask. Other times, elaborate contractual arrangements may be required.

Knowing her project would rely on permission to see and publish various archival material controlled by the Hurston estate, Boyd sought access while still shaping her book proposal. She contacted a niece of Hurston's who, she understood, was the literary executor. They met and hit it off well. The niece gave Boyd a letter to include in the proposal saying she planned to cooperate with Boyd's research.

"Then I had an interesting thing happen," Boyd says. "After the book deal was announced in *Publishers Weekly*, I got a call from another niece saying, 'Well, actually *I* represent the Hurston estate, and you need to be talking to me if you're doing a book on Hurston.'"

Fortunately, it all worked out fine: "And that's been helpful, because I've needed college transcripts and those sorts of things of Hurston's, which you can't get without permission from a descendant. The estate and the agent for the estate, Victoria Sanders, have been wonderful about getting me whatever paperwork I need to speed up this research process."

In addition, Boyd searched out court documents: "In 1948 there was a child molestation charge that was filed against Hurston by the New York Society for the Prevention of Cruelty to Children, and I had to find the court documents relating to that case. That just took a lot of archival digging, one thing leading to another. I started in the National Archives and ended up being directed ultimately to the New York municipal court system and was able to find court documents that really explained the case—she was not guilty."

Previous scholars had relied on thirdhand accounts, newspaper stories, and an interview with Hurston's attorney. Boyd found irrefutable documentary evidence to restore Hurtson's good reputation. "It's very clear that there was no guilt on her part. It's very clear in the documents, and I'm happy to have those documents that settle it once and for all," Boyd says. "You get a little document and you file it away. It's not a big thing to celebrate, but in a way it is, because it proves beyond a shadow of a doubt a fact that is important to the book as a whole and the authenticity of the book as a whole."

Proving any single fact beyond a shadow of a doubt is one of the hardest things you can do. When a document can do that for you, it is indeed a big thing to celebrate.

Interviewing

Like many biographers, Boyd was anxious to interview people who had known her subject personally. She felt some urgency to conduct these interviews since Hurston died in 1960, and therefore anyone who had known her would be very old. She studied Hurston's own somewhat fictionalized autobiography, *Dust Tracks on a Road*, and picked out names.

"I would interview one and ask them about others," Boyd says. "Initially, my ideal approach was to do all the interviews first. But that didn't work out because some people just weren't available—they would say no. Also that wouldn't have been as cost effective, because I would have been running all over the country to interview these people who live in various places. So I made the list of the people who were left to interview, and I contacted them, but I didn't just immediately start running around the country interviewing them as I had expected at first."

And some of those she contacted simply declined to be interviewed. Just because you want to talk to somebody doesn't mean he or she wants to talk to you. Some people have been burned by journalists or simply value their privacy.

Boyd encountered another unforeseen problem: "In the process of doing what few interviews I did up front, I realized that those interviews weren't as helpful, necessarily, as I had thought they might be, because a lot of time has passed, and these people are very old, and their memories of Hurston were dimming. Or in some cases their memories seemed to be influenced by what they had read. She's become famous. So people would say stuff to me, and I could tell they had read it—that it didn't really relate to their own personal experience with her."

Boyd came to rely less on such interviews. She remained steadfast in her determination to examine Hurston's life as thoroughly as possible, but flexible about how best to learn what she needed to know.

Even when an interview is reliable, you may have to push a little, to "work" the interview. DeBlieu describes her visit to Belmond, Iowa, a town that had survived a tornado in 1966. She interviews resident after resident who tells stories of stoic survival, of people pulling together and getting on with their lives. But something isn't quite right—nobody is talking about the children who were injured. DeBlieu tracks down a woman whose two children were trapped under their caved-in house.

It does not begin as a pleasant interview.

DeBlieu and the woman are in the deli of the local supermarket. "Lots of people can tell you more than I can," the woman says warily, and, "I don't even like to talk about it." But DeBlieu keeps gently pressing her for details, and the woman at last tells her harrowing story: Not only was she buried with her children under the house, but she was traumatized for years afterward—terrified to let her children play out in the yard even on a sunny day, lest another tornado strike out of a clear blue sky.

DeBlieu says, "When everybody was giving me their pat stories, it would have been easy to leave and say well, okay, that's the end of it—isn't it nice that this town has such a good attitude toward living through the tornado. But by pushing a little bit more, by standing there and basically pushing through a situation that was very uncomfortable personally—this woman did *not* want to talk to me. I knew she didn't want to talk to me, and my instinct was to just turn around and leave—and leave her in peace. So by standing there and sweating through it, I got to the bottom of things. I got to the grit of the story, which was that she suffered an emotional breakdown after her children were injured during the tornado."

It's a fine but important line: You don't want to bully a subject into saying things she'll regret, but you can't back off too easily. DeBlieu had prodded about as long as she could stand. Another moment or two of silence, she admits, and she'd have left without ever learning the woman's story—and both would have been poorer: "She became so forthcoming that it was almost as if, by telling the story again, it was helping her. It was therapeutic for her."

Creative Research

Research can spark ideas, even suggest new directions for the project.

For DeBlieu, an initial piece of background research provided the paradigm that would define her book. Like most breakthrough discoveries, it was obvious—in retrospect: "I was amazed to learn that wind is what physicists call a 'viscous fluid.' It's a fluid, a liquid, and it behaves like water. When it forms a current, a current of air behaves just like a current in a rushing stream. So if you want to feel what it's like for a bird to be flying through an air current, put yourself in the ocean or put yourself in a creek somewhere and feel the tug of water flowing around you—what does that feel like? That's what animals who live and move through wind experience every day. In learning that, I was able to understand the wind a lot more, because I could look up and see clouds being moved along the way flotsam would be moved along in a stream or on the ocean. I could see ripples in the clouds, or places where there would be shooting long strands of clouds, that was some sort of a weird, shearing current. Making that analogy really helped me understand the whole world of wind, the world that's sitting on top our shoulders, a lot more clearly."

It was an analogy not available from her personal experince; it came only in turning outside herself.

What You Can't Find Out

Shoumatoff's *The World Is Burning: Murder in the Rain Forest* investigates the murder of Chico Mendes, a rubber tapper who had achieved world renown in trying to save the Brazilian rain forest. Shoumatoff writes, in a foreword entitled "Caveat Emptor":

> In many ways this is a book of opinion, because the "facts" of this story, which I have diligently and impartially endeavored to set forth, sometimes don't add up. . . . As with everything in history, no one will ever know exactly what happened. But then again, to what extent can you believe in anything? Especially in a place like Brazil, where the general outlook on the passing scene is so fluid, where so many things—culture, attitudes, even the continuously changing currency—conspire against the vision of a stable, fixed reality. It's different down there.

One of the ways in which it is "different down there" he discusses in a section called "The Amazon Numbers Problem": "As I have written elsewhere, numbers are a temperate-zone precision trip. In the tropics they are flourishes thrown out for effect—the figures are figurative."
He goes on:

> People will tell you something happened "fifteen days ago" or that they shot "forty wild pigs." It would be a mistake to take these numbers literally. There are a dozen reasons that someone in the Amazon might give you bad information, intentionally or not. One of the most common is politeness. If you ask a question that anticipates the affirmative, the *caboclos* and the Indians are so humble that they will automatically tell you yes, because you, the *civilizado* (civilized one), the white *doutor* (doctor), must know best. So you learn, in trying to ascertain a particular piece of information, to ask as many people as you can, even to ask the same person several times. You circle, double back, play dumb: what was that again? You gather layers of versions, weigh them against each other, blend them and work them into a whole, until at last

the piece of information begins to acquire a kind of burnished sheen, and the semblance of credibility.

So in conducting your research, a measure of humility and skepticism is in order. Things may not be what they seem. People may tell you what they think you wish to hear. You may misinterpret what you see and hear. However conscientiously you work, you are bound to get something wrong.

Establishing even the most basic fact of your subject with 100 percent certainty may defy your best efforts.

Boyd explains, "I'm going to Alabama next week. Hurston was actually born in Alabama and we don't really have a birth certificate for her—I don't know that one exists. But I'm going to see if one exists. I also have a 1900 census that gives her birth date as 1891. Her birth date has been a subject of controversy, because she lied about her birth date numerous times."

Imagine trying to write a definitive biography of a figure for whom you can't even establish the most fundamental vital statistic: date of birth.

Remember Junger's tale of a lost boat: He began by assuming—based on reasonable evidence—that the boat went down but knowing virtually nothing else of the circumstances of the sinking.

Only the very fortunate writer finds all the important facts somewhere indisputably in the record. More often, the writer must negotiate the truth from the incomplete archive of the world, striking the best bargain for the reader.

Integrating Knowledge Gracefully

It's not enough to know a lot. If you dump it on the reader in great heaps, you'll bury him.

Like the temptation to use extended research as a means of actually avoiding writing, there's also the temptation to just cram information into a chapter, hoping it will add up to something, rather than to carefully structure the dramatic order in which knowledge unfolds toward a climax of accumulated meaning. You must weave research into your book unobtrusively, with grace, without slowing the pace of the story.

DeBlieu uses one method—alternating scenes of personal experience with more reportorial scenes: a wind tunnel test in Colorado, an aeolian geologist excavating a sand dune at Nags Head Woods, a team of engineers from Operation Blue Sky systematically destroying a house to determine how much wind pressure it takes to tear off a roof or knock down a wall.

The narrative stance backs off a little whenever she takes on the role of reporter. The shift alerts the reader that we are off on a little expedition of research.

Johnson, as we've seen, uses a kind of telescoping narrative stance—moving closer and closer in from the objective reportage that establishes the facts of the case.

Two principles serve those writers and others:

1. Present factual information in bite-sized pieces, not massive doses.
2. Integrate statistics, descriptions, science, police records, courtroom testimony, history, and so on into the context of the *story*. It's not just free-floating information but rather information that heightens the drama of the scene, the chapter, the overall story being told.

The information can't be dry, abstract, and dead: It must be alive and connected to the people and events of the story. Each new fact must heighten the reader's appreciation of the next moment of the story.

Steve Twomey of *The Philadelphia Inquirer* won the Pulitzer prize in 1987 for a piece on the future of war as seen from the flight deck of the *U.S.S. America*. He begins the piece at a tense moment: An F14A Tomcat fighter jet is lining up for a landing, but the runway is blocked by an A-7E Corsair bomber straddling the No. 4 steam catapult, the "cat" used for launching jets.

> "What's taking 'em so long down there?" Air Boss growled. He had left his leather armchair in his glass booth in *America*'s superstructure. He was standing up for a better look, which he always does when the flight deck crunch is on.

The ship's 79,724 tons suddenly shuddered. Steam billowed from No.4. The A-7 had vanished, rudely flung out over the Mediterranean by the "cat stroke," like a rock from a slingshot. Finally.

"Launch complete, sir!" said Mini Boss, his assistant.

"Clear decks!" Air Boss boomed into the radio to his launch crews. It would be close, maybe too close. "Secure the waist cat! Prepare to recover aircraft! Hubba, Hubba!"

We're squarely in the middle of the dramatic ballet of flight deck operations. We learn two of the types of planes on the carrier, the role and habits of the Air Boss, the jargon of the flight deck, where the ship is operating, and what it feels like when an airplane is shot off the deck. We know the Air Boss sits in a leather chair in a glass booth. We even learn the tonnage of the carrier. Not as a catalogue of specifications, but all in a moment of decision.

In a later section on the aviators, notice the use of statistics to quantify the experience.

The men who fly the $38.7 million F-14 fighters are just about as smug and smooth as *Top Gun* portrays them. . . .

"Yeah, that's us," said a 28-year-old pilot from Drexel Hill. "We're *cool*. We're *fighter pilots*."

Most are in their late 20s or early 30s. Handsomeness seems to be a job requirement. Catapulting off a carrier, which subjects them to a jolt seven or eight times the force of gravity, "is a lifetime E-ticket at Disneyland," said the Drexel Hill pilot.

"To be sitting in that machine and to know that 300 feet later you'll be going 200 miles per hour and the whole thing takes 2½ seconds? Well—the level of concentration in sports or whatever has never reached *that* adrenaline high," said a 42-year-old pilot from Philadelphia, who has done it 1,250 times.

The numbers emphasize the incredible feat of acceleration and the stress on the human body; the ages draw attention to how young these top guns are to be handling machines of such power and cost;

the last statistic is the clincher: This is a once-in-a-lifetime thrill that one aviator has achieved *1,250 times.* All of this leads to the final comment of the piece by a landing-signals officer, voicing the reader's awe at the unreal nature of the carrier routine: " 'Sometimes,' said an LSO, 'I can't believe what we do out here.' "

Knowing When to Stop

"One of the challenges of writing creatively is knowing when to stop," DeBlieu says. "The less disciplined writers, the ones who just run on and on, to an extent they're hurting the genre."

The well-meaning but inexperienced writer tries to include absolutely everything he has learned—every fact, every impression, every quote. He may do this out of exuberance, sheer fascination with the material, or lack of perspective on a project in which he has been immersed for months, maybe years. He may not trust the strength of his writing, the power of the single concrete example, so he offers dozens of illustrations where one or two would suffice. The motive may be pure: to make sure the reader *gets* it. But the method can overwhelm the reader and drive him away.

"The challenge is always to find that one story or anecdote that will portray all you want to portray," DeBlieu reminds us.

In fact, any writer taking on a big subject will leave out most of what he or she learns in the course of research. It's inevitable. The transcript of a half-hour interview may run to thirty pages. The transcript of a court case may run to thousands—never mind the appeals. Your research doesn't belong in the book simply because you learned it.

There's a test for every fact, impression, quote, and anecdote you've gleaned from your research:

- Is it essential to understanding the subject?
- Does it move rather than impede the story?
- Does it amplify an important theme without causing confusion?
- Is it unique rather than redundant?

It takes discipline to leave out what we've learned from hard, imaginative, and costly research. The easy part is leaving out the dull interview, the aborted trip, the disappointing experiment. What's harder is leaving out the spicy quote, the provocative anecdote, or the surprising fact—because it is redundant, slows the story, or confuses the reader with too much diverse knowledge.

"It was very tempting to go on and on," DeBlieu says. "It required some control on my part, and on the part of my editor as well."

One of the many stories she collected came from a woman who had been trapped in a hurricane in Hawaii: "She was in this cinder block school with a bunch of other people who had taken shelter there, and she just began pacing around and around and around this big room, the cafeteria or whatever she was staying in, trying to keep herself sane. And it went on and on and on. And she began to feel like a war victim, a refugee. She had these wonderful descriptions about that experience. And I cut it out, because I felt it was too much."

By cutting that anecdote and others, she was able to concentrate on those stories she kept in the book—like the scene in Belmond, Iowa, among the tornado survivors: "By cutting out a couple of other stories that I thought were very compelling and choosing to concentrate on the tornado story, I was able to flesh out the details, to really put in more, and I think in the end give the reader more, because I brought the situation more to life."

Less can be *more*: By carefully selecting which parts of your research to include, you can create fuller, more lasting impressions of them. They won't be summarized, glossed over, lost in the thicket of other less compelling parts.

"I don't like to saturate the reader," DeBlieu says. "I like to have a reader come away saying, Wow, that was really interesting—I wish I knew more. I think that's the measure of a work that's successful: the reader comes away wanting to know more about the characters, more about the world that the writer has created."

Thus the writer has not just satisfied an appetite for knowledge of this subject but created a hunger for more.

Exercise

1. Identify a subject close to your heart. Develop a research plan to investigate it, including key questions, resources that might hold the answers, a timetable, and a budget.

2. Using the Internet, conduct a search for books on the same subject as the one you plan to write. Ask yourself, How will my book be different?

3. Visit an archive that holds primary documents and browse.

4. Using any sources you need, *try to prove one fact beyond a shadow of a doubt.*

5

Discovering Themes as You Write

Tim O'Brien observes in "The Lives of the Dead": "The thing about a story is that you dream it as you tell it, hoping that others might then dream along with you, and in this way memory and imagination and language combine to make spirits in the head." As much as you might plan, research, ponder, design, even outline a piece before you begin writing, in fact the thing will come alive only in the process of actually writing it.

Writing well is an act of discovery.

You begin with a fascination, an excitement about subject, an anecdote that won't let go of your imagination, a problem that keeps you up at night, a real-life event, an incident from your past, a character—real or fictive—you can't get out of your head, and you start writing. The unfolding piece may surprise, baffle, delight, or frustrate you—or do all those things by turns. The writer knows what topic or experience she is burning to write about but in the act of writing will discover new layers of meaning, maybe even a more genuine topic.

Maxwell Perkins, Hemingway's editor, writes in a letter to James Jones, "Hemingway didn't know, except in the most general sense, the story he was going to unfold in *For Whom the Bell Tolls*, and, by the way, it took him five years, I think, to write that."

The process can be trying, in all sorts of ways. Long into *East of*

Eden, Steinbeck wondered whether the book had grown in conception since he had begun it—and fretted that it had not. "I planned it as a huge thing," he writes in the *Journal.* "I have been afraid that it narrowed down from the big thing rather than expanded. As a matter of fact I've wondered whether it was not becoming little. I want it large. What I would like would be for it to read little but to leave a vast feeling."

Not a bad aspiration for any writer—"to read little but to leave a vast feeling."

Assaying the First Draft

The indispensable habit you must cultivate is the habit of being able to recognize what you've got in your early draft, even your early notes. That's when the real writing begins.

Start by presuming that a first draft is just that—a draft. You "read" a first draft in a very special way: *paying attention to what it's trying to reveal about the nature of the story.* You presume it's going to change, that parts of it are all out of order and must be rearranged, that there are many mistakes, redundancies, omissions, clumsy transitions, spongy parts, mistaken turns, failed experiments—some trivial, others significant.

Some of the work you refashion as you go, just to make it possible to continue with some coherence; some of it you climb across to get to the other side, where you discover the next significant moment—knowing you will have to return and shore up the makeshift bridge.

Hemingway reminds us, in a letter to Charles Poore, editor of *The Hemingway Reader,* "There's no rule on how it is to write. Sometimes it comes easily and perfectly. Sometimes it is like drilling rock and then blasting it out with charges."

The first draft is a chunk of ore—with any luck, high-grade ore. It will take some refining, some chipping and molding, maybe even some blasting—hard, sometimes dirty work—to turn it into pure gold. You have to roll up your sleeves and be a stonecutter before you can become a sculptor—command of craft always precedes art: apprentice, journeyman, master.

Forster observes, in his discussion on the most prosaic of all structural considerations, plot: "We noted, when discussing the plot, that it added to itself the quality of beauty; beauty a little surprised at her own arrival: that upon its neat carpentry could be seen, by those who cared to see, the figure of the Muse; that Logic, at the moment of finishing its own house, laid the foundation of a new one."

Careful plotting leads to beauty—one of the many paradoxes by which we write.

And the habits of craft, developed day in and day out over a working lifetime, create moments of astonishment, sublime and magical effects, precisely because the writer is not thinking overtly about making art. Perkins goes on in his letter to Jones, advising him not to be too self-conscious about creating his effects: "A deft man may toss his hat across the office and hang it on a hook if he just naturally does it, but he will always miss it if he does it consciously. That is a ridiculous and extreme analogy, but there is something in it."

When you read a first draft, you're looking for what sparkles. You're conducting an *assay* of the raw material you've generated—trying to determine, as a metallurgist might, the proportion of precious metal in the ore. (The word derives from the same Old French root as *essay*: *asaier* or *essaier*, "to try.")

Then in revision, you separate the gold from the slag.

You're asking some basic questions of your own words:

• What story have I written? (How does what I've created match up with my intention?)

• Where does my interest lie? (Among all the competing subjects, themes, and characters, which one is primary, the engine that drives the book? Is it the one with which I started?)

• What underlies the triggering circumstance? (Beneath the apparent subject—the surface of the story—what is the deeper subject being explored?)

• Why does this character or problem fascinate me? (How does it connect with my passion?)

• Will it hold anyone else's interest? Why? (Hemingway: " . . . don't think anything is of any importance because it happens to you or anyone belonging to you.")

• Have I created all the essential parts? (What's missing—in the logic of the story, the completeness of the imagining, the depth of character and feeling?)

Reading the first draft also requires the ability to recognize obvious pitfalls: Where does the gravity of the cliché want to pull this? Have I fallen into that cliché? How do I avoid falling?

At this stage, you're not a critic—you're an anthropologist. Your job is not to judge, to praise or censure, but simply to *observe*: closely, thoroughly, honestly. Reading your own first draft, it's as if you've been set down inside a strange, exotic culture, and your job is to determine as precisely and comprehensively as you can just how that culture works.

• What are its assumptions, rules, hierarchies, belief systems, patterns of behavior?

• Which persons (characters) have status, and how is that status measured?

• What do the people do and what are their motives?

• Who are the enemies of the culture, and how is warfare—conflict—conducted: overtly through physical violence, or covertly, perhaps symbolically?

• What is its history—and its future?

• At this moment, what important matter is at issue?

Not until you thoroughly understand the world you yourself have created on the page can you begin to exercise aesthetic judgment.

Observing Your Patterns

In other words, *you read your first draft to find out what you have written.*

As simpleminded as that sounds, it's both true and profound. You can't revise intelligently until you have an accurate and comprehensive sense of what is actually on the page, and the difference between what you *intended* to write and what you *actually* wrote can mean the success or failure of the project.

Don't assume that you wrote about what you set out to write about.

Don't read your draft in self-congratulatory appreciation. Read it instead for what *is* there, not what you *intended* to put there.

One easy trick that can dismay a writer in a hurry and teach a valuable lesson: After you've dashed off a wonderful scene, listen to a friend read it out loud. Most often, you'll cringe at the dissonances, the unintentional rhymes, the muddy syntax, the confusing dialogue, the missing words. Your friend will stumble over passages that confuse her, laugh reflexively at unintended puns or jokes, and—absent cues—misread the inflections of your narrator so that an innocent line becomes arch or a wise observation sounds like nonsense.

What's true at the level of syntax is true at the more panoramic level of story. It's complete in your head, but on the page it is rough and incomplete. And true at the more subtle level of theme, the underpinning of the whole enterprise.

Don't fool yourself: Read what is actually on the page, not the brilliant unwritten story in your imagination.

If you haven't got an obliging friend, read your scene out loud, *slowly*. Record it, if possible. Hear what's missing.

Even gifted, successful writers often feel as if they have somehow not quite captured the things they set out to capture in a first draft. In his *Journal*, writing at the finish of *East of Eden*, Steinbeck quotes Cervantes' prologue to *Don Quixote*, harking back to the birth of the novel: "Idling reader, you may believe me when I tell you that I should have liked this book, which is the child of my brain, to be The fairest, The sprightliest and The cleverest that could be imagined, but I have not been able to contravene the law of nature which would have it that like begets like."

Steinbeck then adds his own coda: "Although some times I have felt that I held fire in my hands and spread a page with shining— I have never lost the weight of clumsiness, of ignorance, of aching inability."

Conversely, your draft may reveal a far more interesting story direction than the one you planned. It's not always better to force the story back to your intention. Sometimes the most fruitful course is to change your intention for the story—now that you see what you have wrought.

When F. Scott Fitzgerald submitted the original draft of *This Side of Paradise* to Scribner, Maxwell Perkins recognized Fitzgerald's talent but declined the manuscript as incomplete and disorganized. But Fitzgerald clung to a stubborn faith in the rightness of his original version. At the author's request, Perkins passed it along to other publishers, all of whom declined it. At last, following Perkins' critique, Fitzgerald drastically rewrote the book. Upon accepting the revised novel, Perkins wrote to Fitzgerald: "Viewing it as the same book that was here before, *which in a sense it is* [italics mine], though translated into somewhat different terms and extended further, I think that you have improved it enormously."

In improving the novel, Fitzgerald made his career. Had another editor published the early draft, we can only speculate whether it would have earned him such recognition.

There are some techniques for discovering what you're really writing about:

• Observe repetitions—of words, ideas, locales, and so on. These are the surface emblems of the deep driving ideas of the piece— the themes. In *Gatsby*, each of the five locales carries a thematic identity: Daisy's mansion is careless Old Money; Gatsby's garish palace is vulgar New Money; Nick's cottage is ambitious Middle Class—literally in the middle between the properties of Daisy and Gatsby; the Valley of Ashes is a barren field of death—of dreams of love, of characters; New York is the Outside World—accessible only by braving the Valley of Ashes. Each time a scene happens in a given locale, it comes backlighted, as it were, by that thematic identity: Love will never blossom in the Valley of Ashes. We visit each locale several times, and with each visit the story cuts deeper toward the thematic core. In the end, for instance, the Valley of Ashes is the scene of literal death. Nick, the middle-class man who lives in the middle, is literally caught in the middle of the deadly affair. In his final meeting with Tom Buchanan on Fifth Avenue—out in the world removed from East and West Egg—he sees how completely aloof Tom and Daisy are from the human wreckage they caused. It is the very repetition of a finite number of locales that clues us in to their thematic resonance—and allows them to grow into their full thematic promise.

• Observe motifs of images—how the mood is set with images of light and dark, physical descriptions, the sense of place. The first line of Johnson's *What Lisa Knew* reads, "There was an absence of light." She continues to remain preoccupied by light and shadow and darkness throughout the book: Steinberg's dark sinister apartment where black deeds are committed in secret played against the glaring fluorescent lights of the police station and the hospital emergency room, where Steinberg and Nussbaum are revealed for the monsters they are, their evil exposed. The truth, almost literally, comes to light.

• Observe resistance from characters to do what you want them to do. In trying to make the plot come out neatly, you may be pushing them to act in an unnatural way. In *Libra*, DeLillo uses this resistance to great advantage. Since two of his core themes are conspiracy and plotting a novel, each rebellion by a character who won't fit neatly into his or her assigned role furthers both themes—demonstrating implicitly how both kinds of "plots" go awry and revealing the tension between art and life. Art, like a conspiracy plan, is tidy, elegantly organized to its best effect; life is messy, unpredictable, sabotaged by free will and human fallibility.

• Allow early drafts to simmer so you can return with a fresh perspective. You need time to forget what you've written so you can be surprised, delighted, or dismayed enough to recognize the true quality of the work. If you've read it so often that you've practically memorized it, the work is no longer plastic but fixed, a hardened fact.

• Review earlier work in search of common themes: What do you keep coming back to in your writing? I find myself, for instance, continually returning to the theme of a community under threat, fascinated by the volatile moment when a crowd becomes a mob, when the social contract breaks down and law gives way to anarchy. This is not obvious at first glance from the books I've written, set in several historical periods, with different surface plots and characters—yet one way or another, the stranger always comes to town, disrupting the order of things and inciting the community to crisis.

• Observe what is conspicuous by its absence: What are you deliberately *avoiding* writing about? Where are the holes in the story, the difficult unwritten scenes papered over by space breaks? Listen to the admonition from Tim O'Brien's "Notes" in *The Things They Carried*, in which one of the characters in the stories writes him a letter about his own story: " 'It's not terrible,' he wrote me, 'but you left out Vietnam.' " Did you leave out Vietnam?

• Most important of all, ask: Where does the energy lie? Which scenes or characters instantly rev up the story? Which characters or scenes are wooden, lifeless? In which passages is the story enslaved to your intentions? Listen to the story tell you *its* intentions. Which themes are really coming through?

What's Left Out

Cutting is the easiest kind of revising.

You can, for instance, have a strong intuition that a draft is just too long, and you can arbitrarily decide to cut it by 10, 20, even 50 percent just to quicken the pace, to lighten it, to establish a cleaner line of story. If your instinct is right—and usually if you think a work is too long, your reader will agree with you wholeheartedly—then the leaner draft will probably be an improvement. If nothing else, you will achieve a more accurate sense of where your interest lies—all the parts you couldn't bear to cut. The piece will draw down to a tight focus.

Much more difficult is trying to fill in what's missing. What's missing may be a discrete scene or expository summary or a paragraph of close description—a complete segment, in other words, that can be inserted at the appropriate place, once you recognize the shape of the hole. That, of course, means comprehending the shape of the *whole*—the book's larger intention, how all the parts fit together to reinforce that intention.

Commonly, this missing passage is the difficult scene you shied away from writing—because it was too painful, too emotional, too technically challenging—marked by a space break. Such a space break is like a bottomless crevasse into which the drama has fallen without a trace. Less may indeed be more—sometimes—but more often you just have to write the hard scene. The story has made a certain promise, the action has built to a defining moment, and you can't just dodge out the back while the reader's not watching, leaving the scene unplayed—*because in this scene will lie the heart of your theme, your meaning.*

A naive writer will protest: "But I wanted to leave the story open to interpretation—let the reader decide what happens." The lady or the tiger syndrome.

But the reader should never be in doubt about the literal action of the story—what he has seen and heard. The reader needs to know all the facts clearly. Otherwise he can't enjoy his most satisfying prerogative, interpreting what he has just witnessed. Intelligent readers can argue whether Steinbeck's ending to *The Grapes of Wrath* is a gesture of hope or despair, but they can't argue whether Rose of Sharon suckles a starving man at her shriveled breast: Steinbeck has written the literal action of the scene with lovely clarity.

Remember, you started this Big Book with a passion to get to the bottom of something. It's up to you to set the thematic agenda for the reader: Here's what this book is interested in. Here's what it's not. Here's what happens in this story. Get it?

So if what is missing is a discrete passage, for heaven's sake roll up your sleeves and write it—clearly, without being coy or ambiguous.

On the other hand, what's missing might be the back story of a main character woven into a dozen scenes, one thin strand at a time; a thematic preoccupation that must inform all scenes of a certain type; the proper tone to achieve the intended effect in a whole chapter; the most effective narrative stance.

This is the most difficult kind of revision, because it calls for you to completely reconfigure part or all of the work. It's like rewiring a house that's already been built: You have no choice but to tear out walls, open up ceilings, dismantle and reassemble.

It's always more complicated to retrofit integral systems—particularly when you want to preserve the integrity of the original house.

It's an imperfect metaphor, but the architecture of your book, like the architecture of a house, reflects thematic choices—in fact, a systematic series of choices, all mutually reinforcing.

As you open up walls and ceilings, don't lose sight of the larger effect: your overall theme. Don't install baroque moldings on a Frank Lloyd Wright staircase. Don't put stainless steel countertops in a Victorian kitchen. Match your diction to the gravity—or levity—of a scene. Reinforce the scene's underlying ideas with resonant images that remind us of the scene's connection to other scenes in other chapters—the way Fitzgerald uses various automobiles to link scenes in *Gatsby*. The cars are functional as actual transportation that sets the novel firmly in the 1920s, but various cars also convey extravagance, ridiculousness, greed, manipulation, carelessness. And one of them figures directly in the climax of the action—the fatal hit-and-run in the Valley of Ashes.

There's no shortcut. So one of the most important things to accomplish in a first draft is *completeness*—the sense that it's all there, in some form or other, however rough, waiting to be shaped, arranged, and polished.

The ability to answer yes to the final question of the assay: Have I created all the essential parts?

If there are holes in the logic of the story, the completeness of the imagining, the depth of character and feeling, then you haven't yet got all the pieces. You have two choices:

1. Invent the rest of the missing pieces before beginning to revise the whole.

2. Proceed with the revision, mindful of the gaps, inventing the necessary pieces as you go.

Option number one is easier, naturally, if the need is for set pieces—discrete scenes or passages.

Option number two is usually the only choice if there is some thread missing from the whole work, or a large piece of it.

Again, there are always several ways of meeting any narrative challenge. The crucial requirement is that you recognize that something is missing and meditate effectively on what it is and how to introduce it into the story.

Planning Your Revision

A lot of writers don't revise in any systematic way. They tinker, nipping here, tucking there, generally smoothing out the prose, excising awkward phrases and purple flights of metaphor. This intuitive tinkering may work fine for short stories and articles, which often can be apprehended all in a piece—though it takes a certain kind of writer with well-developed, trustworthy instincts to pull it off. Many of us who go about revising this way are just fooling ourselves—acting lazy but putting it down to our artistic sensibility. Tinkering is a relatively painless process, and that sends up a red flag. Good writing is harder than that.

Tinkering will surely change the manuscript, but there's no guarantee it will improve it. Don't confuse *different* with *better*.

In any long piece—from an extended magazine article written in subheaded chapters to a book—there are at least three kinds of "global" revision *before* the writer gets to the happy stage of *pointing* the prose. (That is, just as a mason "points" a hearth by carefully filling in mortar around all the joints of the cemeted bricks or stones, leaving clean edges and a finished look, at this stage the writer fills in all the gaps between words, solidifies the grammatical joints within sentences, smooths out the transitions between sentences, and makes the whole artifice look straight, clean, and beautiful.)

Global revision takes in the following points:

1. Revising for structure (integrity of whole, transitions, integrity of parts).
2. Revising for story (narrative stance, text, and theme).
3. Revising for quality (clarity, tone, emotional impact).

Obviously, all three are so interrelated that they're hard to unbraid, and after much practice they can become almost intuitive. Nonetheless, it's useful on a large scale to revise in a singleminded way, layering the three major revisions to result in a sound, coherent Big Picture.

Like designing your research plan, or outlining a book by chapters, such a method creates a pleasing overall shape, leaving you the freedom to revise locally—inside chapters and scenes—with imagination, even daring, discovering still more surprises, teasing even more secrets out of the material.

Start with structure—good editors do. During his long, distinguished career, Stanley Colbert worked as a literary agent (Lord & Colbert, The William Morris Agency, The Colbert Agency), senior editor at Henry Holt, and CEO of Harper-Collins Canada. Now he teaches what he learned all those years to M.F.A. students at the University of North Carolina at Wilmington. As he worked with writers as varied as Jack Kerouac, Robertson Davies, and James T. Farrell, he never underestimated the importance of sound structure: "I would love to have a writer who's got a good fix on the material and knows what's working and can identify what isn't. It calls for a writer to totally understand structure, which most writers don't understand." The first thing he would address in any book was its structure.

Most long works conform to an implicit three-act template. (As with any general principle, there are plenty of variations and exceptions to this structure.)

- Act one, the setup—one quarter of the book.
- Act two, the main action—one half of the book.
- Act three, the finale–one quarter of the book.

Each act ends with a climax; the climaxes escalate toward the act three climax, which is also the climax of the book. In practice, act three tends to be the shortest—sometimes very short—the fastest paced, the most extreme action at the highest emotional and dramatic pitch. So the proportions are not absolute, only a guide. Sometimes the three acts will be nearly the same length. Sometimes—as in melodrama—acts one and two will be the same length, with act three much shorter.

Of your own book, ask the question that Colbert or any savvy editor would ask: What's the first act curtain? The second? The finale?

Realize that structure creates the surface design that carries theme.

Until the surface design is coherent and dramatic, themes are just abstractions without meaning.

Formally, we've inherited the three-act structure from classical Greek tragedy. Informally, storytelling just seems naturally to favor it. Our Paleolithic ancestors probably stumbled upon it while hunkered around the communal campfire spinning yarns, as E.M. Forster wryly speculates in *Aspects of the Novel*: "The primitive audience was an audience of shock-heads, gaping around the campfire, fatigued with contending against the mammoth or the woolly rhinoceros, and only kept awake by suspense. What would happen next? The novelist droned on, and as soon as the audience guessed what happened next, they either fell asleep or killed him."

In the early stages of telling a story—act one—we must introduce our characters, assign them their roles in the drama, and reveal something of their makeup; we must set them down in a particular time and place, then develop a dramatic situation around them; we must teach the reader how to read our book. And we must open up a promise, an expectation, a reason for suspense that will compel the reader to read on.

We need a curtain and a compelling promise to close the act.

Only then can we go on to act two, the main body of all the action, proceeding inexorably to climax.

"You know, almost every play we ever see, the biggest problem is the second act curtain," Colbert says. "So what's your second act curtain here?"

So like playwrights, we have to deliver on the promise of the opening, fulfill the main action of the middle, and pay off the reader's time and effort with a memorable ending to act three that leaves the reader with a sense of accomplishment, of enlargement. There's nothing that says you have to write it this way, but the structure is intuitively right and has stood up in many cultures over the ages.

"This is the transaction you're entering into with me and the reader," says Colbert, who diagrams the three-act structure as a series of overlapping inverted triangles, each new act taking as its springboard a piece of critical information or action leading up to the climax of the act before. Each broad promise focuses into a moment of truth, the end-of-act curtain. The following diagram illustrates that the setup for act two actually comes late in act one; for act three late in act two.

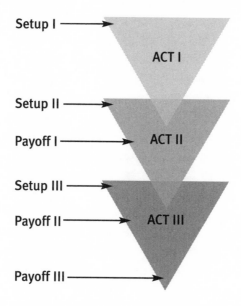

"You set something up, and that creates an anticipation," Colbert explains. "And if you pay it off, that creates a satisfaction. Setup without payoff, no satisfaction. Payoff without setup, no anticipation."

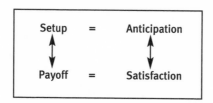

"While you're at it," Colbert says, "Conflict equals drama."

Testing Structure

Try this test. Pick half a dozen great novels—or nonfiction novels, such as Capote's *In Cold Blood*—off your shelf (you get to choose what's great, but I've already referred to some obvious choices). Flip to the back of the each book and find out how long it is. Then observe the structure.

Say you've picked Steinbeck's *The Grapes of Wrath*. In the Bantam paperback edition, it's 404 pages long. Act one, one quarter of the book, should be about 100 pages long. You flip to page 100, and there you find the climax to act one: Forced off their land, having made all their preparations, fought the inevitable as long as possible, the Joads have at last finished loading the old Ford truck and now climb aboard. The chapter—and act one—end on page 101: "And the truck crawled slowly through the dust toward the highway and the west."

The setup is over, and the journey is underway. The adventure is joined.

Now skip ahead through act two, one half the book or about 200 pages, and you find the climax to act two exactly where you expected it—right after a section on Rose of Sharon's pregnancy: The local police thugs try to start a riot in the government migrant camp in California—the only safe haven the Joads have found on their heart-breaking road to the promised land—to give them an excuse to enter the camp in force and close it down. The men of the camp, led by Tom Joad, capture the thugs and narrowly avert disaster. It's a climax of suspended violence, a riot that doesn't happen, full of intrigue and the thrill of suspense: Is this the end of the road? And it sets the stage for the crowning violence of act three, as those thugs return and Tom kills one of them in mad revenge for the murder of his friend Casey, the preacher and seer.

Since we're only roughing out a loose, traditional structure, you could move the curtain of act two forward to the end of the scene in which Tom kills Casey's killer, making Tom once more an outlaw. Remember, as the novel opened, he was returning home from prison, on parole for killing a man in self-defense.

Act three, of course, climaxes with the flood waters rising around what is left of the Joad family, as Rose of Sharon gives birth to a stillborn child and then suckles a starving stranger at her breast.

The three-act structure is complete, thematically: A family of ordinary folks, smitten by hard times, drives west in search of the Great

American Dream, battling the armed agents of capitalist greed, sustained by courage, loyalty to family, and the generosity of other plain folks, and winds up broke and starving in a foreign place, the family all but dismembered—but retaining to the last its sense of hope and human dignity.

And, since this is a road story, the structure is also complete geographically:

- Act one—On the family farm preparing to leave.
- Act two—On the road to California, as family members die or abandon the quest.
- Act three—In California, where the dream is revealed as a tragic hoax.

The Great Gatsby, a much shorter novel, is also structured in three acts:

- Act one, the first forty pages or so, has narrator Nick Carraway insinuating himself into the lives of Tom and Daisy Buchanan, Jordan Baker, and other Gatsby hangers-on in East and West Egg. Gatsby emerges as a creature of legend and mystery, endlessly talked about but never present, until Nick finally meets him at the close of act one.
- Act two, about eighty pages, plays out Gatsby's seduction of Daisy. The curtain is the blowup at the New York party at which Gatsby and Tom openly quarrel over the affair, and as the scene ends they are all piling into cars for the reckless and fatal drive back through the Valley of Ashes.
- Act three, the final forty pages, plays out the accident, climaxing in Gatsby's murder, then allowing a short anticlimax before the curtain.

Thematically, in act one, Gatsby has been "created" by the narrator in much the same way as Gatsby created his own identity out of the remnants of Jay Gatz. In act two, he courts Daisy with his ill-gotten material wealth, and that leads to a tragedy of crossed purposes—Gatsby has bought into his own fiction, believes money can buy happiness, or at least love. In act three, he falls, a victim to his own misbegotten ambition. The structure serves the themes.

Now apply the same test to your long manuscript.
- Does it break naturally into three acts?
- What is the progress of the plot through the acts?
- What is the thematic progress?
- Or do you discern another structure at work?
- Or do you realize with a heavy heart that there is no discernible structure?

If the reader doesn't recognize any structure, that's okay—structure is supposed to be so intrinsic that it becomes invisible to anyone not searching for it. The reader should simply feel a natural, almost inevitable movement toward fulfillment. But if you can't discern the structure of your own work, you've got a problem. Until you understand your own organizing principle, you probably can't go any further, because you haven't established the integrity of the whole.

But let's say you've X-rayed your draft and found the structure—imperfect, perhaps not a textbook example of the three-act template, but that's fine. Most big books overwhelm any neat structure—remember?

Now determine the integrity of the parts. If you have three recognizable acts, do they accomplish their respective purposes of setup, main action, and finale?

Within the acts, examine parts, then chapters, then scenes. Each part should have a definite purpose in the scheme of the story, add the next necessary element of knowledge to the unfolding drama, all the while captivating us.

In *Journal of a Novel* Steinbeck observes, "But I like a chapter to have a design of tone as well as of form. A chapter should be a perfect cell in the whole book and should almost be able to stand alone. If this is done then the breaks we call chapters are not arbitrary but rather articulations which allow the free movement of the story."

A scene is a miniature drama in which a single issue is decided in specific circumstances. A sequence of scenes moves toward resolving the issue of the chapter, while opening an even more intriguing question. The chapters accrue into acts, with escalating climaxes—curtains—till at last the book accumulates its final momentum, climaxing into a meaning larger than the sum of all the parts: the final curtain.

Revising Out of Context

One reason to survey the structure of your manuscript is to free you to revise it in parts. Just as you can't write a book all at once, you can't revise it all at once. It's too big to comprehend all in one sitting. The bigger it is—conceptually and in terms of sheer page length—the harder it will be to wrap your mind around. Once you can rely on the overall shape and movement of the book, you can relax your grip on the big picture and begin to revise locally.

Colbert recognizes the challenge this poses for the writer: "The most difficult thing in dealing with structure is to get a writer to be able to think comfortably out of context—out of linear context—because they've written it in a linear context generally: start at the beginning and then write all the way through. And now I'm at this scene on page eighty-five, which I'm lifting out and want to talk about."

If the novel is the house, Colbert explains, that little scene on page 85 may be only the fireplace in the house, but if it's out of proportion, it ruins the structural design and needs fixing. "Many writers, before they can think of the fireplace, have to reconstruct the whole house to get to the fireplace."

Colbert offers another reason against taking on the whole manuscript at once: "When I talk about revisions with a writer, I never talk about a whole manuscript. I never talk about *everything* that has to be done. And the reason I don't is because too much that has to be done starts to sound like it *can't* be done."

The key, he says, is setting goals that are *attainable*. The first twenty pages. The first act. A key scene. "Because what I've found happens," Colbert continues, "is that the writer is prepared to deal with that short thing, and in doing so the obvious things start to appear to him: you know, I did this, but what it means is, in the next act, I'm going to have to do that—and you say, right!"

Transitions

Now that you have established the integrity of the whole and of each component within the whole, you have one more structural inspection to make: *transitions.* Transitions are the friction points between bearing surfaces—scenes and chapters.

For the book to have continuity—for the themes to carry over from one section to the next, building force, blossoming into their full meaning—you need graceful, logical transitions. More, you need to establish a systematic way of making transitions—a pattern your reader can recognize early on and follow throughout the book. You have to teach the reader how to follow you as you move from one scene to another.

Sometimes you want an abrupt transition—a chapter break, for instance, might pick up with a new character or a jump in time. Many books derive their suspense from the reader's anticipation of *convergence*: the sense that all these disparate characters, scenes, and themes will come together in an interesting way later on in the book. Thrillers often work in this manner, ending a chapter with a minor cliff-hanger, then in the next chapter deliberately disrupting the continuity of point of view or locale with a new one, teasing the reader to stay with the story long enough to return to the solution to the earlier suspense.

We begin in Baghdad, say, in the close third-person limited point of view of a CIA operative spying on a missile site in the company of a local guide. But the guide has betrayed him, and the chapter ends with the operative about to be captured by Republican Guards. The next chapter takes us to Amsterdam, where a gemologist is cutting a diamond of remarkable size while an Arab sheik looks on. The cutting tool slips, and the diamond—is it ruined? We turn the page and are spirited off to a cabinet meeting in Washington addressing a terrorist crisis. . . .

We don't know yet what the connection is between the CIA, an Iraqi missile site, a Dutch diamond cutter, an Arab sheik, and the White House, but we assume there must be a logical connection—they are in the same book aren't they? There are some implicit connections already between the White House and the CIA, between an Arab sheik and Iraq, between terrorism and the Middle East—and we stay tuned to learn just how all these elements come together.

Authors who use this technique successfully often hint at the meaningful convergence in some subtle way: Perhaps the new character is talking to a minor character we just met in the earlier chapter, or says something that resonates with the earlier situation, or is in some predictable way implicitly connected to the issues of the story—when we switch from the point of view of the crook to that of the cop trying to catch him, for example. In genres such as the thriller, one of the rules is that everything must contribute directly to solving the main plot, so the reader assumes convergence as one of the rules of the genre.

One of the great satisfactions of reading such books is trying to figure out just how in the world the writer is going to bring all those far-flung elements together in some way that makes perfect sense. The masters of the genre play to this and create ever more unlikely convergences—which seem perfectly inevitable in retrospect. The more unlikely the elements, the more satisfying the effect.

But usually we want to ease the reader from one scene or chapter to another. The simple technique for testing this is to compare the ending of a chapter with the beginning of the next and ask, Which element continues? Which element will keep the reader oriented? If you employ a constant first-person point of view, for example, some basic continuity is achieved through the unifying personal voice. There are other ways.

Tom Wolfe begins *The Right Stuff* with a chapter entitled "Angels," in which he introduces first the young wife of a test pilot, Jane Conrad, as she waits for word of whether it was her husband, Pete, who has been killed in a crash. The scenario is repeated: Every few weeks it seems yet another crash leaves her waiting in dread to learn if her husband is dead or alive. Then Wolfe moves naturally to Pete. After each crash, he dons his Navy bridge coat, "the most stylish item in the Navy officer's wardrobe," with its double row of gold buttons. The flyers wear it only to funerals. The bridge coat becomes a repeated emblem of both death and camaraderie.

The chapter ends with Pete buttoning on the bridge coat one more time for a comrade's funeral, then, for a brief paragraph, skips ahead seven years to the dawning heyday of the astronauts, of which Pete is now one, to a reporter asking Jane, "Are you scared? America wants to know!"

"Why ask now?" she wants to say but doesn't, since only those inside the sorority of expectant widows can ever understand—harking back to the first lines of the chapter: "Within five minutes, or ten minutes, no more than that, three of the others had called her on the telephone to ask her if she had heard that something had happened out there." And all the dread that we have experienced with her since.

We turn the page to chapter two, titled "The Right Stuff": "What an extraordinary grim stretch that had been. . . . And yet thereafter, Pete and Jane would keep running into pilots from other Navy bases, from the Air Force, from the Marines, who had been through their own extraordinary grim stretches."

We're still with Pete and Jane, still pondering the deadly danger of flight test, transitioning into a discussion of the actual Right Stuff—the main theme of the book. The voice and point of view remain constant, the characters make the jump to chapter two with the reader, then fade into the broadening discussion of other pilots, the training of pilots, their evolution as men with the Right Stuff. Jane and Pete's experience is part of a larger picture. The book's aperture opens up.

We turn the page to chapter three, "Yeager," and the evolution is complete: "Anyone who travels very much on airlines in the United States soon gets to know the voice of the *airline pilot* . . . coming over the intercom . . . with a particular drawl, a particular folksiness, a particular down-home camlness that is so exaggerated it begins to parody itself (nevertheless!—it's reassuring). . . ."

The persona that began as a response to sheer terror now outwardly embodies the Right Stuff—and the laconic, understated, modest hero who best embodies it is Chuck Yeager.

The transitions make the story feel like all one thing, even though now the earlier characters have retreated into the background and a new character has taken the foreground. The connections make sense. There's a kind of argument being worked out in the developing story: Out of danger and terror emerges a certain breed of remarkable character, brave and slightly crazy, who has the Right Stuff America needs to conquer Space. The book will go on to follow through on that theme, chronicling the exploits of the astronauts and their wives.

So what creates a natural, logical link between your chapters? The main character? The central action? A continuous setting? Which element makes the jump to the next chapter, bringing the reader along with it?

If the answer is "nothing," think hard about how you might achieve that link without compromising the intention of your book. Remember, you're not just moving the story along smoothly; you're also moving along the ideas that underlie the story—the big themes that drove you to write it in the first place—as Wolfe moves along the theme of the Right Stuff.

Sometimes the best tactic is as straightforward as announcing the new locale, naming the new character, reorienting the reader to a new set of circumstances—that is, recognizing that the transition may seem abrupt and giving your reader a little help staying with the story. Like Wolfe, DeBlieu titles her chapters in *Wind* ("Creation's First Flood," "Guiding the Hand of History," "Of Body and Mind," and so on) so that each chapter title clues the reader to the direction her story will take—into myth, history, psychology— shifting gears, smoothing out the transition, while supporting her main theme: The invisible wind becomes visible through its myriad and profound effects.

Michael Shaara, in *The Killer Angels*, is even more categorical. His four main sections follow the chronology of the Battle of Gettysburg, dated June 29, 1863; July 1, 1863; July 2, 1863; and July 3, 1863. Within each section are numbered chapters named after their respective viewpoint characters: "Lee," "Buford," "Chamberlain," "Longstreet," and so on. We follow the action chronologically, according to a particular explicit perspective in each scene.

The organizational logic is simple, but also brilliant. It allows Shaara to present a sprawling, complex chain of events with a hundred and fifty thousand participants as a human story on a scale we can comprehend: Here's the timetable; here are the few characters you need to pay attention to; here's when to pay attention to them on their little corners of the battlefield. Forget about keeping track of the panoramic spectacle of events. Shaara provides an easy-to-follow narrative map.

His organizational design also supports his principal theme: War, like any great enterprise, finally comes down to individual choices made by fallible men in the lonely stillness of the human soul—Lee, Buford, Chamberlain, Longstreet.

What's the logic by which your chapters lead naturally one into the next?

Once you've established that the chapters dovetail smoothly into one another, apply the same test inside the chapter to scenes: How do we get from here to there?

The novice often dodges the issue of interior transition and inserts a space break. Used sparingly, a space break can function as a switch, alerting your reader to shift to a new locale, time, or point of view. But a space break is not a transition; it represents the *absence* of a transition.

A transition fills in the gaps between discrete scenes, bridges the distance between then and now, there and here. A transitional passage creates the necessary illusion that your story is not just a selection of a few moments in the lives of your characters, but rather a comprehensive account of everything they've ever done or said that matters: description, summary of intervening events, reflection by the narrator, a montage of quick images to indicate progress forward in time or space. The magic lies in creating that illusion of completeness—and it's the same illusion in both fiction and nonfiction: persistence of vision.

So now you've got a sound structure, each of the parts linked through clear, graceful transitions.

Revising for Story and Quality

You've already figured out that while you've been revising for structure, you couldn't help getting tangled up in the story—which also means the themes. A graceful transition often requires a good hard look at the logic of the story: What would such a person really do? What would the next event be in real life? Does nature really behave this way?

Now is the time to explicitly review the elements of the story:

- Narrative stance—Who is telling it, in what tone, and from what psychic distance?
- Plot or text—What big events actually happen and in what order?

- Theme or subtext—What underlying themes are carried through the book consistently?

If one of your chief themes, as is Steinbeck's in *The Grapes of Wrath*, is the injustice of want in the midst of plenty, then each scene will somehow incorporate that want: hunger for a meal, striving for a job, longing for greater spiritual fulfillment. Each chapter will play out the drama of the have-nots struggling to have, in a particular locale along the road, with the consequences escalating: Family members sicken, lose hope, desert, even die. And the chapters accrue into acts whose curtains form around the defining moments of the conflict between want and plenty, between haves and have-nots, sometimes violently, culminating in the emblematic final image of a childless young mother suckling a starving man, an ironic reversal of the natural order.

If your theme is going off track—if you began preoccupied by one idea and then switched in midstream—now is the time to catch the shift. Do you need to follow through on the earlier theme, or jettison it altogether and pick up on the one that evolved in its place? Which is the mistake? Is there room for both—or does one undercut the other?

Often it's a case of simply helping the story to remember its themes, adding a resonant image here, a line of dialogue there, a touch of description in between, to keep the story—and the reader—conscious of the underlying business of the story.

The two most common revisions are likely to be for *story logic* and *order of event*.

Story logic includes all questions of plausibility, psychology, and fact: Would this really happen? Would this character think like that? Is this true to the laws of nature?

Order of event is the key to all narrative, because the order in which you tell the events, true or fictive, is the order in which they happen for the first time to the reader. So the order must make sense and accumulate the urgency of suspense. If the reader can't figure out the larger pattern because the events happen in a mixed-up way, or if crucial knowledge is left out, the impact of the story will be blunted.

By the time we get to Steinbeck's Rose of Sharon, lying in the barn shortly after giving birth to a stillborn child among her doomed family and suckling a starving stranger, we've experienced a whole series of events that built inexorably toward that outcome. The ending is contained in the beginning: A paroled killer (Tom Joad) and his naive family, pushed to the limits of survival by drought and Depression, set out in an overloaded car with virtually no resources searching for the promised land, which, in their fantasies, they endow with childishly exaggerated virtues.

We know they haven't got a chance in hell of succeeding on their quest.

Tom already killed once—so it's no big surprise when he kills again. We've struggled through Rose of Sharon's difficult pregnancy as the family lives on starvation wages—we know prenatal malnutrition doesn't bode well for a newborn. The logic is all there, the order, in this case chronological, moves us toward an outcome that becomes more and more inevitable, as one after the other, the family's options are closed off.

Each of the plot elements is underpinned by a theme: want in the midst of plenty, faith in America, the class violence inherent in the capitalist scheme, family loyalty, hope in the face of doom.

Revising for quality, you pay attention to the texture of the story. You make sure the action is clear, the emotion hits the right pitch, the narrative stance is appropriate to the effects you are after. You may have to back the narrator out of a scene, or urge him in closer. You may have to address tonal inconsistencies—moments when the reader is unintentionally jarred by the narrator's sudden shift in attitude.

By now you are beginning to point the prose—the final stage in which you work with language as a poet does. You home in on scenes, paragraphs, sentences, phrases, finally individual words. You put to work all your hard-earned craft of sentences.

Cutting the Good Stuff

While you are writing, you are listening to your story. Listen closely and you'll discover astonishing things—things you never dreamed of when you started. That's the mystery of writing: We don't know what we know until we try to say it in words. At that stage of the process, write and listen, but don't judge.

But inevitably the moment arrives when you must determine where your interest lies. The book is all there—but too much of it is there. You have already let it simmer and steep awhile—a few weeks or months—so that when you go back to it, the awkward sentences, the clumsy metaphors, the improbable scenes stand out as though written in different-colored ink.

You cut them with pleasure.

But you're not really cutting until you're cutting the good stuff.

Any old hack can recognize an eyesore. But it takes a disciplined professional to recognize a lovely but redundant sentence, a clever but inapt metaphor, an arresting but distracting image, a beautifully crafted—and utterly incongruous—scene.

By this stage, it is crucial to know exactly what you are trying to achieve: What is your main theme? Serve that. All else is expendable. All the writing is strong, even beautiful. All the scenes are well developed, all the description lovely, all the exposition articulate, even witty. That's not the point now. The point is: Which parts serve the theme *best*? Which scene merely replays a drama that was already played out more effectively? Which amusing or instructive anecdote digresses too far from the main stem of the book? Which character, delightful as he or she comes across, is merely a distraction from the main business of the book?

I'm not suggesting that something as complex and multifaceted as a book should be—or even can be—corseted into a tight, linear format with a myopic obsession on a single explicit theme. But the writer can't afford to indulge the writing. Every part must be measured against the main thrust of the whole. Every part must give you a good reason to keep it in—justified by its participation in the large purpose of the book.

There's always too much: Any good book spills over the sides, overwhelms the structure created to contain it. Now you have to have some backbone and keep the book honest to its cause.

That's where the heartbreak comes in. That's the stage of the process when you feel blood on the cut tissue. It hurts. But the wounds heal over, and the book is stronger, more focused, more intensely what it is. At last, you realize what you're writing about, and that even beautiful writing must serve the cause.

Exercises

1. X-ray the "bones"—the structure—of your manuscript. What is the arc of story (the main progress from equilibrium toward crisis, followed by resolution and a return to a new equilibrium)? Does it break into three acts? What are the "curtains" for each act?

2. Lay out the chapters of your manuscript with the first and last pages showing. Check the first sentence of each chapter against the last, and the last sentence against the first sentence of the next chapter. Are the transitions logical? If you change point of view, locale, or story line from chapter to chapter, what is the pattern of the changes? Is it regular enough that the reader will catch on to your design?

3. Take an early draft of a piece of your own writing and state briefly what you *think* it is about: state your main theme as you perceive it. Now circle all the abstract nouns (e.g., *love, anger, frustration, joy, shame*), and list as many of them under a general rubric—a defining category—to see if there are any congruities. Compare the list to your stated theme. For example, if your list contains *liberty, independence, self-determination, autonomy, freedom,* and *right to privacy,* you can recognize a consistent theme under the rubric "politics" or "political rights." If you need many rubrics—many lists—to contain, for example, *obscenity, market volatility, introspectiveness, geopolitical perspective, seaworthiness,* and *compassion,* you may have some sorting out to do in order to identify your main thematic interest.

4. List the elements of your plot—the surface action of each act. What themes are actually being communicated by the action? How do you know?

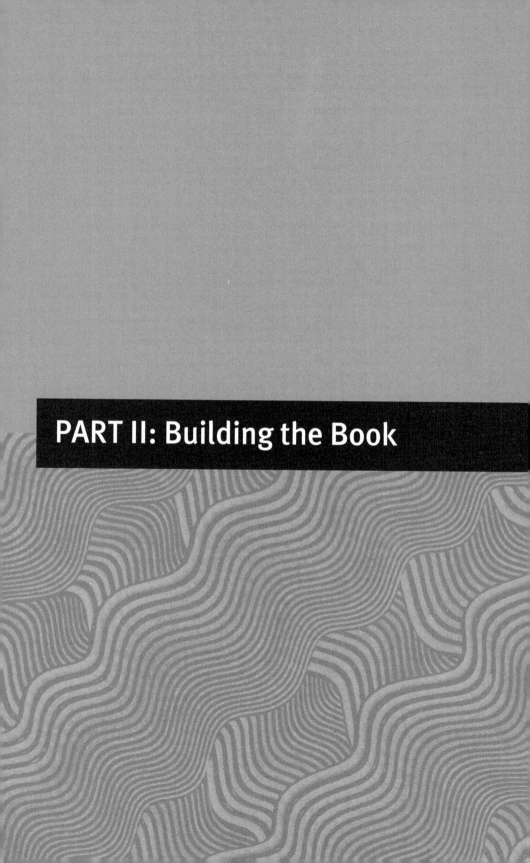

PART II: Building the Book

6

Developing Theme

So a writer, captured by a subject, really knows what his themes are going to be only after he has meditated at some length upon his work—usually in writing. You start with a *mystery*—an unknown outcome: a character in a predicament, a subject that fascinates you, a circumstance that intrigues you, a phenomenon that captures your curiosity. And as you explore it, as you assay your draft and recognize its structure, you discover where your interest lies—your real subject, your resonant themes.

Once you have discovered the theme or themes at the core of your work, hone and *develop* them the way a photographer develops film—clarifying, sharpening, creating nuances of highlight and shadow, composing the elements so that the eye is persistently drawn back to the center, by a variety of techniques:

• Creating repetitions and motifs consciously: that is, deliberately looking for opportunities where resonant images, words, even lines of dialogue would advance your story and opening up a space for them, thereby creating rhythm.

• Bringing them to the foreground with subtlety.

• Creating and manipulating *resonance*—as they play off other images, other scenes, other dialogue.

• Creating effects of scale—that is, effects that are purely the result of the length and scope of your project, impossible to create in a short story or article (see chapter eight).

- Accumulating meaning over the time of the narrative.
- Deciding what to leave out.

A good bit of this work is done intuitively—at least with practice. Sometimes you are captured by a feeling, a mood that colors the work implicitly. Sometimes it's best to look at thematic subtext out of the corner of your eye rather than straight on. You see more, and it doesn't disappear so readily. It's the unconscious of the story.

But at least in the beginning stages of a project, it's useful not to fool yourself about what you have, what you are after, and how to get there from here.

Repetition

The simplest tool of the writer is repetition.

Repetition creates emphasis: Just reading a phrase several times magnifies its importance. We notice it. We presume the writer is not senile: If a thing is repeated, there must be a good reason. So we pay attention to the thing repeated, tuck it away for future reference. Repetition also provokes memory: Rote learning may be out of vogue, but how do you think actors learn their lines? By the simple expedient of saying them over and over.

It works that way in a long story, too.

Tom Wolfe, the master of repetition (critics would contend that he's mastered it all too well), repeats his signature phrase "the Right Stuff" scores of times throughout the book of the same title, which chronicles the evolution of the military's flight test program into the NASA space program—and makes heroes of the flyers and astronauts. He turns technological history into a breathtaking adventure story— and the phrase "the Right Stuff" helps focus the legend of the daring young men in their jet-propelled glory.

Early in the book, he goes to great lengths to define the concept, which begins with unquestioned physical bravery:

But it was not bravery in the simple sense of being willing to risk your life. The idea seemed to be that any fool could do that, if that was all that was required, just as any fool could throw away his life in the process. No, the idea here (in the all-enclosing fraternity) seemed to be that a man should have the ability to go up in a hurtling piece of machinery and put his hide on the line and then have the moxie, the reflexes, the experience, the coolness, to pull it back in the last yawning moment?—and then to go up again *the next day*, and the next day and every next day, even if the series should prove infinite—and ultimately, in its best expression, do so in a cause that means something to thousands, to a people, a nation, to humanity, to God.

The book opens with the young wife of a naval aviator anxiously awaiting word from the squadron—will it be word that her husband is safe, or notification of his death? The early chapters of the book recount, in dramatic detail, the harrowing exploits of test pilots. One after another, aviators "screw the pooch," "auger in," fall from the sky and are "burned beyond recognition."

Fail at the last crucial moment to have the Right Stuff.

The catalogue of disasters imbues the term with a deadly connotation. Whenever it is repeated throughout the book—in the context of Mercury, Gemini, Apollo, even in training—it conjures an exact association with that killer proving ground for hot fighter jocks: flight test. And reminds the reader again and again that, for these men, the test of courage is not one test "but a seemingly infinite series of tests."

The Right Stuff. "A man either had it or he didn't! There was no such thing as having *most* of it."

The simplest tool of the writer is repetition.

Resonance and Cumulative Meaning

I've just finished a manuscript of a novel I've been burning to write for years: a fictional memoir about a generation of boys waiting to go to war—to Vietnam—which is how I spent my teenaged years. It opens at St. Dismas-of-the-Cross Preparatory Academy in Maryland, where the headmaster is indoctrinating the new boys in the founding myth of the school.

The first line: " 'Beginning not in slaughter but prayer,' Father Leo said."

He goes on to recount the annihilation of the Knights of St. Dismas-of-the-Cross on the Jerusalem Road during the Crusades—a slaughter made possible only by their extreme valor and unquestioning loyalty unto death to each other and their God.

The duel between slaughter and prayer—the sacred and the profane, redemption through physical sacrifice—forms the paradoxical theme of the book.

The theme is developed in at least three ways. First, in background, through references to other wars:

• The slaughter of the original crusading knights comes back from time to time.

• The boys play a violent war game called Storm the Castle on the hill behind the school, borrowing tactics from Napoleon—and remember even in adulthood the wounds they inflicted on one another.

• A rich boy named Wiley Chute Beauchamps III from Charleston converts his room into a virtual Shrine of the Lost Cause—complete with busts of Robert E. Lee, a wall-sized battle flag, and a legion of miniature Union and Confederate soldiers with which he replays bloody set-piece battles—until a cadre of other boys steals all of his memorabilia and sinks it in the nearby lake.

• The boys study Wilfred Owen's "Dulce et Decorum Est" in English class—a bitter evocation of World War I—from an eccentric instructor whose brother, unbeknownst to them, was killed in the Vietnam War.

• The father of the narrator, Tom Lovett, survived the retreat from the Chosin Reservoir in Korea. The only time he ever strikes Tom, he permanently scars Tom's face with his souvenir Marine ring.

Second, in background and foreground, through specific, concrete images of the lovely and terrible violence of boy culture—the intense, gentle, emotional attachments side by side with the cruel hazing. Every act, large or small, contains both violence and grace:

• After a brutal soccer practice played in bare feet, a boy named Peter washes another boy, Tom's, blistered feet—and Peter once split open Tom's skull with a blow from a field hockey stick during Storm the Castle.

• A soccer game—played in the memory of a coach killed in Vietnam—turns into a bloody brawl.

• A nocturnal canoe outing on a hauntingly beautiful lake nearly ends in drowning.

• A hockey game during a postcard Christmas homecoming ends with a boy deliberately crippling his younger brother—to keep him out of the war.

And so on. Every piece of knowledge is hard-fought, won through fierce competition and pain—the willingness to inflict it and to absorb it—all under the vigilant eyes of the brothers and their sacred, dangerous honor code. The school motto: "Being a good loser takes practice—DON'T."

Third, in foreground, right on the surface of the story through the intrusion of the Vietnam War itself:

• "Twenty-six St. Dismas boys, some of whom we'd known as underclassmen, had already died in Vietnam, and seven more would die that year, in the final spasm of the war. Their names would be chiseled with the rest into the marble slab at the left of the altar, behind the pulpit where Father Leo stood giving the new boys their lesson in Crusader-priests. Every war had its marble wall of names, a roll-call of the dead, so that being in chapel was like being entombed inside a sepulcher, surrounded by restless spirits who had died too young amid the violence of foreign battlefields. Because they were St. Dismas boys, they had, almost without exception, died officers."

• After evening bull sessions spent reading aloud letters from one of the boys' brothers who is fighting in Vietnam, ogling his grisly trophy photos by flashlight like *Playboy* centerfolds, the narrator dreams violent nightmares of cowardice and mutilation: "We had the sense that we were preparing to go out into a lethal world, where we would strike like matches, flare brilliantly, and then be used up in an instant."

• Peter Albemarle, the main character, yearns to fly jets in Vietnam, and eventually becomes a deadly hero in the Gulf War: "He wanted to zoom over that jungly nightmare and light it up with tracers, rockets, automatic cannon fire, make it bloom with napalm. His convictions were not political but visceral—he craved the thrill."

None of this is the plot. The plot is the story of how the narrator is called upon by Peter Albemarle, twenty-five years later, to recover the body of his wife, who dies in a diving accident in the Caribbean under questionable circumstances. To solve the mystery of how she died, the narrator must solve the mystery of what happened at St. Dismas all those years ago. To determine how Peter is implicated in her death, he must ultimately solve Peter's enigmatic character, and to do that he must relive their shared boyhood, reinterpreting events he has completely misunderstood all this time—including the suspicious disappearance of one of the brothers. And most of those events have to do with the cultural habit of violence and the mystery of how it forged friendships as passionate and heartbreaking as true love.

As it happens, the narrator, Tom, must descend into the darkness of a different kind of sepulcher—an underwater cave wherein the dead woman's body is trapped—before he can rise toward the light of knowledge. Thematically speaking.

At the level of literal action, it's just a spooky cave. Tom's mission is just a grim favor for an old best friend. But if I've done my job right, the reader remembers that chapel, that marble roll call of the dead, and all the nightmares of cowardice. That's what we mean when we say that a certain image or idea *informs* a scene: The memory of it colors the meaning of the scene, gives it force, spins it with irony.

Every literal action should be ballasted with an underlying resonance that plays upon memories of other moments in the novel. Just below the surface of the plot, triggered by the images of what is actually happening at the moment, the reader should feel a resonance like overtones in music, a sympathetic vibration of themes. The same chord struck in different octaves, in major and minor keys, echoing through memory, calling up associations of other incidents earlier in the novel.

That's what narrative is: a chain of deliberate memories.

And it's not enough just to repeat similar thematic moments: There must be a sense of development, an escalation of tension and consequence, of movement toward a moment of truth after which things can never be the same. The culture of violence creates irreversible consequences. So what begins as a lecture on Crusader-priests and a mock schoolboy battle on a muddy hill ultimately ends in actual war and death: All those years later, Peter Albemarle winds up on the cover of *Time* for shooting down three Iraqi fighter jets on the same day; he also winds up as a suspect in the murder of his wife.

The consequences ratchet up: Fear and desire become action, with higher and higher stakes.

I don't know if it works. That will depend ultimately on the quality of the writing, the urgency and coherence of the story as the reader experiences it—which all comes down to execution, how well I've actually done what I think I've done. That's the maddening part of this writing business. All I know is how I tried to make the reader feel what I felt writing it—the old fear and exhilaration, the guilt and absolution—by repetition with spin, variations on a theme, by a relentless lexicon of violence, by a chain of invented memories, by a little bloody history of the sort that seduces impressionable boys on the verge of manhood.

Like I used to be.

Text and Subtext

With all this talk about developing themes, it's crucial to remember one precept: Before you can have meaningful subtext, you have to have compelling text.

That is, the plot has to be plausible and interesting; the surface action coherent and compelling; the characters real, active and captivating; the shape of the story pleasing and suspenseful, escalating toward a defining moment after which things can never be the same—

before you can lead the reader into the deeper themes. There has to be a good story happening on the page before that story can mean something deeply significant between the lines.

And if it is what the old scribes used to call a good yarn, it probably already has underlying significance, waiting to be recognized, heightened, emphasized.

Time and again, a young writer will say, "I'm writing a novel about how faith triumphs over adversity," or, ". . . how a woman realizes she must lead her own life," or ". . . how a boy grows up and realizes he must leave home." There's usually a lot of "realizing" going on, thoughts and reflections and memories, but it's usually fairly abstract; the writer has a firm grasp of his or her theme—the subtext—but no sense of concrete action.

So ask: What's the actual test of faith in the story? What crisis causes a woman to take control of her life? What specific event jolts a boy into a longing to leave his loved ones and strike out on his own? What do these people look like? Where do they live? What is the immediate source of tension in their lives? What do they want more than anything in the world? What actions will they take to get it? Who or what is out there to stop them? What are they afraid of? How is that fear manifest in the action of the story? How will they confront that fear in an actual scene? What resources can help them face that fear, perhaps even overcome it? What's the moment of truth—not what does it *mean*, but what actually occurs in a literal, physical way? Why will any of this matter to us?

Before you can mount an epic battle between good and evil, you have to create a plausible Ahab and a great white whale and set them loose on an ocean of story.

Story Elements and Melodrama

Novices often have a misguided impulse to cram in all sorts of melodrama—to be interesting: rape, incest, murder, suicide, child abuse. But because they lack the craft, we assume the fault lies in the material, what they've chosen to write about. In fact, each of the subjects and themes individually may be compelling, but combining them all in the same narrative frequently causes two things to go wrong: First, the writer doesn't take the trouble and space to delve deeply enough into any particular subject or theme in order to make it original, and it winds up being a surface gloss, a generalized or summarized version, and therefore a cliché; second—and related—the many subjects and themes compete for the reader's attention, just as they do for the writer's diffusing focus, detracting from one another.

The ambition to pack the book full of interesting material is right, but the execution is flawed. Three strategies will serve the writer in this predicament:

1. Select story elements wisely. Cull those elements that carry the action "over the top." If you have a story in which a young woman is raped, her friends all experience sexual abuse, a child is killed in a drive-by shooting, an AIDS victim suffers discrimination, while various TVs replay images of famine in Somalia, civil war in Bosnia, and Chinese human rights abuses, you probably have about six too many loaded subjects on the burner. Where does your interest lie? Which is at the center of your story? Which was the subject that ignited your passion? Choose the one you really care about—the one you feel most keenly, the one you know about most deeply—and work it out in human dimensions.

2. Flatten the language. The hotter the action, the cooler you want the language, to a point. (Exaggerated understatement also can sabotage a serious passage with an over-the-top hard-boiled effect that makes the reader laugh at exactly the wrong moment: "The kid was dead. She cried. Joey cried. I cried. We all cried. . . .") Anytime you are writing about sex, violence, war, torture, genocide, child molestation, nuclear annihilation, any subject that carries great weight and is loaded with emotion, stay away from lurid language. Plain language and dramatic restraint will allow the action to claim its own importance—not because the adjectives and adverbs are shouting for attention, but because what is going on in the piece is profound and moving. You are removing the narrative personality and the high-profile language that might obstruct the reader's view of the story.

In *In Cold Blood*, Truman Capote describes the hanging of multiple murderer Perry Smith, whom the reader has come to know intimately, in a restrained, journalistic fashion, partly through the reaction of Kansas Bureau of Investigation Agent Alvin Dewey: "Steps, noose, mask; but before the mask was adjusted, the prisoner spat his chewing gum into the chaplain's outstretched palm. Dewey shut his eyes; he kept them shut until he heard the thud-snap that announces a rope-broken neck."

The careful reporting of the mundane last details of a man's life— the chewing gum—quiets the scene. And the reader is invited, like Agent Dewey, to close his eyes to the actual execution, waiting for the telltale sound—which, of course, is more startling. The fact that even the man who hunted the murderer down, who earnestly believes Smith deserves to be executed, can't bear to witness his actual death lends it a human dignity. There's no gloating, no celebration, just a reluctant sense of doing what must be done, however unpleasant, to satisfy justice.

3. Recognize the subtext. Never write a love scene that is only about love, a sex scene that is only about sex, or a scene of violence that is only about violence. The key to writing scenes that might otherwise be trite, lurid, or sentimental is *subtext*: the crucial action happening under the scene. This is what critics mean when they speak of gratu-itous sex and violence—sex and violence for their own sakes, lacking subtext to give them artistic meaning.

Elsewhere in *In Cold Blood*, Capote recounts the horrific murder of the entire Clutter family in excruciating detail, letting the killers tell most of the story through their confessions, but not for the pruri-ent thrill of replaying the event. He's after a deeper purpose, an answer to the mystery of the event. Capote writes, "But the confessions, though they answer the questions of how and why, failed to satisfy his sense of meaningful design. The crime was a psychological accident, virtually an impersonal act; the victims might as well have been killed by lightning. Except for one thing: they had experienced prolonged terror, they had suffered." Were it not for that deeper purpose, a reader with conscience would feel guilty, embarrasssed, sullied by what he has just witnessed.

In *For Whom the Bell Tolls,* Hemingway writes a sexual love scene between Maria, a Spanish partisan, and Robert Jordan, his main character, a soldier of fortune whose mission is to blow up a bridge held by the Fascists. As they make love in Jordan's sleeping robe, "For him it was a dark passage which led to nowhere . . . now beyond all bearing up, up, up and into nowhere, suddenly, scaldingly, holdingly all nowhere gone and time absolutely still and they were both there, time having stopped and he felt the earth move out and away from under them."

The passage has been widely satirized for the expression "felt the earth move." But notice the context more carefully: ". . . he felt the earth move *out and away from under them.*" He's not talking about an incredible orgasm; he's talking about two people, one a refugee who has been gang-raped, the other an expatriate with profound doubts about the morality of the killing he is about to do, coming unmoored. They seek in each other not just sex but context, a place to belong, an absolution from past and future shame.

Their lovemaking is an act of desperation, a last bid for human connection—that's the subtext. Their connection can exist only unconnected to the real world in which they live and fight.

A scene may work through *indirection*—that is, characters talk about one thing out loud but are really talking about something else much more significant. A husband and wife argue about the money he's spent on a set of new titanium golf clubs, say, but what the wife is talking about is loneliness; what the husband is talking about is frustration.

Frequently, the subtext plays *against* the text: A scene of violence reveals tenderness; a love scene evokes loneliness; a sex scene unlocks a psychological dimension to a key character; a funeral becomes an opportunity for humor.

A war story becomes a love story.

Time and the Story

In any story, time matters in at least two basic ways:

   1. Sense of duration—how much story time is covered.

2. Sense of the clock—of time passing, counting down toward an outcome.

The second obviously depends on the first: If the story covers a summer, then as the weeks and months go by, we anticipate the end of the summer and therefore the outcome of the story.

The longer the story, the more it matters.

Beginning a book not knowing its chronological span is like starting out on a long journey without a clue as to how far you must travel. How will you know if you're making progress? How will you fall into the right pace? How will you know when you are closing in on your goal?

You will be able to count how many pages are left, but you miss an important element of storytelling: suspense. Suspense is made up of a crucial question and the delay in answering that question. So literal cues about passage of time become important in creating that sense of delay—because the more time that's passed, the less time is left. The drama is becoming more urgent. The solution finally becomes imminent.

Memory and Emotion

In O'Brien's terms, " . . . memory and imagination and language combine to make spirits in the head."

The long prose forms use memory in a complex way. The words are meant to trigger associations from the reader's own life—to act as emotional cues—much as a Method actor deliberately recalls a personal experience that parallels the scene he is acting in order to simulate the emotion that a person in that scene would be feeling. The difference is, of course, that the experience is inverted: When the prose is working, the reader recalls the parallel experience unconsciously and instantaneously in response to the cue, and the writer, unlike the actor, has no control over which particular memory the reader recalls.

The writer describes a failed love affair, and the reader feels the pang of his own broken heart over a woman he broke up with in high school. The writer tells of being a scared child, and the reader recalls how she felt as a little girl away at camp for the first time, lying awake, scared of the dark. The writer is after emotional congruence—trying to provoke the reader's participation in the story.

Of course, the writer can have no idea which actual details the reader's memory will supply, but if the emotion is truly universal, he can count on the reader's having some experience that parallels the one in the story in at least a passing way, though often the story takes on the extreme case. Every reader has known, in some form, fear, love, doubt, betrayal, faith, hope, despair, panic, pride, pain, outrage, terror, depression, exhilaration, the urge to violence, shame, longing, happiness—even if he has not fought in a war, solved a major crime, pitched in the World Series, lost the family farm, emigrated to Ireland, fought off a rapist, won the Nobel peace prize, survived cancer, lost a child, fled slavery, run for president, or landed on the moon.

The typical reader's life has been full of small crises, everyday drama. Opportunities for public heroism don't come to everyone. And most people don't run the affairs of nations; they run the affairs of their townships, their parishes, their PTAs. But their emotional equipment is the same as that of princesses and heroes. The writer taps into that congruence of emotions. The reader can feel the emotional truth of extraordinary action. Through the words on the page, the reader can participate emotionally in the experience.

The fiction or nonfiction novel uses the reader's memory in another way: it relies on the reader's ability to recall the gist of the story and the specifics of character and event. As the novel accumulates, the requirements of memory become daunting.

Realize just how much this is asking of a reader: By the beginning of the last chapter of, say, *The Grapes of Wrath*, Steinbeck is counting on the reader's ability to remember 388 pages—more than a hundred thousand words' worth of names, places, events, nuances of character, historical background, physical descriptions, past action, dialogue, and narrative reflection. All of it, every word, is essential context for the final scene. Forget any important part of it, and the power of Rose of Sharon's gesture at the end of the book is diminished.

And all that material has been learned over time—perhaps weeks or months of reading, with varying degrees of concentration and comprehension, with interruptions in between, with time to forget. And each thing has colored the way we read and remember the next thing—it's a chain, the links connected in a certain precise order.

The narrative is like one of those strands of Christmas lights wired in a series: If one light goes out, they all go out.

We've stopped reading.

That's the main reason why, if we read a hundred pages of a book and are then interrupted for a long time, we rarely go back to it: We can no longer remember what we've read as part of a chain of events; we have only a vague impression, but no urgency to continue, no sense of expectation—suspense—about what's to come, unless we reread up to the point of interruption. Suspense depends on at least a short-term memory of the events in their order.

But a curious thing happens *after* we've finished reading: We no longer remember the order, only the accumulated effect. That's another paradox about reading: The order of the telling is crucial to our interest as we read, but it becomes irrelevant after we've finished. Then all events exist together in a single moment of time, the "moment" of the book—we recall them out of order, they blend into one another, impressionistically.

It's as if we've returned from a journey, a vacation trip to Bermuda, say. On the kitchen table, we've got dozens of snapshots of faces, events, monuments, museums, in no particular order. We've forgotten the anxiety of almost missing our connecting flight in Dallas, the suspense about what exactly Bermuda will look like and whether it will rain during our week there. We can't exactly retrace our steps to that quaint little shop off the beaten track. Yet amid the random glimpses of favorite scenes, characters, and events, the trip has left a single strong impression. It means something in our lives.

Of course, without the right ordering, we never would finish—we would not feel the compelling vector of story driving us forward, playing on our curiosity and memory, promising and paying off, but not before another, more intriguing promise has been made.

And without some substantive, cumulative effect that stays with us after we've read, the deft ordering, the quickening pulse of suspense, would be an empty exercise, the book instantly forgettable.

The book relies on the accumulation of scenes, images, ideas, emotions, landscape into a larger whole impression.

But does the reader really remember all of it? Clearly no—not in the sense of being able to retell it in verbatim detail. What the reader remembers are moments, effects, and a general impression of the arc of the story and the texture of the writing.

So as he reads, the reader is never really remembering everything at once—any more than the writer can write everything at once. He is experiencing movement through time and space, a movement resonant with memories of what has gone before. A subtle and implicit way to create the sense of time passing, informed by memory, is through *rhythm*.

Rhythm

Rhythm exploits not just the memory of the writer, returning again and again to a key image, an emblematic phrase that unlocks a rush of associations, but also the memory of the reader. The reader remembers parts of it as he reads—the parts necessary for the current scene to have power. Rhythm is one tool the writer uses to cue those exact parts the reader needs to have in the forefront of his mind to comprehend the scene in front of him.

E.M. Forster defines rhythm in a novel as "repetition plus variation." He cites Marcel Proust's repeated musical phrases in *A la recherche du temps perdu* (Remembrance of Things Past) as elements of a rhythm developing "toward the establishment of beauty and the ravishing of the reader's memory."

Beauty and memory, two ingredients essential to a great work.

In the case of Steinbeck, the rhythm is not created by a succession of musical phrases but by weather: Rain and drought are the heartbeat of *The Grapes of Wrath*. It opens with the paradox of rain that does not refresh—because it comes too late: "To the red country and part of the gray country of Oklahoma, the late rains came gently, and they did not cut the scarred earth."

All along the Joads' journey, images of drought and refreshment recur like music, underscoring the theme of want in the midst of plenty but also creating unconscious links to memory. At each mention of dust, the reader is reminded of the Oklahoma Dustbowl, the reason the Joads have been forced on the road in the first place. Every mention of rain is a taunt, a reminder of the one ingredient that eluded them, that could not be conjured by hard work, dedication to family and land, even faith in the Lord.

When the drought is broken and rain finally arrives—all at once in torrents—the timing is disastrous.

As the last chapter opens, "In the boxcar camp the water stood in puddles, and the rain splashed in the mud." The flood waters engulf the boxcar, and the Joads flee to higher ground. But the rain is relentless, the flood unstoppable. Their doom, begun by drought, now is to be completed by the rain they have awaited for so long.

Even the word *rain* takes on a reverse talismanic value in the novel. It is always the thing just out of reach, an emblem of the promised land, the saving element that changes into an agent of destruction. An unlucky charm. It reminds us how often we are outdoors in the novel, how exposed the Joads are to the vicissitudes of weather—and every other force, natural or man-made.

The idea is expressed as a physical reality, a vivid image that recurs time and again in a great variety of circumstances, setting a rhythm, stimulating memory.

The fact of rain takes on different local meanings in specific passages, but always the paradox of rain and drought, feast and famine, verdure and desert, fertility and barrenness (think of Rose of Sharon, her baby stillborn, her breasts secreting milk)—all literal, in this book—swims just under the words.

This is a book that could only have been written by a man who slept on the ground, lived in the fields, studied the sky with apprehension and wonder. The themes are authentic because the writer's experience of them is authentic—the visceral memories of his own hard-luck days leach into the words. That's where his passion began, and the rhythm of weather developed naturally out of that physical knowledge.

In Frank McCourt's *Angela's Ashes*, food references set the rhythm.

Again, we are acutely aware that the authenticity of the rhythm comes from the writer's own experience—even more so, since this is a nonfiction account. Hardly a scene goes by without a mention of bread, buttered potatoes, tea and biscuits, fresh eggs, apples and bananas, toffee and butterscotch sweets—usually because they are lacking. On a long nighttime drive, I listened to the audio version of McCourt reading the book, and by the time I was a hundred miles from home, I had a nearly overpowering hunger for a baked potato.

The book is about hunger: the physical hunger of young Frank and his brothers and sisters—who go to bed hungry, yearn for food, dream about food, talk about it, even steal it—but also a hunger for security, for love, for respectability, for a better life. The rhythm of hunger is so powerful—inflecting scenes about play, war, politics, religion, family strife, sickness, even death—that after reading only a few chapters, the reader is famished.

"Done badly," Forster warns us, "rhythm is most boring, it hardens into a symbol and instead of carrying us on it trips us up." It can't be planned in a rigorous way to fit some preconceived design but "has to depend on a local impulse when the right interval is reached."

Tom Wolfe, for instance, does many things well, but he often overdoes what he does well, spoiling the rhythm of a scene with overstatement.

A Man in Full, his novel about a millionaire Atlanta businessman bankrupted when the bubble burst on the "Decade of Greed," is preoccupied with distinctions of class, with the correlation—or gap—between appearances and reality. This is a familiar theme for Wolfe, who as a social chronicler is a genius: He understands that the outward trappings of material culture—cars, furniture, clothes—can be profound indicators of our values. In particular, Wolfe is preoccupied with clothes. Since nearly all characters have to be dressed somehow, this would seem a natural, subtle way to constantly remind the reader *sotto voce* of some of the concerns of the novel.

But in this novel Wolfe seems incapable of subtlety. Here is one of his characters, an African-American attorney name Roger "Too" White (get it?!), appraising a roomful of folks at a press conference.

> The older men's taste, if it could be called that, ran to gray beards consisting of out-of-control ten-week stubbles that had spread like crabgrass on the undersides of their jowls and

practically down to their Adam's apples. Made you itchy just looking at it. They wore baggy polo shirts, completely unbuttoned at the neck, with short sleeves hanging down to their elbows. There were no neckties; not one. There were two jackets, one on the hunched-over back of a paunchy white man, a newspaper reporter, judging by his notebook. He had on an ordinary cotton button-down shirt—the dignity of which had been subverted by the fact that he had been one button off when he buttoned the shirt, causing the right side of the collar to wind up two and a half inches lower than the left. One was a woman, the only decently dressed person among the whole bunch of them.

Where a stroke here or there would give us the intuitive impression of shabbiness without interrupting the action of the scene, Wolfe paints the whole wardrobe—not in his character's voice, but in his own. He does this again and again throughout the novel so that instead of the reader accumulating a distinct impression without realizing it, the reader finds himself skipping whole passages of such description to get on with the story.

Even particular articles of clothing, such as Roger "Too" White's expensive crêpe de chine neckties or the bank enforcer's skull-and-crossbones suspenders, are repeated over and over without variation, highlighted, called attention to, hardened into symbols as plain as varsity letters.

Wolfe's chief flaw lies in his unwillingness to allow the reader the pleasure of discovery: He must connect all the dots, not just once, but over and over again, in case the reader missed the obvious. This is why the novel eventually becomes tiresome for the intelligent, energetic reader who craves the "aha moment," as Wolfe himself titles one of his chapters. That delicious feeling of discovery is always foreclosed by Wolfe's irrepressible authorial narrator butting into the story and spoiling the suspense—like the nervous party boor who blurts out the punch line of a great joke before the setup is finished.

In addition to a habit of restraint, that local impulse depends a good deal on your own visceral memory—the authentic experience you bring to the work—as well as on which memory you want to tweak, which associations you want to recall to the foreground, which part of the past informs the present.

The rhythmic resonance derives from the intersection of private passion—personal emotional experience, such as Steinbeck's experience with extreme weather or McCourt's with hunger—with the larger world: big ideas, public subjects, universal themes.

Don't belabor the technique: If it doesn't come naturally, instinctively, out of your own deeply felt emotional past, you'll be like Wolfe, pasting symbols onto characters. Or like Max Perkins' self-conscious hat tosser, trying way too hard, missing the hat rack every time.

Exercises

1. Take a short scene from your writing that contains "loaded" action, and excise all adjectives and adverbs. Rewrite it, letting the action, in spare language, carry the drama.

2. In your long manuscript, identify an image or a phrase that recurs frequently. Why does it recur? How does this image or phrase resonate with your own experience? What is the effect you are after? Can you heighten the effect even more with judicious repetition and development of the image or phrase?

3. Turn to the key scene of your long manuscript. What does the reader have to remember about the characters, story, past action, and theme to appreciate the full significance of the scene?

7

Connecting With the Reader

Nobody likes to be preached at—including your reader. *Especially* your reader, who has just plunked down $29.95 for a thrilling, thought-provoking ride through your imagination. The reader craves a voice he can count on—persuasive and sincere, a voice that doesn't shout at him like a car commercial, yet one that carries a quiet authority.

Even Jesus, a powerful orator who addressed themes as consequential as sin, redemption, and eternal life, understood that these monumental themes were best presented in stories, rather than as abstract exhortations. He was the consummate preacher who, if the Gospels are accurate, shied away from sounding preachy every chance he got. Hence the parables—simple in design, complex in interpretation.

In most parables, there is no unambiguous answer to the issue being treated—as in the "Parable of the Prodigal Son" (Luke 15:11–32), for instance. The son who has demanded his inheritance early, then squandered it, winds up broke and lonesome in a foreign land. He's savvy enough to go home, hoping for the best.

The father celebrates his return by slaughtering the fatted calf and inviting all his neighbors in for a great feast—the kind of feast his loyal son, who stayed behind to manage the farm and work beside his father, never got.

The subject is simple—a wayward young man returns home. But the issue is not so simple: What do we think is the right action for the father to take? Should we feel gratified that the spoiled young man gets himself into trouble and then counts on his rich daddy to bail him out? It's clear that, had everything been fine, the prodigal son would have forgotten all about family and home, and his responsibility to both. It's only when he falls flat broke and begins reflecting on how well even his father's servants are treated at home that he comes crawling back: "And when he came to himself, he said, How many hired servants of my father's have bread enough to spare, and I perish from hunger!"

The prodigal is not exactly a sensitive and repentant son.

Is it fair for the loyal stay-at-home son to be deprived of any special recognition, to be rebuked by his father for craving it? Or does that just make him a chump? Where's the justice? What in heaven's name is the lesson?

The ending is not much help. After the elder son objects, "Lo, these many years do I serve thee, neither transgressed I at any time thy commandment: and yet thou never gavest me a kid, that I might make merry with my friends," the father retorts, "Son, thou art ever with me, and all that I have is thine"—though apparently that doesn't extend to fatted calves. Then he repeats the joyous exclamation with which he welcomed home the prodigal son: ". . . thy brother was dead, and is alive again; and was lost, and is found."

The father dodges the good son's question. He answers logic with emotion.

It turns out that the *theme* of the parable is the overriding theme of all the New Testament parables: a shift in the paradigm by which a whole people interpret their sacred stories. Previously, the efficacy of a story was determined by the criterion of justice—that is, under the law of Moses, were a person's actions fairly rewarded or punished? Did he get what he deserved?

This is actually very close to the paradigm of justice that drives Greek tragedy, designed to evoke pity and fear from the actions of exemplary public figures in extraordinary trying circumstances: pity that a noble character suffers too greatly for his transgression; fear that if it could happen to a king, it could happen to us. The punishment is disproportional, which allows us to feel compassion rather than condemnation for an Oedipus or an Iphigenia. They've been punished too much, so *we*—audience and reader—can go easy on them, endowing us with a warm feeling of humaneness, especially because our fear identifies us with them. The Greek playwrights counted on their audience sharing a strict sense of justice.

Jesus' thematic twist is to substitute mercy for justice—forgiveness instead of punishment. The emotion of love triumphs over the logic of retribution. That's the new deal, the whole reason for his ministry. His great theme.

So theme is what the story is thinking about underneath the apparent subject.

In telling the parables, Jesus displays expert storycraft:

• He presents the issue not as a simple all-or-nothing dichotomy but as a *choice* that will always carry certain contradictions—in this case, that to grant mercy and forgiveness, one must sacrifice a little justice. He respects his material.

• He *personalizes* the issue, casting a giant abstract absolute into the particular human lives of a man and his two sons (characters), concretely and specifically evoked. None is a villain or a caricature—he respects his characters.

• He gets his message across through *indirection*: There's no outright mention of Jesus' intention to introduce a new standard for moral judgment and divine salvation—he's just telling us a story about a man whose son once left home and then came back. We have to ponder its meaning for ourselves—and therein lies our satisfaction. The storyteller implicitly trusts that we are smart enough and our judgment is sound enough that we can makes sense of his story without his spelling out everything. He respects his audience.

Honor Thy Reader

The overriding principle: *Trust your reader.*

Your reader wants the writer to respect his intelligence, to make him feel included, not to show off your erudition at his expense. Don't talk down to your reader, but don't make him feel stupid, either, by slinging around jargon or technical knowledge that the average educated person is unlikely to know. When in doubt, explain technical matters as precisely and readably as you can. Use a glossary, a map, an appendix, if you have to—anything in service of clarity.

Your reader wants to be clear on the literal action of the story—who is actually doing what to whom, where, when, and in what real-world context. Your reader hates to be confused, insulted, deliberately offended for no good reason.

John Gardner makes the case in *The Art of Fiction* that how the writer treats his reader is directly related to how he writes about his characters—real or imagined: "Sanity in a writer is merely this: However stupid he may be in his private life, he never cheats in writing. He never forgets that his audience is, at least ideally, as noble, generous, and tolerant as he is himself (or more so), and never forgets that he is writing about people, so that to turn characters to cartoons, to treat his characters as innately inferior to himself, to forget their reasons for being as they are, to treat them as brutes, is bad art."

Your reader craves a sense that the story is leading somewhere interesting and important. Your reader wants to be challenged, put on his mettle, encouraged to use his wits. Most of all, your reader does not want to be bored. He wants to feel suspense, excitement, a sense of discovery, an eagerness to read on—not merely for entertainment, though entertainment is part of the experience, but for a deeper sense of involvement, a complete immersion in a world more vivid and compelling than everyday reality.

Your reader wants to learn things he never knew before, to feel a sense of satisfaction and accomplishment and enlightenment for having read your book.

The reader wants to feel elevated rather than debased by reading your book—which according to Gardner begins as a matter of taste: "To write with taste, in the highest sense, is to write with the assumption that one out of a hundred people who read one's work may be dying, or have some loved one dying; to write so that no one commits suicide, no one despairs; to write, as Shakespeare wrote, so that people understand, sympathize, see the universality of pain, and feel strengthened, if not directly encouraged to live on."

For Gardner, writing well is a matter of life and death—your reader may be desperate for the truth of your book. Gardner recognizes that great books—like all great art—*are* great precisely because they change lives. They have an indelible effect on the imagination, the conscience, the intellect of those who experience them.

This is thrilling—and terrifying.

Storycraft and the Reader

Plenty of strategies are available to the writer for giving greater weight and impact to the theme and connecting more powerfully with the reader:

• Repetition—for emphasis and to jog memory—establishing rhythm. We've talked about this already, but it's worth reminding ourselves that all long narrative relies on memory, and anything the writer can do to make a story memorable—scene by scene or across the grand sweep of the whole—gives it that much more chance to succeed.

• An accurate story sense: telling a story that somehow hits a nerve. This is partly instinctive and partly based on honesty—asking yourself whether the story you are telling is big enough, important enough, universal enough to warrant the reader's attention. Nothing is significant merely because it happened to you or to one you love, Hemingway reminds us.

• Choice of the right diction to create the most effective voice and proper tone. Language has some of the dynamic qualities of music. Forster recognized this in Tolstoy's work. Poets worry over their words. Prose writers can benefit from some "word discipline."

• Clarity of style—using active, precise verbs, focused sentences, definite referents, graceful transitions, accurate terms.

• Signature detail as a shorthand for both establishing the "reality" of a scene on the page and reminding the reader of something he read one hundred pages ago.

• Tasteful handling of rough material.

• Humor. The hardest effect to achieve, one that relies on an innate sensibility and timing.

• Metaphor—the expression of one thing in terms of something else.

• Narrative candor—admitting when a "fact" is actually speculation or opinion, or when a thing cannot be explained sensibly. Again, this gives credit to your reader, trusts him to make up his own mind about sketchy parts of the story. But you get to supply the context, creating a voice the reader trusts.

Accurate Story Sense

This covers two matters: knowing which story to tell and knowing which parts are essential to the story.

It often takes awhile to discover the story within a subject. For Steinbeck, all the social and natural evils of the Great Depression expressed themselves at last in the journey tale of an ordinary farm family. McCourt realized that the story of a generation, its virulent politics, stifling religion, and heartbreaking social fabric, was the story of the small boy he used to be struggling to escape Ireland, the church, even the hold of his family.

Once you recognize the story within the subject, which parts belong to it?

As my father-in-law, a former aerospace engineer, is fond of saying, "Systems don't fail—*parts* fail."

Literature is full of great books with weak or inessential parts—we can each nominate our own. (Mine would be the textbook whaling industry chapters in *Moby Dick*.) Any weak part interrupts the line of the whole. If the reader doesn't get beyond the weak section, the whole book has failed. Everything on the other side of the weak part will remain unread, unrealized in any imagination but your own.

So inventory the parts of your book.

• What is the function of each?

• How is each connected to the whole?

• Which ones—honestly—are not essential to the business of the book?

The converse is also true.

After Ron Hansen had completed his long novel *The Assassination of Jesse James by the Coward Robert Ford*, a fellow writer questioned whether Hansen needed the second half of the book, which recounts Bob Ford's fortunes *after* killing Jesse James. The conventional reading was that the story ended with James' murder. Hansen had a whole different structure in mind: Ford's fate mirrors that of his hero and victim. And the book is structured along classical lines: When the ghost of Jesse James haunts the Ford brothers after his betrayal and murder, the reader feels the hand of Shakespeare, deviling Brutus in his tent with the ghost of the murdered Julius Caesar.

That was the story Hansen wanted to tell.

Clarity of Style

Writing a good story that has a beginning, a middle, and an end without confusion and with a sense of suspense during the tale and significance afterward is one of the hardest things in life to do.

A lot of writers hide behind pyrotechnics—flights of lyrical language, avalanches of fact or philosophy, a barrage of high-powered words. There are a few intellectuals who have such a command of language and ideas—Gore Vidal comes to mind—that the drama of their books is the drama of a fine mind at work, the suspense of an idea forming and opening to possibility and consequence.

But it's easy to be lyrical—any well-read undergraduate can spin whole pargraphs of lovely descriptions of nature, or romantic ruminations on love and death. Telling a good story is hard.

"The hardest thing in the world to do is to write straight honest prose on human beings," Hemingway writes. "First you have to know the subject; then you have to know how to write. Both take a lifetime to learn."

Style lives in the sentence.

If you can take control of your sentence, then you can write your whole book. There is no such thing as an unimportant sentence: Each sentence must contribute to the effect of the book. Each subject—the doer of the action—ties in to your greater subject; every predicate—the action itself—is a mini drama. Every direct object completes a thought.

So whenever you use passive voice, the doer of the action recedes into the background—or may not be known at all. Whenever you use a static verb—*is, feels, involves, senses*—the effect is static. You may want a static effect to create a contrast to more dynamic verbs, but you probably don't want an entirely static scene—again, unless the effect you're after is to contrast the stasis of a certain scene with the lively movement of another.

Whenever you clutter a sentence with verbs, you risk diffusing the focus, undercutting the power of the one verb that matters.

Whenever a pronoun has no clear referent, the reader is at least momentarily confused. Likewise with a phrase or clause that seems to have no clear point of attachment in the sentence.

Don't skate along on top of the prose, painting with a broad brush and hoping for the best. Climb down into the gears of the sentence: What do you mean to say, and have you said it without ambiguity?

Grammar is not a set of arbitrary rules concocted by a committee in Zurich. It's a system whereby words can be combined in the head to make magic.

If you have any doubts about how to use a comma, a semicolon, or a rhetorical fragment, or what the difference is between a compound and a complex sentence, get hold of a handbook and bone up. It is not hard—there is a logic to it. With only a little disciplined practice, you can master it once and forever. If you have to think about whether your sentence is correct, you're not ready to write that sentence, let alone your big book.

If you don't know the rules so implicitly that they're second nature, what chance have you got of pushing beyond them, stretching them to make room for your great story?

Signature Detail

Pick out any random passage of Cormac McCarthy's *All the Pretty Horses*, the first of his Border trilogy about a couple of twentieth-century cowboys, and you'll be transported instantly to the desert West:

> They rode slowly up through the open country among scrub mesquite and nopal. They crossed from Tom Green County into Coke County. They crossed the old Schoonover road and they rode up through broken hills dotted with cedar where the ground was cobbled with traprock and they could see snow on the thin blue ranges a hundred miles to the north.

The signature details capture the story: These boys are always on horseback. The country is hard and desolate—full of "scrub mesquite and nopal," "broken hills," and "traprock"; it's also a land of immense space, of grand scale, of breathtaking beauty glimpsed a long way off—"snow on the thin blue ranges a hundred miles to the north." A glorious place, but hard on people:

> In the afternoon they passed through the ruins of an old ranch on that stony mesa where there were crippled fence-posts propped among the rocks that carried remnants of a wire not seen in that country for years. An ancient picket-house. The wreckage of an old wooden windmill fallen among rocks. They rode on.

Stones, rocks, wreckage, remnants, ruins, a few fenceposts sticking up out of rocks.

We're absolutely *there*. The details are realistic and true to the actual ground on which the novel is played out. At the same time, the deliberate choice of words to express those details resonates with the tone of harshness, of a dead-end life with little solace but the beauty of the open country, a good horse, and a friend you can trust.

Tastefully Handling the Rough Stuff

Almost by definition, big books—long stories that have a public dimension and strike a universal chord—often treat rough material: war, death, suffering, genocide, crime, mental and physical illness, injustice, and so on. Not always, of course: One can write about physics, as James Gleick does in *Chaos*, or other technical subjects without confronting the question of taste.

But even in a biography of Mother Teresa you'd have to make some decisions about how to portray the disease and squalor of Calcutta in such a way that it lent dignity and meaning to the story and the life, rather than merely disgusted your reader.

As with most decisions of craft, the most important thing is recognizing that there's a decision to make—being aware that certain subject matter may be repugnant to your reader. What you do about it will vary with the case at hand, but if you're aware it's an issue, you're halfway home.

Gardner offers some exercises to train the writer in making such decisions. In *The Art of Fiction*, he advises: "Without an instant's lapse of taste, describe a person (a) going to the bathroom, (b) vomiting, (c) murdering a child."

Why would the writer want to write about such matters? Any memoir about degenerative illness must convey an accurate sense of the progress of the disease, including its effect on bodily functions. Joyce Johnson, in *What Lisa Knew*, must reconstruct the murder of Lisa in order to bring her to life and evoke a sense of outrage; and McCourt writes a hilarious scene of throwing up his First Communion breakfast, including the consecrated Communion wafer, as a way of exploring the naive terror instilled in him by the church.

Mostly, it's a question of attitude—and attitude reflects itself in the tone of the writing. Ask yourself some basic questions:

• What is it about the material that might offend or repel the reader?

• Why am I writing about this material—what is my passion, my goal?

• What is my attitude toward the material—and how will I signal that to the reader?

• What effect am I after—what reaction am I trying to evoke from the reader?

• How graphically must I present it in order for the reader to get an accurate sense of the truth of my subject?

Lurid, gushing language can signal the reader that you're infatuated with the material in a way that makes him nervous—the way some filmmakers turn brutality and carnage into a gleeful feast for the eye.

By contrast, in recounting the worst details of Lisa's murder and Hedda Nussbaum's injuries, Johnson cools off into a flat, reportorial style, keeping a dignified distance. She's no voyeur.

Or consider this scene from *Schindler's List*, in which Thomas Keneally portrays the wanton murder of a Jewish engineer by Amon, the camp commandant. She is helping to construct the new concentration camp, and has been arguing with one of the German overseers, Hujar, about how to dig the foundations.

> She went on arguing the case, and Amon nodded and presumed she must be lying. It was a first principle that you never listened to a Jewish specialist. Jewish specialists were in the mold of Marx, whose theories were aimed at the integrity of government, and of Freud, who had assaulted the integrity of the Aryan mind. Amon felt that this girl's argument threatened his personal integrity.
>
> He called Hujar. The NCO returned uneasily. He thought he was going to be told to take the girl's advice. The girl did too. Shoot her, Amon told Hujar. There was, of course, a pause while Hujar digested the order. Shoot her, Amon repeated.
>
> Hujar took the girl's elbow to lead her away to some place of private execution.
>
> Here! said Amon. Shoot her here! On my authority, said Amon.
>
> Hujar knew how it was done. He gripped her by the elbow, pushed her a little to his front, took the Mauser from his holster, and shot her in the back of the neck.
>
> The sound appalled everyone on the work site, except—it seemed—the executioners and the dying Miss Diana Reiter herself. She knelt and looked up once. *It will take more than that*, she was saying. The knowingness in her eyes frightened Amon, justified him, elevated him.

It's a chilling scene, one of many such scenes in the novel. Like Johnson, Keneally restrains his language—the scene is nearly bare of modifiers. This doesn't mean that he abbreviates the action or summarizes it. He recounts the actual murder in clinical detail—the gripping of the girl by the elbow, the drawing and firing of the Mauser.

He does something else that reveals his attitude—tone—in the scene: He puts it in context. Amon is a racist. His "logic" is that of a paranoid bigot. His own subordinate is surprised at the order—"There was, *of course*, a pause"—revealing by his reaction that the order has no basis in justice or morality, even to an SS officer. When Hujar tries at least to shoot the girl in a private place—a feeble attempt at recognizing the gravity of the moment—Amon begins shouting at him. We know this because of the exclamation points—Amon is losing control.

The context is closed by the look in Diana Reiter's eyes—a defiant look that will haunt Amon at that moment and also much later, "for by evening the fullness of this hour would be followed by such emptiness that he would need, to avoid being blown away like a husk, to augment his size and permanence by food, liquor, contact with a woman."

Amon is the scared, pitiable one after all.

It's a complex scene—starkly horrifying, but also enlightening. We see beneath the evil. The point is not to glorify sadism, but to comprehend the nature of evil in our time.

Handling rough material with grace does not mean soft-peddling it. There are occasions when you have no choice but to present your reader the unadorned truth, the scene he would rather turn his eyes from.

I faced such a decision in writing *Cape Fear Rising*, a novel based on a racial massacre that actually happened. The book opens with a lynching: Six black men are made to run a gauntlet, shot, then beheaded, their heads stuck on poles on the roads leading into town. Time and again, sensitive readers have chided me for writing such a gruesome scene—especially at the beginning of the book, before the reader has any chance to prepare.

But there is far worse to come in the book. The opening announces that the book is going to be rough going for the faint of heart. It also happens to be about a true episode. To soften the details of the event would be to damage the truth of the horror—and one important theme of the book is how such grisly behavior can happen in the middle of a "civilized" society.

Know what you are doing and why.

A Word About Profanity

There was a time, not much more than a couple of generations ago, when profanity beyond *hell* and *damn* simply didn't appear in books. Writers even of the stature of Hemingway were forced to resort to absurd euphemisms when writing rough dialogue: "Obscenity on your mother's obscenity." Defending his use of swear words, Hemingway advised his editor, "I'm not the little boy writing them on the wall to be smart."

Several landmark court cases later, profanity is so ubiquitous the contemporary reader scarcely notices it anymore. It's lost its edge, the sharp needle of shock—which is a shame.

Not because I'm a prude or a moralist—though plenty of intelligent readers will sigh and put down a book that is all rough language. That's their choice, and while you must respect your reader, you can't soften those things that need to be hard without doing damage to the truth.

But voice and tone are matters of control, and control is a matter of discipline. And discipline in language—in the diction of a story— requires restraint, the holding back of your first instinct. Your first instinct may be to present realistic dialogue or action for the sake of mimicking real life accurately. But art does far more than mimic life. It mimics and also transcends it, casts it in some new light so that we may comprehend its meaning. For the fiction writer, this means creating artificial dialogue—*artificial* in the best sense of *artifice*, a created thing of beauty.

It's not enough simply to record the way people actually talk. The dialogue must be concentrated, shaped, dramatically moving, in a way that real-life conversation seldom is.

The same principle applies to the artifice of narrative voice: If you merely mimic a real voice, with all its digressions and stammerings, you achieve one fairly trivial effect at the expense of all the crucial ones—interest, focus, suspense, thematic coherence, and so on.

We know all this as it applies to other elements of the writer's craft, but somehow we tend to forget it when it comes to diction, expecially profane, vulgar, or obscene language. Probably this is due in part to the fact that it is so widespread in our culture that we hardly hear it anymore.

But as soon as it appears in print it takes on a permanence, a finality, that amplifies its effect in a way that rarely happens during casual conversation between friends at a bar.

Amplify it one step further—through oral performance—and the effect becomes obvious. Time and again I've watched young writers read in public for the first time a work that contains profane language. Some of them relish it, smiling with a kind of in-your-face satisfaction. But many others—even the majority, and especially if young children or family members are present—suddenly balk and begin an impromptu editing session right at the lectern.

Some of this is no doubt due to timidity, a novice's reasonable embarrassment that the seasoned writer will learn to recognize and overcome. But some of it, I think, is the result of a sound instinct— the instinct that says, "I wasn't careful enough in how I worded this."

Think always of what you are doing and why. What effect are you after? Is this the best way to achieve that effect? Be aware of the words you put on the page. In the case of profanity, realize the opportunity it offers to add texture, shock, even humor to a piece—but not if it turns up willy-nilly.

Tim O'Brien probably couldn't write about Vietnam without using the word *fuck* in all its permutations. Yet he does so rather sparingly— at least from the point of view of mimicking the combat soldier's conversation. He's absolutely aware of when he's using the word and why—creating a dramatic lexicon for men living on the edge, coping with death every day. Whole pages go by without any profanity, and when we hear it, we notice it.

For his characters, the word is not just a profanity but a blessing. Abracadabra, hocus-pocus, Dominus vobiscum. The way to add voltage, turn up the heat on a sentence. It can function as any part of speech at all—noun, verb, adjective—a word that carries its own syntax in the eternal present tense.

And the profanity works in part because other moments of his stories are tender, even lyrical. The dialogue, the action doesn't stay at one pitch. It modulates. Sometimes profanity is a way of expressing joy, humor, even love.

The nonfiction writer faces a different challenge. Clearly, the reportorial narrative voice doesn't require profanity: Profanity indicates an attitude, a judgment, so as soon as it enters the story, the reporter has given way to the interpreter, the commentator, the memoirist.

The exception to this, of course, is when the writer is *reporting* profanity—written or spoken: the banter of construction workers, an argument between inmates at the county jail, a client berating her press agent. I would argue that in this instance, some degree of profanity is probably necessary to accurately portray the scene. Deleting it would create a false picture—would not serve the truth.

But what do you do when a subject speaks in profanities during an interview? Accuracy dictates that you include it, but what if the subject says, after you've turned off your tape recorder, "Oh, by the way, please take out all the cursing—I don't want to offend anybody"? The subject would never publish such words under his or her own name— recognizing that informal and formal speech are different.

There's not a good answer. It may be a matter of simply politely editing your transcript—just as a journalist would correct basic grammatical errors that are not material to the story. The key word is *material*: does it affect the truth of what I am writing? If a cop I'm interviewing for a book about the criminal justice system uses the word *nigger*—one of the most obscene words in our language—then I'd quote him. He's a cop. It's material.

If, on the other hand, an angry biologist is explaining the life cycle of a freshwater mussel being extripated by pollution, I'm after the information, not a portrait of the biologist, so I would be inclined to ignore a profanity.

We're talking about diction—a special case, an extreme case perhaps, but one that illustrates that every sentence is the result of a hundred local decisions, and the sum of those decisions creates style. Nothing is minor. Every word counts.

Humor and Reassurance

Humor is based on a simple principle: reversal of expectations—we expect a certain result, a certain tone, a certain reaction, but we get something entirely different.

Unlike comedy, it derives from a fatalistic realism, the knowledge that humans are fallible and often ridiculous in their pride, that we all eventually suffer and die. The humorist illuminates human nature by finding levity in dark moments—lightening the heaviness. All of us being in the same human boat, we find that ability to make light reassuring. Even the expression "to make light of" carries a tone of comfort, like a candle in the dark.

McCourt's *Angela's Ashes* is a pretty grim book—or it would be, were it not for humor. He writes, for instance, of his childhood pal in Ireland, Mickey Spellacy, "whose relations are dropping one by one from the galloping consumption." As a boy, McCourt envies Mickey, because each time a relative dies he gets a week off from school.

> But this summer Mickey is worried. His sister, Brenda, is wasting away with the consumption and it's only August and if she dies before September he won't get his week off from school because you can't get a week off from school, when there's no school. He comes to Bally Campbell and me to ask if we'll go around the corner to St. Joseph's Church and pray for Brenda to hang on until September.
>
> The boys balk: "What's in it for us, Mickey, if we go around the corner praying?"
>
> "Well, if Brenda hangs on and I get me week off ye can come to the wake and have ham and cake and sherry and lemonade and everything and ye can listen to the songs and stories all night."

McCourt's response: "Who could say no to that?"

Taken out of context, the humor may seem a bit gruesome, even twisted: A little girl is dying, and her brother and his friends are scheming to profit by her death. They're even trying to manipulate their church for gain. But the book is all about hunger, and death has become so commonplace among children that they develop strategies to take out the sting—treating it as an opportunity to ditch Catholic school, which is a nightmare of rote learning and corporal punishment.

Throughout the book, the humor does at least two things at once: It makes the unbearable—including the frequent deaths of children—bearable. And it serves the themes—the hunger for both food and story; the omnipresent, mysterious, and often terrifying role of the Catholic Church; the struggle to escape the misery of McCourt's circumstances.

The story of Mickey Spellacy takes another twist: Brenda lingers until the second day of school, Mickey gets his week off, but when McCourt and Bally show up at the wake, they are turned away: "We'll go back to St. Joseph's and pray that from now on everyone in Mickey Spellacy's family will die in the middle of the summer and he'll never get a day off from school for the rest of his life."

That gets another grim laugh, until the finale: "One of our prayers is surely powerful because next summer Mickey himself is carried off by the galloping consumption and he doesn't get a day off from school and that will surely teach him a lesson."

The lesson is ambiguous, but it is McCourt's: Humor is not quite enough to transcend the dangerous and hopeless world of his childhood.

Metaphor

David Quammen's *The Song of the Dodo: Island Biogeography in an Age of Extinctions* tackles an extremely technical subject: the mechanism by which evolution operates. He delves into such complex matters as natural selection, biodiversity, genetic mutation, gigantism, dwarfism, and extinction. His book is 625 pages long—plus glossary, author's note, acknowledgments, source notes, bibliography, and index. A daunting volume.

Yet it reads like a novel—full of suspense and movement, fascinating characters and dramatic scenes. And the highest praise I can give it is what I wrote when I reviewed it: I never understood evolution until I read this book.

The general principle had been more or less clear since my days as an anthropology undergraduate, but whenever the discussion focused on the actual evolutionary moment, that split second in time when a new species is born or a new adaptation changes forever an existing species, that golden instant when the rubber meets the road, the blackboard went all swimmy.

A complex idea requires a simple eloquence in the telling, and I had never encountered an eloquence equal to the mystery of evolution, until Quammen's book.

His most effective tool is metaphor—expressing one thing in terms of something else. Usually, the "one thing" is a complex idea, an abstraction, and the "something else" is a concrete expression of the abstraction in analogous terms.

He begins the book with a metaphor to express the concept of unraveling ecosystems—habitat chopped up by development, roads, farms.

"Let's start indoors. Let's start by imagining a fine Persian carpet and a hunting knife. The carpet is twelve feet by eighteen, say. That gives us 216 square feet of continuous woven material." We cut up the carpet into 36 equal pieces. "When we're finished cutting, we measure the individual pieces, total them up—and find that, lo, there's still nearly 216 square feet of recognizably carpetlike stuff. But what does it amount to? Have we got thirty-six nice Persian throw rugs? No. All we're left with is three dozen ragged fragments, each one worthless and commencing to come apart."

Then Quammen deftly connects the metaphorical to the actual habitat: "Now take the same logic outdoors and it begins to explain why the tiger, *Panthera tigris*, has disappeared from the island of Bali."

Time and again, Quammen explains the complex natural world in terms of simple metaphors. He does not "dumb down" the subject matter; on the contrary, because of his manner of telling, the reader has access to some rather sophisticated science and history. But he does make an effort to find common ground with the reader who is not a scientist—but certainly understands how to cut up a carpet. Then he leads the reader through a simple exercise that illuminates a difficult concept. In fact, his most useful metaphor is the island itself—a small, isolated, finite stage on which to act out the drama of evolution on a scale we can comprehend, a metaphor for the whole planet.

Narrative Candor

Voice is one of the most elusive qualities in any story. We recognize it when we hear it, but it's hard consciously to create an authentic voice. Somehow voice seems to be the natural manifestation of all the narrative decisions we've made so far. We discover it more than we fabricate it.

McCourt says that his many earlier attempts at a childhood memoir all failed until he found himself one evening writing in a child's naive voice—which he immediately recognized as the voice that would carry the book. The voice required that he give up a persona of worldliness, of the dignified teacher's wisdom, and become the fumbling student again. In a sense, it was a decision to let the joke be on him. In writing from the perspective of one in the act of discovering what his life will turn out to be, rather than from that of a man who has mostly achieved his life, he was able to bring the material alive.

In that sense, *Angela's Ashes* succeeds because McCourt can remember what it was like *not* to know what he now knows. A true memoir.

The child's voice also created the opportunity for humor through irony—the distance between what the narrator perceives to be the truth and the actual truth. Kids get all sorts of things wrong, and their wisdom is the wisdom of earnest innocence. The voice is disarming and vulnerable.

Nobody trusts a know-it-all—in life or in books. Part of McCourt's discovery about voice was to allow himself to be ignorant, unsure, misled, and sometimes just plain wrong. Your reader wants to trust your voice, but he also wants a human voice that admits to mistakes, limitations, character flaws, whose humor is at its own expense—not that of the characters or the reader.

And of course the voice is formed partly by McCourt's Irish diction and syntax, including slang, that lends it a somewhat exotic flavor for Americans.

Voice really depends on the answer to the question, Who is telling this story? Which persona are you as the narrator adopting? Are you the conversational buddy on the next barstool, or a reporter? Are you inside the psyche of a main character who is an intellectual, a cop, a nun, a serial killer, a painter, an AIDS victim? That will color your diction—and determine your metaphors, your sensibility.

Are you writing fiction or nonfiction? In fiction, you have almost limitless choices of voice. In nonfiction, you have two: the reporter or the memoirist. Both are versions of yourself. But even that choice isn't simple. As we've seen with McCourt, the memoirist can be retrospective or mostly in the moment.

In *The Tennis Partner*, Abraham Verghese sometimes speaks as a doctor, sometimes as a father, sometimes as a tennis aficionado, and sometimes as a plain old friend. His voice is confidential and sensitive to matters of the heart, but it can also be beautifully clinical in describing medical procedures and tennis shots.

So figure out who you are to be telling your story. Determine this in an exact way: Which part of your personality are you engaging? Which role are you playing?

You're also asking the question of narrative stance again: What's the technical point of view (first person or third person), what's the psychic distance (level of emotional identification with characters), and what tone am I after (narrator's attitude)? You will not read voice on the page; you will *hear* it in your head. So one good way to find your voice is to write a key scene in the voice that seems instinctively right, then listen to it out loud. Then write it in a different voice and listen: *Is* it different? What is the effect of the difference?

Whatever other attractions your book holds, your reader will read it largely because the voice he hears in his head as he reads is one he trusts, a voice he likes listening to over the long haul, a voice that does not grate or annoy or bore, a voice he can count on to tell him the truth.

Find the passage in your work that sounds most like that voice, then measure the rest of the work against it.

Exercises

1. Write a short parable that addresses a contemporary theme: Tell a story that does not yield to easy interpretation.

2. Select a sentence from a book you admire. Rewrite it at least three ways.

3. Consider a great book you admire. List at least three reasons why a reader might resist engaging the story. Next to each item list at least two tactics the author uses to overcome this resistance. (For example: In telling the story about his miserable childhood, Frank McCourt anticipates some readers' reluctance to participate in such a depressing story and so takes the edge off the heartbreak with a sense of humor.) Now apply this test to your own manuscript.

4. Select a short passage from a book you admire. Then:

- Rewrite it in the voice of a brilliant liar—someone you like but don't trust.
- Rewrite it in the voice of a stand-up comic—making all the jokes you can.
- Rewrite it in the voice of your best storyteller friend recounting it to you out loud at your favorite hangout.

5. Write a short scene between characters who, in real life, would express themselves in a string of profanities. Write the scene without any profanity.

8

The Cathedral of the Novel

It astonishes me that intelligent people who would not hold a wedding, plant a garden, or even slap together a utility shed without exhaustive planning nonetheless regard the novel as a spontaneous literary event that just *happens* onto the page—a suspenseful, thrilling, long story arising full-blown and unraveling flawlessly in chronological sequence without any planning whatsoever. All the writer needs is inspiration.

I choose these examples advisedly: wedding, garden, shed.

A novel, like a wedding, *is* an event—a celebration even. A book is just a wad of wood pulp until a pair of intelligent eyes scans its lines, and then it begins *happening* in a cognitively literal way inside a stranger's imagination. It's a marriage, if you will, between writer and reader—both are on for the long haul. But it's a marriage that nobody is sure will actually succeed, either as a memorable event or a long-term partnership of mutual trust and passion.

You cannot just announce a wedding and wait to see who, if anyone, shows up. As in a wedding, the author approaches the event with some definite hopes about how things will turn out, what shape the event will take, what promises will be made to which sort of suitor. There are no guarantees, but there is a meaningful shape to the ritual—and the anticipation of a seduction to follow.

To plant a garden is an exercise in preparation—choosing good ground and then preparing that ground. Just so, the novelist must search out an area fertile enough to promise a story of a certain scale and then must prepare it to yield something grown from a seed, something that wasn't there before on the bare ground: a long fiction. It will grow under the husbandry of the author—good old-fashioned word, *husbandry*, whose linguistic roots include both *freedom* and *bondage*. That's the central tension of writing the long form: creating boundaries within which you can invent freely.

This is useful to remember: If the thing is organic, it will grow beyond your designs for it. But you must have designs for it, or it won't grow at all.

And the utility shed metaphor comes from Henry David Thoreau, who reminds us that writing, after teaching, is the humblest of professions: "The youth gets together his materials to build a bridge to the moon, or perchance a palace or temple on the earth, and at length the middle-aged man concludes to build a wood-shed with them."

The novel, like the shed, is functional. However fine the art of it, whatever lovely ideas, characters, and lyrics inhabit it, the novel must *work*. It is, in a dignified sense, utilitarian. We'll talk later about the very special work it does.

So the novel is an organic event that requires prepared ground to do its work.

Being an Extraordinary Storyteller

Another way of saying it: I believe the novelist must have a pretty definite idea of what the novel is to be about, what shape it will take, where her interest lies, even where it is liable to wind up. As novelist John Irving reminds us in "Getting Started": "If you don't know the story before you begin the story, what kind of storyteller are you? Just an ordinary kind, just a mediocre kind—making it up as you go along, no better than a common liar."

This is an old-fashioned notion but one that we tend to forget in an era when many novels are really more like novellas—single-character stories of barely one hundred pages, limited in time and scope and concern, that follow a single thread out to its end without *War and Peace*-style complications—and so perhaps can be approached like the short story, which reveals itself to the writer as it unfolds. In the short story, as Edith Wharton puts it, there's almost no delay between the flash and the bang; like a painting, it can be apprehended nearly all at once.

But in a novel—especially the kind of novel you're trying to write, a novel about a great subject—there are likely to be many flashes and bangs, lots of noisy characters scurrying about, clamoring for attention, making a mess out of things, a long wait between the author's promise and the reader's reward. So you must orchestrate that distance, make the best use of that delay, keep the characters and events sorted out, keep the reader reading (persuasion of continuity), save the biggest bangs for last, and make the reader feel, after much time and labor, that he has apprehended all of it and the experience has been worth it.

You can't just wing it: A good part of writing the novel is done before you start writing it.

It's not a paint-by-numbers exercise by any means: The novelist's deep preparation begins long before she sets out the scope of a particular long story. "Fiction is inventing out of what knowledge you have," Hemingway says. "If you invent successfully, it is more true than if you try to remember it. A big lie is more plausible than the truth."

The Problem of the Cathedral

Whenever I teach Forms of Narrative Prose to my graduate students, I begin the first session with a riddle: If the cathedral is a solution, what was the problem it was meant to solve?

"To give glory to God," my students say, wondering if they have blundered into the wrong seminar, or, "To create a majestic object of beauty." They're caught in our narrow Romantic aesthetic so reflexively that they are not even aware of it: Beguiled by the stunning inspirational effect of the finished cathedral *on them personally*, they fail to imagine themselves in the place of the artisan contemplating how to build the damned thing.

That is, they are reacting like *readers*, carried away by the majesty of the finished artifact—rather than like *writers*, charged with creating that effect.

From the architect's point of view, the prosaic problem solved by the cathedral is most significantly not a problem of faith, ego, legacy, or even beauty—there is nothing either personal or sublime about it. It is a problem of *architecture*—of *structure*, not *beauty*; of *craft*, not *art*. But if it is solved with sound engineering, art and beauty are made possible.

For thousands of years, builders were obsessed with the problem of creating a large interior space. This sounds simple, but think about it again, and you'll understand the challenge of the novel.

It was easy enough to construct a gigantic roofless space—like the Roman Colosseum. Walls are easy. But how do you hold up the roof on the cathedrals of Chartres and Notre Dame? How do you hold up the middle?

A corollary problem that distinguishes the cathedral from, say, a granary: The space must be *lighted*—something important, some *sacred communication*, must occur inside it. In an age before electric or even gas lamps, this was no small challenge. And if you are depending on load-bearing walls for support—walls that must be very thick indeed if you're building a tower to heaven—you have to figure out ways to cut large, high windows without making the whole shell so structurally weak it topples from the sheer weight of itself.

Usually, by a series of my primitive blackboard drawings and some lively discussions, in my seminar we rediscover that a whole series of innovations, from the Roman arch to the flying buttress, and including the cruciform shape of the cathedral itself, are all engineering inventions to help hold up the roof—the middle.

So let us refine the problem solved by the cathedral: How do you build a large indoor lighted space?

Answer: You create an architecture of light. Which is exactly what the novelist must do.

One-Line Novel

In other words, you've got to create a large, durable, multifaceted story structure that will illuminate what's inside: the characters whose actions and interior lives tangle and disengage, sprawling across continents and years.

You've got to stop being a romantic and think hard about *structure*—how you're going to organize the space inside the novel, which pattern will create which effect. Just piling on more of everything—building thicker and thicker walls—won't do. You've got to do some close figuring, some careful calculations, to arrive at a blueprint that makes possible mystery and beauty.

One useful place to begin is to encapsulate the thrust of your novel into a *signature*—as in music: defining the key, the pace, the range of tonal possibilities.

Think of *Moby Dick*: Madman goes hunting for a white whale. *Anna Karenina*: Beautiful woman marries the wrong man. *Huckleberry Finn*: Two guys float down a river on a raft, trying to escape to freedom. The signature, expressed as one simple defining sentence, may sound trivial, but it can focus your effect.

It doesn't slight the larger, complex concerns of the novel, the twists and nuances of character and action. It does not *summarize* the novel—it will take your whole novel, every chapter, scene and word, to tell your large story. But it does define the structural arc of the story, the blueprint for holding up the long middle. Such a signature declares, as Captain Ahab might, "The path to my fixed purpose is laid on iron rails, on which my soul is grooved to run."

It's your purpose, the driving line of the novel. Every other creative decision you make derives from that purpose. It's not for a second what we're interested in on a deeper level, but it will drive the surface tension, which will pull along all the other tensions: Jim and Huck's raft is a vehicle for moving Mark Twain's story down the river. It carries the characters places where interesting things happen, and it causes an alliance that matures into friendship, complicated by the social fact that Jim is black and Huck is white, that their world is full of pretenders and hypocrites, and so on.

Sometimes, in the course of the novel, Huck and Jim stray too far from the river. But whenever the story digresses too far and the reader's interest begins to flag, you can practically hear Twain's panicked voice shouting, "Back to the raft!" and the characters scramble aboard to resume their journey—and their story.

Think of the signature as the cable that hauls the roller-coaster cars up the long, slow hill of suspense, around the hairpin turn of reversal, down the stomach-clenching fall. We don't care about that cable—we probably don't even realize it's there. But it makes the ride work. Without it, none of the thrills would be possible.

Outlining

One way to write a novel is to outline it first. A lot of writers don't, but I maintain that once you have conceived a structural template, you have much more freedom within that to relax and allow the story to surprise you—since you're not struggling so hard to make sure it has dramatic coherence. In your outline, you have already established an overall coherence. The arc of the story hangs together. You've framed your cathedral.

The kind of outline I mean is basic and spare, and consists of six parts:

1. Working title (you can change this later: *The Great Gatsby* started out as *The High-Bouncing Lover*), which helps you focus on the main concern of the novel.

2. Signature (your roller-coaster cable: Poor boy, Gatsby, tries to win heart of rich girl, Daisy).

3. List of major characters (who: In *Gatsby* there are only three who matter to the story, four more who matter to the plot, and a handful of bit players).

4. List of major locales (where: in *Gatsby*, five locales serve all the action).

5. Numbered chapters, each containing a one-sentence description of the central event (Chapter 1: Nick meets Daisy, Jordan Baker, and Tom).

6. Your concept of the ending—not in exact terms, but a recognition of what the ending must address (does the poor boy win the rich girl?).

With practice, you can construct such an outline in your head.

As you write, and as your understanding of your own story develops, almost everything will change. Locally—within chapters and scenes, moment by moment—you will be surprised and inspired, events will take remarkable, unexpected turns; new characters will arrive out of nowhere. That's as it should be. You should be writing for the same reason your reader is reading: to find out what happens next.

The Architecture of Chapters

This takes two forms: the arrangement of chapters within the larger framework of the novel, and the progress of scenes within each chapter.

Dramatically, the "rule" of chapters is the rule of scenes in any fiction: Each one should have a clear reason for inclusion. It should not just provide more information, a more thorough resume of character, or lush descriptions of place. It may do all those things, but first it must have an indispensable role in moving the story along.

In chapter one of *The Great Gatsby*, we meet the narrator, Nick Carraway, and get a mixed message about how much to trust him. We are quickly spirited away to Daisy Buchanan's mansion, where, in a setting that seethes with restlessness, trouble waiting to happen, we meet Daisy and her cohort Jordan Baker, about whom (Nick teases us) he once heard a "critical, unpleasant story," and Daisy's husband, Tom, a rude, bigoted man who receives a mysterious and upsetting telephone call.

Chapter two lets us in on the secret of the call: It was Tom's mistress, Myrtle, and now we're riding the train with Tom, Myrtle, and Nick through the Valley of Ashes under the watchful billboard eyes of Dr. T.J. Eckleburg, toward New York City and a very bad party.

It's not till chapter three—more than forty pages in—that we actually meet Gatsby, though everybody we've met has remarked on him, adding gloss to his legend. By now we have all the players on stage, all the significant relationships laid out—including the adulterous affair that will lead to tragedy; we've even been over the literal road where the tragedy will happen. When the tragedy unfolds in fast, confused flashes, we won't have to stop and take in mere description, or become oriented to a new locale. Every scene has had its own minor tension—Daisy and Tom spatting, Jordan throwing a tantrum, Tom driving too fast—and we can already see the dramatic convergence of the parts in the mystery of Gatsby's identity.

Storytelling is the art of unfolding knowledge in a way that makes each piece contribute to a larger truth.

Unlike a short story, a novel chapter must be both complete and unfinished—that is, it must seem to be one discrete thing, a self-contained dramatic whole, or there would be no reason to separate it out as a distinct chapter, and yet it must create enough new anticipation to make the reader carry his interest over to the start of the next chapter.

Each chapter seems to accomplish its "business" and then asks a question, raises an issue, piques a curiosity, that introduces other "new" business and teases the reader to turn the page rather than stop: Tom and Daisy are having a rocky marriage—we know that for sure now—but who was that on the phone?

Suspense

Remember: Suspense is made up of curiosity and delay. There's a question we really want to know the answer to, and the writer doesn't allow the answer to emerge until the interest has been heightened, the reader knows enough to appreciate the significance of the answer and to fret over it, and can't bear to wait any longer.

Here is how suspense works in a novel: Your wife says, "I've bought you something, but you can't open it until Christmas." Anticipation.

She lets you ponder that for a whole week and then says, "You know, the thing I bought? We really can't afford it. But what the hell." Mild anxiety.

Another week goes by. She says, "You know that present I told you about? Well I hope you like it, because I can't take it back." Greater anxiety—and curiosity. More is at stake.

A week later, she says, "I'm wondering if I ever should have bought you that present." A touch of panic? What does she mean? You lie awake counting the possibilities, worrying each one through. In the context of marriage, they matter. What's she trying to tell you?

A week before Christmas, she places your present, wrapped in beautiful paper and ribbons, under the tree. You pick it up and shake it, curious. She says, "Oh, no! I hope you haven't broken it!" So you place it gently back under the tree—feeling guilty, resentful, a little foolish.

Suspense is what's going through your mind, every minute from the moment you learn of the present until the moment you open it, and every teasing worry brought on by the new information. Every emotion—frustration, gratitude, anger, anxiety, love, doubt, impatience—is part of your experience with suspense.

Christmas Day arrives. She makes you wait till after breakfast, till after you've opened all the other presents, till after she's opened hers from you (will it measure up?). You take a deep breath and pull at the ribbons, tear the paper. Inside is—paper! And something else—a plane ticket. For Paris, France! You're baffled—you don't even speak French and have never expressed a desire to go to Paris. As you're about to say thanks anyway, she looks at you and smiles slyly. "No, no," she says, "that's not your present! Your present is *in* Paris!"

Are you *not* going to get on that plane?

And when you do, are you *not* going to say to yourself, "Wait a minute—how could I have broken it by shaking the package?" and start worrying all over again?

Finishing

While you're inside the novel working on it, day after day, month and year after month and year, it seems more real than the world beyond the page. Scenes and characters take on a vividness that is almost painful, often exciting, and quite beguiling.

When it is working.

When your novel is not working, it just lies there in pieces on the page, leaking vital fluids all over your desk.

In either case, your course is clear: If it's working, just let it keep working. Keep plodding on, accumulating the pages. If it is not working, you'd better pause and remember what it was you were trying to do in the first place (your signature) and then do some hard diagnostic work to figure out where it has gone wrong. If you set out to send two guys down the river on a raft and they've wound up in a salon in Copenhagen discussing Kierkegaard for no particular reason, then perhaps you took a wrong turn somewhere. Trace the line of the story back to the wrong turn, and take a different turn.

The most common reason, I think, why writers get stuck in first drafts is that the line of the novel just peters out. It wasn't a large enough scenario. It didn't contain a big enough possible world. The characters weren't interesting enough to sustain deep reflection on their interior lives. There just wasn't enough *there* there.

A false start. Better to find out after fifty pages than five hundred.

As Hemingway confides to A.E. Hotchner, "I never set out with a plot in mind, and I never yet set out to write a novel—it's always a short story that moves into being a novel. I always make it prove that it can't be written short." Only when the story proved it could sustain long reflection did he begin to envision the arc of the novel.

So the first big challenge—and don't underestimate it—is simply sustaining a long, interesting story from start to finish. Not just linking together a bunch of scenes or anecdotes or ruminations or slice-of-life moments, but building a big story that is all one thing, that finishes what it starts, that arcs convincingly from clear beginning to recognizable end—a big, luminous creation in which you've managed to hold up the roof so the people inside can conduct their sacred communication with the reader. If you've done that—even if the novel is dreadful, predictable, hackneyed, overwritten, and full of missed chances and ragged threads of unsolved story—you have written a novel. You've done something most people can't do. Will never do. Wish they could do and had done. Would trade their drawers full of great beginnings for.

Celebrate. Take your loved one out to dinner and splurge on a good bottle of champagne.

Next, write a *good* novel.

So the novel that is working and the one that is an utter dead fish present clear paths of action. The tough one is the draft that *sort of* works but also has dead spots, riveting scenes and flat scenes, a plot that seems plausible one day and ridiculous the next, characters you love and then grow tired of and then love again, until tomorrow when they seem utterly uninteresting.

I don't know what to do about such a first draft, except to finish it and find out for sure where it ends up and then try to reenvision the thing. Some writers will tell you to stop right there and not write another word until you've figured out the design flaw—but that may stop you for good. Sometimes you just have to struggle through to the other side, building whatever makeshift bridges you can out of soft scenes and tired sentences until you can replace them with sounder stuff.

Probably this is an indication that there is something basic wrong with the conception of the novel, but exactly *what* is wrong may be impossible to recognize until you've arrived at either a right or wrong ending and can read the novel whole. If you're lucky, the flaw will stand out in sharp relief. If you're luckier, it will be fixable.

If the novel is based on autobiographical experience, the flaw is probably in staying too close to what happened, instead of what, in the most interesting of all possible worlds, *might have* happened.

Almost as big a trap is trying too hard to force your novel to a preconceived ending. That's the central paradox of writing the novel: You have to know where it's going, but when it speaks to you, shows you a better direction, you have to be ready to abandon your plan and listen to the story. It's enough to drive you crazy.

The other obstacle to finishing is again a prosaic one: *continuity*.

This affects the writer in two ways. First, as we've seen, memory plays large part in creating the effects of a novel; it's extremely easy to lose track of complex turns of plot, the life histories of characters, the dramatic logic of the story. The famous example of this occurred in Raymond Chandler's *The Big Sleep*, in which the murder of a chauffeur springs all the other links in the chain of plot. When filmmakers were adapting it for the screen, they came across a curious fact: on close reading, it's never clear in the novel *who* killed the chauffeur or why, yet the entire plot of the book depends on it. So they called Chandler and asked him, and he obligingly looked at his novel again.

Beats me, he said.

William Faulkner hung a map of Yoknapotawpha County over his writing desk, to keep his fictional geography clear. He even changed the population count from time to time, to keep up with the migrations, births, deaths, and lynchings in his novels.

Most of us have faulty memories, and simply keeping track, in a precise way, of the intricacies of what has happened so far—especially as the book grows into the hundreds of pages and several layers of drafts—is difficult. Again, it's not a matter of art but of the working craft. Like an outline, it's scaffolding you dismantle after you've built your cathedral.

For the big stuff to work credibly, you've got to get the little stuff absolutely right.

The second way in which continuity challenges the novelist is through real-life time: A novel will typically take years to complete, and the writer will change. At some point, a major change may mark a before-and-after transition in the writer's life—the death of a loved one, a gain or loss of faith, marriage or the breakup of a marriage. The writer of chapter seventeen may not be the same writer who wrote chapter one—the writer may need to scrap the old pages and work from a new vision entirely.

Whenever I begin a novel, I always feel a clock being started. The catch is that I have no clue how long the clock will run till the alarm bell goes off, but there is a certain urgency *that must be ignored*, since the only way to write a novel well is to proceed as if you had all the time in the world.

Likewise, mundane interruptions to the daily habit of writing the novel can pose serious threats to finishing: a job, family obligations, illness, jury duty. Anything that keeps you away from the pages for more than a day or two can impair your ability to keep track of the thing, let alone to do something wonderful and artful with it. One solution is to "visit" your novel in progress even on those days when you are prevented from working on it—remind yourself of the last few pages you wrote, or of a scene that's been nagging you. You're just touching it to make sure it's still there, poking your head inside that little universe to remind yourself how the air tastes and of the quality of the light.

Effects of Scale

In *The Fiction Dictionary*, Laurie Henry writes, "Because of its greater length, a novel will have more characters, take place over a longer period of time, and involve more movement among settings than a novella or short story." This expression of the causal relationship between the novel's length and its other characteristics has always struck me as backward—based on a fundamental misconception about how the novel operates.

The novel does not have more characters and scenes *because* it is bigger—as if the novel were just a bigger bin in which to throw more stuff. Just the other way around: The novel's length is an artifact of the different way scenes, characters, and events are used in a novel. The novel encompasses a broader scope, which may require a longer period of time, a deeper reflection into the back stories of characters and the histories of events. It's not a sprint toward a goal that is in sight from the starting line but a marathon toward a point somewhere out there in the invisible future, arrived at not straightforwardly but through many twists and climbs. It requires the pace of the long haul, a different sort of faith on the parts of writer and reader.

For instance, *War and Peace* is commonly regarded as a big, sprawling novel; in most editions, it runs at least seven hundred pages. Yet scene by scene, the novel is not crammed full of detail and chatter. To the contrary, the party scenes that open the novel are almost minimalist in style. We get a brushstroke for each character, not full descriptions and resumés. Likewise, in the battlefield scenes, we don't get complicated military detail: We get Prince Andrei glimpsing a single cannon here, a commotion over there. We know one thing only about the Russian foot soldier: He is barefoot. And all the scenes take place in a very few locales, to which the action returns again and again: the drawing room, the country estate, the barracks, the battlefield.

Yet consider the progress of the first three big scenes in the novel:

1. Anna Pavlovna's society party, at which the main business is the women's relentless politicking for appointments in the army for sons, brothers, and cousins, where we meet Pierre, huge and out of place, the illegitimate son of the famous Count Bezukhof.

2. The Horse-Guard barracks where Pierre visits his dissolute friend Kuragin in the midst of a debauch: An officer named Dolokhof wagers he will guzzle an entire bottle of rum while balanced on a windowsill high above the stone courtyard and not holding on, as his drunken companions tease a chained bear.

3. Old Count Bezhukof's deathbed chamber, where the underhanded fight for his inheritance is won accidentally by his bastard son, Pierre—the same Pierre we have seen in high society and at a drunken debauch—who is then certified by the Tsar as the new lawful Count Bezhukhof.

A character's fortune has changed completely before our eyes without even being the main business of the book so far—though it does reflect that business: the reckless Russian nobility preparing for a fall. Shortly thereafter, we go off to war, and the drawing room characters are now in the army, making a mess of the campaign, as we suspected they would, careening merrily toward the debacle at Austerlitz. The novel oscillates (surprise) between scenes of war and scenes of peace, and the implicit, tragic joke is that the pampered nobility can hardly tell the difference—until it's too late and their own estates are burning.

The line of development is unmistakable and large in scope: from career politics, to debauchery, to the illegitimate legitimized, to disastrous war. It is this line of development, the revisiting of scenes and characters, each time with a new twist, a new insight, a new variation, that requires a large canvas—you just can't fit Austerlitz into a short story without overwhelming the form. The scenes are used in succession to create this line of development, which requires many scenes— reprised with new information and variation—and thus many pages, to play out.

The effect is of accumulation—not of sheer detail, but of detail meaningfully augmented by repetition, which deepens our understanding of the events. As in a symphony, motifs reemerge in minor keys and in variations, creating a sense of movement and return. No wonder Maxwell Perkins, the famous editor, once wrote to author James Jones of the remarkable structural virtues of *War and Peace*: "I think it would be much better to read that book over and over, to the neglect of books on the art of fiction."

In *Aspects of the Novel*, Forster remarks on Tolstoy's terrifying and exhilarating sense of space in the novel, which "leaves behind it an effect like music": "After one has read *War and Peace* for a bit, great chords begin to sound, and we cannot say exactly what struck them. They do not arise from story . . . they do not come from the episodes nor yet from the characters. They come from the immense area of Russia, over which episodes and characters have been scattered, from the sum-total of bridges and frozen rivers, forests, roads, gardens, fields, which accumulate grandeur and sonority after we have passed them. Many novelists have the feeling for place . . . very few have the sense of space, and the possession of it ranks high in Tolstoy's divine equipment. Space is the lord of *War and Peace*, not time."

In other words, the grandeur of the novel is partly an effect of scale, an effect created by the scope, depth, and thoroughness of the imagined vision. We've lived with it a long time, during which it worked on our imagination through repetition with variation, like a symphony, and its effect on us is more profound.

The material itself makes it large, not just long.

Manners and Eternal Verities

The novel is the cathedral of great subjects, which, like a mountain, makes its own weather through effects of scale; indeed, it can support issues and subjects that would overwhelm a short story. The novel operates through a process of accumulation of scenes that reprise characters, details, actions, images, settings, and themes in such a way that each repetition adds new dramatic information to the story, furthers the progress of the plot, and deepens the reader's engagement with the novel's central mysteries—the great paradoxes that form its themes.

In an overall way, the novel works like a symphony, through an artfully composed narrative of regression and return, with each return bringing new insight, new meaning, to the larger story.

Forster notes the natural affinity between the novel and the symphony: "Music, though it does not employ human beings, though it is governed by intricate laws, nevertheless does offer in its final expression a type of beauty which fiction might achieve in its own way. Expansion. Not completion. Not rounding off but opening out."

Of *War and Peace,* he observes: "Such an untidy book. Yet, as we read it, do not great chords begin to sound behind us, and when we have finished does not every item—even the catalogue of strategies—lead a larger existence than was possible at the time?"

A novel is the ideal arena in which to recover what Faulkner describes in his Nobel prize acceptance speech as "the old verities and truths of the heart, the old universal truths lacking which any story is ephemeral and doomed—love and honor and pity and pride and compassion and sacrifice." In the novel, there is the space to explore, deeply as well as broadly, the preeminent theme of all great literature, which, according to Faulkner, is "the human heart in conflict with itself which alone can make good writing because only that is worth writing about, worth the agony and sweat."

All novelists are really novelists of manners: They chronicle the interaction between the private soul and the public society. Their characters are connected to time, history, politics, culture, things often missing in short stories, which may be more prone to tune into private, self-referential subject matter, since the story is a more lyrical form, the novel by definition a more prosaic one. One can argue that the novel (not the contemporary stage play, teleplay, or screenplay) is the direct descendant of classical tragedy, since frequently it seems to take for its subject the public anguish of exemplary figures and how their downfall affects the life of the community.

The Work of the Novel

So what is it that a novel does, exactly? Milan Kundera (*The Unbearable Lightness of Being*), in *The Art of the Novel*, defines the novel as "the great prose form in which an author thoroughly explores, by means of experimental selves (characters), some great themes of existence."

Great—you don't hear that word much anymore. But the novel is great—in the sense of being larger than other things of the same kind, namely novellas and short stories. Not just longer—*larger.* Because the reader lives with it for an extended period, the novel comes to take on an accrued reality, like a snowfall. The fully realized world of the novel is a big undeniable fact operating in the reader's mind. It deeply engages the reader on every level—intellectual, emotional, artistic, and spiritual.

It leaves a broad, deep footprint on the reader's imagination.

In other words, the novel is the only fictional form that takes advantage of a particular and powerful aspect of narrative time—the real time out of the reader's life devoted to its reading—time during the reading of the long story in which the reader's mind is already processing that story, coming out of it and going back into it repeatedly, feeding real life back into the experience of reading and also feeding back in the experience of reading the earlier chapters.

An effect of *scale* is operating—one of many such effects in the novel. The story must be of a certain size and scope to accomplish its themes, and once it is that large it creates effects simply by being large, the way a skyscraper in Chicago or New York City can actually change the pattern of wind on the street. We experience its largeness as a fact separate from but related to the story it tells. There's a sense of duration, of weight, of deep and complex experience too large to grasp in an instant. We may come away with a secondary memory of the time in our life we spent reading the novel, so the experience of reading itself creates a textured memory of the novel: an episode in our life—a summer at the beach, a convalescence from an illness, a snowbound winter, an airplane trip to a job interview—intermingled forever in our memory with the action of the story.

War and Peace leaves us with a sense of exhilaration and exhaustion—as if we have survived something dangerous and meaningful. It has the heft of history—the way a cathedral has the soaring luminous height of the miraculous.

A cathedral, complete in every detail but only as large as a country chapel, might evoke admiration but it could not evoke grandeur, the breathtaking realization of interior space created on a larger-than-life-scale. Indeed, the effect would likely be the opposite: the somewhat ironic appreciation of the miniature that makes models so appealing for their fine fragility, or for their implicit joke about scale, as in the case of the ship-in-the-bottle.

The novel doesn't deliver the hit-and-run satisfaction of the short-short, or even the brilliant flash of insight or grace that a short story offers. The form presents a prosaic challenge in literary engineering. Executed well, it makes us gape, openmouthed, awed and captivated. It does not astonish so much as it overwhelms us. It makes us raise our eyes, because the ceiling vaults so high, almost out of sight, suspended by an ingenious, invisible structure, and there under the vault live its most memorable secrets.

The Novella

The novella shares more in common with the short story than with the novel: Ordinarily it is characterized by a unity of character, place, time, and action unusual in the traditional novel. A novella commonly follows the fortunes of a single character through a limited time in a circumscribed locale, focusing on a central action. In conceptual terms, it is much more of a long short story than a short novel.

But as soon as we cite the classic example, Joseph Conrad's *Heart of Darkness,* we describe one kind of contemporary literary *novel*—short, focused on a single character, narrated in a distinctive voice, ending enigmatically.

When the novella reaches a length that can be published within covers, it is usually treated as a novel—though structurally it is not really a novel. Otherwise, since most journals can't afford to dedicate so many pages to a single piece, it may anchor a short story collection or be packaged with another novella.

Since it is more like the short story, the writer can afford a more intuitive approach to structure: Knowing the main character and the central action, the author can remain relatively undistracted by subplots and other complications. The challenge is more lyrical than structural.

Writing a Book

It's axiomatic but worth remembering: Nobody writes a book. What you write every day is a piece of a book, a fragment, a scene. But it's just as useful to configure your ambition, early in the process, to encompass the long form, be it a novella, a novel or a story collection. When you sit at your writing desk every day, you are two writers: one who is working closely on the piece at hand, completely immersed in the moment of the scene; the other holding in the back of her mind a large vision of connectedness, of the piece contributing to the effect of the whole.

But you can't apprehend a book all at once, either reading it or writing it, and so of course the writer, like the reader, simply concentrates on what is at hand, lives in it utterly, spellbound to find out what happens next.

Exercises

1. Pick a reasonably short novel with which you are familiar. Forgetting for the moment about content and style, outline the structure in as bare-bones a way as possible. For each chapter, identify the salient event that defines it and drives the story by unfolding new knowledge in a dramatic way. Trace the locales and note which ones are used over and over. Identify the climactic chapter.

2. Read three novels considered successful by reason of either popular success or critical acclaim. Boil each one down to the single sentence that defines its structural signature: "Man goes on a journey" or "Stranger comes to town."

3. Imagine a novel you would like to write, or consider your current manuscript novel. In one short sentence, nail down its central structural signature. Don't say you can't do this. If you can't, you don't have a book yet.

4. Pick a novel you have never read. Read only the first and final chapters. Without reading what lies between, identify what the novel is about—the big issue that will be reflected in its signature. Now read the novel start to finish, making notes on every device that helps "hold up the middle."

5. Take the signature of a classic novel and recast it in contemporary times. Do the themes hold up? Or do they depend on a particular historical circumstance?

9

The Creative Nonfiction Book

Almost by definition, the nonfiction book must have a large public subject at its core, for the authority of the book comes first of all through its allegiance to the truth of a significant event: *This thing I am telling you about actually happened.*

It matters that a real ship named the *Titanic* actually sank with great loss of life because there weren't enough lifeboats and the captain was trying to set a speed record across the ice fields of the North Atlantic. Otherwise, it's just another sea story, with no real-life consequences. So the event must be compelling for its own sake.

Two recent best-sellers illustrate this fact beautifully: Sebastian Junger's *The Perfect Storm*, which chronicles the fate of a swordfishing boat with a crew of six, doomed to encounter the convergence of three storms into a colossal once-in-a-century monster; and Jon Krakauer's *Into Thin Air*, an account of an expedition to climb Mt. Everest that ended in the horrifying deaths of many of the climbers on the expedition. Both stories came right out of the headlines—based on events that captivated and shocked the public.

But not all matters of life and death result in good stories. Some are just catastrophic but predictable cautionary tales of drunken driving or risky living. Others are just sad case studies of death by cancer or AIDS—devastating for the loved ones of the victims but not necessarily for anybody who doesn't know them personally. Still others are just accounts of terrible events happening out of the blue, which no amount of planning or action could have changed, and therefore without any clear meaning.

Part of the importance of such true stories lies in the way you tell them. You need to ponder *choice*: any decision a real character makes that affects the outcome. Usually, without choice, there is no story, just an event. You need to reach beyond the obvious all-too-familiar facts and create a matrix of meaning—connecting these facts with other facts so that they add up to more than the sum of their parts.

For instance, in one of my recent workshops, a student named Sharon High was working on a nonfiction book about the murder of a state trooper in North Carolina. While horrible, the facts of the case themselves do not automatically raise the crime story above the level of a newspaper account. For the event to remain of interest a year or a decade later to people who didn't know the slain officer, never heard of the killers, and have never been to North Carolina, the writer had to recognize some larger context of the crime. In other words, she had to tell about it in such a way as to make it thematically interesting.

She had worked as the court reporter when the case went to trial, so she had the complete transcript. More than that, as the court reporter, she had established her position as the only person involved in the entire case who was professionally committed to writing the complete truth of the event—since she had to certify the account for the court. So her account of a crime was already implicitly informed by the theme of how one cobbles together complete truth from incomplete, adversarial, often self-serving testimony.

Next, she picked details of the event that particularized the trooper and brought him to life on the page:

• He had a premonition that it was a bad night to go on patrol, which he confided to his wife as he made love to her before he left for his shift—yet he went out on patrol anyway.

• On the way out of his driveway, the headlights of his patrol car washed across the tombstone of his son's grave in the backyard—only months before, the distraught teenager had committed suicide.

• Finally, she replayed the sequence of bad choices that led a gang of minor criminals from Washington, DC, to a remote rural part of the South, in what disaster investigators call a "cascade of events": one small mistake leading to the next, all of them accumulating in a final, fatal one—the killing of the trooper.

So by pondering particular themes, she turned a somewhat ordinary crime into an intriguing story that might shed some new light on how humans behave. One of her themes: how a good man's life is taken because a series of choices by strangers, affected by random events, turned out a certain way.

All categories are arbitrary—ways of describing rather than prescribing. And all good books will transcend categories. But it can be useful to figure out which of the four categories below best describes your big nonfiction book, because then you know how to begin to organize it.

• Personal narrative—a story that you experienced firsthand, such as *Into Thin Air*, in which you may be one of the main actors.
• Reportorial narrative—a story you researched in which you play at most a peripheral role, such as *The Perfect Storm*: You are mainly reporting what others do.
• Documentary—the chronicle of a period, an event, a person, a phenomenon, an idea, meant to establish an accurate record, such as Woodward and Armstrong's chronicle of the Supreme Court under Chief Justice Warren Burger, *The Brethren*.
• Extended persuasive essay—a book driven not by story but by the development of an argument, the use of logic and evidence to make a point, such as Paul Fussell's *Wartime: Understanding and Behavior in the Second World War*, which argues that nostalgia, calculated censorship, and revisionism have distorted our vision of World War II into a dangerous lie.

All share this in common: *The book is all one thing.*

The writer has managed to convey the arc of the whole, the connecting line of development. The book is not just a collection of pieces cobbled together, not merely an almanac of loosely related information. It's a sequence of carefully arranged chapters, each fulfilling the last and supporting the next, each connected by graceful transitions, each carrying the reader closer to a larger sense of resolution.

Often the thread is a conventional arc of story: A character we care about wants something, he acts to get it, other people and forces oppose him, and the outcome—win, lose, or draw—provokes consequences that matter.

The Personal Narrative

There's been an explosion of personal narratives onto the contemporary publishing scene. Some argue that far too many people are telling personal stories of limited general interest, but then we come across *Angela's Ashes* and realize all over again the power of eyewitness, of firsthand experience.

This is no accident. Novelists discovered early on that the first-person narrator was a compelling storyteller: *Great Expectations*, *Frankenstein*, *Moby Dick*, *The Adventures of Huckleberry Finn*, *The Great Gatsby*, *The Sun Also Rises*, and *Middle Passage* all masquerade as memoirs. And as we saw in our discussion of point of view, Fielding, Thackeray, Tolstoy, and others used a kind of authorial first-person, while Conrad invented Marlow, the reader's confidant, to tell his tales.

All those writers wanted that personal voice, the one that claims, "I was there and I saw it and this is the honest-to-God truth."

The personal narrative begins in a passion to understand your own experience—an experience that moved you, changed you, enlightened you, scared the hell out of you. In comprehending it, you connect your experience to the world, and other people recognize it as being a dramatic version of their own experiences—the particulars differ, but the emotional truth is the same.

The most powerful personal narratives often are built around a single remarkable main event—something that doesn't happen every day, perhaps happens only once in a lifetime—such as Krakauer's attempt to climb Mt. Everest. A watershed event in the narrator's life, one that provoked epiphany, the recognition of a new and important truth. The narrator is an actor in the drama, making choices, acting as proxy for the reader—who shares the experience and the choices vicariously along with the storyteller. The event itself offers a natural beginning, middle, and end.

When a personal narrative tells a more general tale, such as McCourt's recounting of his childhood, it's often the case that the experience is *extreme* in some way.

In McCourt's case, the family's dire poverty, the loss of one sibling after another to childhood illness, the alcoholic father and "the pious defeated mother moaning by the fire" all make his childhood a horror story. Even McCourt is aware that his story is an extreme case: "It was, of course, a miserable childhood: the happy childhood is hardly worth your while. Worse than the ordinary miserable childhood is the miserable Irish childhood, and worse yet the miserable Irish Catholic childhood."

Even among their poor Irish Catholic neighbors, the McCourts are an extreme case—and it is the extreme case, the exaggerated version of reality, that illustrates the universal. This is one of the paradoxes of nonfiction: It takes a sinking *Titanic* to illustrate everyday matters.

So of your personal narrative, ask:

• Is it built around a single remarkable event?
• What was your role in the event, and how much of a character will you be in your own tale—in addition to being the narrator?
• What was the central conflict of the event, and what was your own greatest inner conflict?
• How did the event change you, and what did you learn from it?

In drafting his manuscript, Krakauer might have answered: Yes, the event was climbing Mt. Everest. I was both a climber and a journalist, and my own exertions and sufferings played an important role in the story and must be part of the telling, though I will focus mainly on my fellow climbers. Reaching the summit and then descending the mountain safely was the physical conflict, and the interior conflict was my own sense of guilt for the part I played in the catastrophe. What I learned from it is that money can't buy experience, that even experience doesn't guarantee survival because nature is awesome in its dangerous mystery, that we can make fatal decisions even when we seem not to be deciding at all.

Of course, that's reducing his magnificent book to a short paraphrase, which can never serve to tell the story. But it can serve to focus the writer.

If your narrative is based on a more general series of events, a time in your life, say, or a long relationship with a person or a place, ask:

• Where does it logically begin and end?
• Which events will you include and in what order?
• Will you be a mature, reflective, retrospective narrator, or will you remain very much in the moment of the action, as McCourt does?
• What is extraordinary or special about your experience that it should evoke universal interest?

The personal narrative addresses an issue on the surface but also a deeper theme or themes. It mirrors this dual structure in its two parts: the experience being narrated and the meaning of that experience, which of course must matter to someone who doesn't know the author personally, who isn't interested in his or her personal history for its own sake but for the larger truth it brings to light.

In the short personal essay, the writer often can relate the experience in the first section and then ponder it in the second, but a book usually requires that the two elements be interlaced throughout. Otherwise, the reader may lose track of why he is reading about the events—and may therefore lose interest

In Krakauer's book, the experience is the Everest climb itself. The deeper theme ponders the buying and selling of a heroic experience; in this case, veteran guides charged tens of thousands of dollars to unqualified climbers with the promise of getting them to the summit. So who is responsible for their deaths, and what does it say about how we earn our accomplishments?

The personal narrative in whatever form depends on a winning and trustworthy *voice*—beginning with establishing your credentials to tell the story. Early on, Krakauer lets us know he was a seasoned climber who always dreamed of scaling Everest, but that he had always considered it out of reach, beyond his abilities. He also confides that he is telling events only as best he can, not pretending to be absolutely certain about details that may never be known for sure. He meditates candidly on his decision to write the book, admits making some mistakes in the original article that inspired it. He knows what he's doing as a climber and journalist; the voice is modestly self-effacing and trustworthy.

In the personal narrative, as in the reportorial narrative, everything I've said about the novel's structure applies, and you can outline in a very similar way, because you've got the same four necessary ingredients: interesting characters, meaningful action toward a goal, obstacles to reaching that goal and an outcome that matters. In fact, you probably know more about the nonfiction book before you start, since you know already how the event turned out. And it still can be expressed as a guiding signature: Will the paying amateurs successfully climb the highest mountain in the world?

But you still have to hold up that long middle, so approach the material as artistically as you would the fictional events and people of a novel, with the same care for shape, transition, and wholeness.

The Reportorial Narrative

This is the journalist's art at its finest.

The writer pursues a compelling subject through the archives, conducts multiple interviews, walks the ground where it happened, uses every available tactic and tool to find out exactly what happened and why, then tells the story as an articulated whole, a complex and moving tale full of intrigue and suspense and culminating in a climactic scene that changes everything forever—not unlike a novel told in third-person omniscient point of view.

Sometimes the arc of story, the character's driving ambition, is the act of discovery itself: The investigating writer wants to find out the truth. All sorts of things conspire against her: time, distance, history, mistakes, absence of records, legal obstacles, knowledge lost in the translation, people who lie or tell conflicting accounts or who simply won't talk, active adversaries who don't want the truth discovered, her own personal limitations. Getting the story can be a drama all its own—as in *All the President's Men*, Woodward and Bernstein's story about getting the story of Watergate.

It's often a detective story, a mystery, and the reader delights in watching the narrator add up the clues and find the truth.

In this kind of book, as in the documentary, the writer may spend far more time researching—finding information and then struggling to comprehend and connect what he has found—than in the actual writing. Composing the words to tell the story depends on having a deep and profound knowledge of the subject. You can't cheat: Your reader will spot you as a fraud.

The genesis of the reportorial narrative is a passionate desire to get to the bottom of something—to know the whole truth of an event outside your own immediate experience. It's being on the *outside* that makes it different from the personal narrative. All nonfictional books are told, of course, in the same technical first-person point of view. But the reporter backs off, at least part of the time, and through thoroughness of research and focus on other characters can create a sense of omniscience—of comprehending the event in its entirety through the experiences of all the major characters in all the major locales—or the closest thing to it in a true story.

And the story is almost never what you expected it to be. You have to approach the story with humility, a sense of your own limitations. You're not too smart to be fooled by a slick interview or a convincing piece of bad information. There's more to most people and events than meets the eye—remember Johnson's discoveries in *What Lisa Knew*.

When Capote first started pursuing the story of the wholesale murder of the Clutter family in Holcomb, Kansas, he was drawn to the "fact" that a sadistic killer was living in such a wholesome small town—the epitome of American family values. The police were questioning everybody, on the theory that a local man had committed the crime for a local motive. The paranoia of neighbor regarding neighbor, the troubling psychological sea change of the community in the wake of the killings, fascinated Capote. Yet it turned out that the killers were the conventional villains, the nightmare of legend and cliché: ex-con drifters looking for trouble.

His focus changed from the psychology of the town to that of the killers, and the result was a classic that founded a new genre.

As you embark on the project, design your research plan: What do you need to know, and what will you have to do to get that knowledge? How will you gain the insider's access necessary to write the story accurately? What will it cost—in money, time, energy, emotion, and lost opportunities to pursue other projects?

Then get started.

The Documentary

The documentary impulse is among the oldest in literature. The biblical scribes, Herodotus, Caesar, Charles Oman and the other chroniclers of the Crusades all left behind elaborate and detailed records of significant people and events.

The documentary book is similar to the reportorial narrative, though probably more diffuse in focus, not as crucially concerned about drama and tight transition as about being definitive, standing as the unassailable record. The subject may sprawl a bit—a war, a social movement, a life—and may not add up to a neatly arced drama.

Frances FitzGerald's *Fire in the Lake—The Vietnamese and the Americans in Vietnam* takes on a huge subject: two cultures at war for a generation. The whole point of her monumental book is to capture the war as seen by both cultures; thus she allows the paradoxes and contradictory interpretations of events to stand. It is not a "neat" book in the sense of boiling down the war into a lesson, or scripting it as a Greek tragedy, as Barbara Tuchman does of World War I in *The Guns of August*. It's a wide-ranging volume that examines the history of the conflict, the politics of various factions, the military conduct of the war, its social and moral ramifications, the personalities of leaders, and the role of the press and the public. The secret she reveals, finally, is that the war was a mess, but it was a mess for important reasons having to do with politics, ambition, national heritage, and the actions of key leaders in both countries.

The documentary may have the flavor of the commonplace book about it—as in Aleksandr Solzhenitsyn's *One Day in the Life of Ivan Denisovich,* which covers the period between reveille and bedtime in a single day for a prisoner of the *gulag* serving a 3,653-day sentence. The book is cast as a novel, yet it reflects in close detail Solzhenitsyn's own experience as a prisoner of the *gulags* for eight years—once again showing the potentially fine line between a work of fiction and non-fiction, and between the personal narrative and the documentary.

The documentary passion is elemental: to create a record of something worth recording. To document it in a way that can be verified by others.

In this respect, other kinds of nonfiction books often have some documentary aspirations—establishing a body of reliable knowledge, a detailed archive, of a significant event. Daily journalism has a strong documentary impulse. So of course does history. Fiction can be highly documentary: *Schindler's List* and *The Killer Angels* reframed important slices of history.

In the 1930s, the documentary film made obvious what had probably always been true in print documentary: It had a point of view, a definite agenda, often political. It was not "objective," though it pretended to be. It was most often a record of injustice and an implicit argument for reform.

Herman Melville prefaces the English edition of *White Jacket; or, The World in a Man-of-War* innocently enough: "The object of this work is to give some idea of the interior life in a man-of-war." He admits that rather than presenting a log of his voyage—a true documentary—he has invented "illustrative scenes, to paint general life in the Navy." He changes names to protect identities and takes other harmless liberties in order to create a compact and dramatically interesting narrative. Arguably, he has created the nonfiction novel. But: "Wherever statements are made in any way concerning the established laws and usages of the Navy, facts have been strictly adhered to."

In other words, the accounts of injustices—especially the routine floggings—are true and abhorrent. Following publication of *White Jacket*, the latest in a series of documentary protests against the abominable treatment of American sailors, Congress reformed the Navy and outlawed flogging. Books can make a difference.

Writing a documentary requires meticulous habits—to observe, research, and record. The dangers are two, and they are the same for both writer and reader:

1. Being overwhelmed with information (Melville presents his "log" only selectively).

2. Having no focus, no thread tying all the information together (Melville uses the time-honored structure of the journey to shape the narrative and give it profluence).

The key to solving both is to separate fascinating indispensable facts from boring minutiae.

Good biographers struggle with this. Even an uneventful life can become infinite on the page. So a biographer searches out those telling moments, the crucial points of decision, that offer a glimpse into the deep personality of the subject. And in doing so, of course, selects the moments that will represent the life—creates not *the* life but *a* life. All the most conscientious documentarist can do is present a truthful *version* of events.

You're following events in a thorough and perhaps even chronological way, but you still have that long middle to hold up. You have to create a shape, or at least a series of links in a chain, or the effect will be a rambling collection of parts, not necessarily adding up to anything larger. Here theme can help create connections.

FitzGerald divides her book into three sections—which might be considered acts according to our dramatic structural model:

1. The Vietnamese.
2. The Americans and the Saigon Government.
3. Conclusion.

Acts one and two are roughly equal in length, and act three is about half as long as the first two. FitzGerald sets up a dramatic dichotomy— two ways of understanding the war—arranged according to a chronology of major events that escalate in intensity and meaning. Act two ends with the Tet offensive by the Vietcong—the beginning of the end—and then act three synthesizes what has gone before, connecting the Vietnamese to the American experience while concluding the chronology of major events.

Even so, it's tough sledding at times. But of course you can't write for people who don't read the kind of book you're writing. This doesn't release you from the obligation to write clearly and economically. If anything, it makes clarity of style more urgent.

FitzGerald begins "Nations and Empires," an early chapter setting the stage for the debacle of the war, as if setting the scene for a suspense novel.

> Saigon in 1966 was, as always, a city of rumors. It breathed rumors, consumed only rumors, for the people of Saigon had long since ceased to believe anything stated officially as fact. Among the stories of comets falling and bombing halts there was that year one rumor that stood out from all the rest. A work of art, a Fabergé among rumors, it was so embellished with circumstantial evidence of murders and secret meetings, so exquisitely crafted of inference, coincidence, and psychological truth, that its purveyors established its value without question.

A simple syntax accumulates a rhythm of repetition with spin, escalating the surreal suspense of wartime Saigon. And the style resonates with one of the book's key themes: the elusiveness of truth.

In Quammen's *The Song of the Dodo*, which tackles an equally sprawling subject, a specific scientist's discovery may come back in another form in a later chapter; a concept played out in one arena is played out in a slightly different way in another. The threads reach back and forth across chapters until we feel the book begin to knit.

The Extended Persuasive Essay

A book can take on the form of an extended academic or reflective essay carried through with a depth and completeness not possible in the short form. Such a book, like its shorter cousin, gives a prolonged glimpse of a mind thinking, marshaling evidence, exploring data, probing positions, asking questions and resolving them. It comes closest perhaps to addressing directly an issue and its themes.

Probably it will be read only by a reader interested in the subject of the book.

If this sounds like a truism, consider: Before *The Perfect Storm*, how many readers combed the bookstores for the latest title about commercial fishing? A gripping tale of death and survival—not the subject per se—carried away readers. Had Junger written the definitive argument for or against factory trawlers, only those who already care passionately about the fishing industry would be likely to read his book.

That is the risk and the opportunity: Certain readers will never open the book, but a finite number will be drawn to it eagerly. And if you can get a reader to sample it, a strong and winning voice can capture a tepid reader.

Of all forms, the extended essay is most transparently an argument, an engine of persuasion, which must focus on logic and not on feelings or opinions that are not large enough. Tone is crucial: A know-it-all stance or an overbearing attitude can push away the reader who might otherwise be won over.

Classic rhetorical techniques apply here:

• Establish your credentials up front: Here's my authority for making this argument. James Fallows can write *Breaking the News: How the Media Undermine American Democracy* because he's earned his bona fides as the Washington editor for *The Atlantic Monthly* and a weekly commentator on National Public Radio, among other journalistic experience: "This book mainly describes the media from the outside, assessing the way journalists' behavior affects our public life. But since I have spent more than twenty years as a reporter, it naturally also reflects my own concerns about the institution."

• Establish your own biases early so the reader is sure of an honest transaction. In his introduction to another book about the media, *News Is a Verb: Journalism at the End of the Twentieth Century*, Pete Hamill writes, "This is not an objective or neutral essay. The subject is so deeply intertwined with my life that I can't write about it in a cold, detached manner. Quite simply, I love newspapers and the men and women who make them. . . . I want them to go on and on and on."

• Marshal convincing evidence, presenting it in escalating importance, saving your strongest evidence for the finale.

• For every abstract assertion, supply a concrete, specific, illustrative example: Make each concept a flesh-and-blood reality.

• Couch the essay in clear, economical language—remember the documentary—elegant in the sense of achieving a large effect with minimal apparatus, as a single strand of pearls accents a black evening gown. Don't get tangled in verbose sentences laced with jargon.

• Anticipate and dispose of the strongest arguments against your position; they will certainly occur to an alert reader, who otherwise will wonder why they didn't occur to you.

• Allow the complexity of the issue to stand, but define the terms of your argument within it as precisely as possible.

• Refrain from direct emotional appeal ("What kind of monster can shoot a gentle deer?") or ad hominem attacks ("So-and-so is a fool and a liar, so you can't believe what he says on the matter").

This kind of book can be both the easiest and the hardest to write well.

It can be easy in the sense of not requiring interviews or some other kinds of research—though it well might. The writer also doesn't have to do the imaginative work of inventing characters and plot and scenes, as in a novel, or following the fortunes of real characters in painstaking detail through a complete arc of story. This kind of book doesn't depend on what other people do, at least not directly.

But it is hard in at least two big ways:

1. You have to develop an original argument that holds together. By its nature, a big subject has been explored before. This is the problem that doctoral students face in conceiving their dissertations— and why they are so often driven to focus on obscure tributaries of large ideas that, until now, no one has deemed worth the trouble. Your best chance at being original is to write specifically and concretely— about real people acting in particular ways—and arguments are about *concepts*, not people. One solution is to make the argument about people—as Fussell and others do. Let stories communicate concepts. But there is a limit to how far this tactic can take you. Sooner or later, you simply have to make your point, connect the dots from your thesis through your arguments to your conclusion.

2. It's human nature to love a story and hate a lecture. Remember, that's why Jesus spoke in parables. Over the long haul of a book, if

you don't have a narrative line, an arc of story, to hold up the middle, you've got to hold up the middle through the dry drama of logic, through thematic connections between ideas. So you had better have some pretty fascinating ideas, and you had better ravish the reader's mind with the power and subtlety of your intellect.

The passion driving this sort of book is intellectual: passion for the beauty of a well-formed argument in service of a worthy idea.

Crossover Books

When you're thinking big, addressing public subjects and universal themes, playing with great ideas, no single category is going to be large enough to contain your book. In that sense, all good big books are crossover books.

Melville's "documentary" is shaped as a voyage and salted with knowledge from other sources—and he is the voyager. So it's both a personal narrative and a reportorial narrative.

Writers of personal narratives often delve into the archives so they can inform their stories with facts and events outside their own experiences, thus placing them in larger contexts. Thus Krakauer relates the fatal history of mountaineering on Everest along with that of his own ill-starred climbing expedition.

And it works the other way, too. At intervals throughout *What Lisa Knew*, a largely reportorial narrative, Johnson relates her personal connection to the story as a mother, a New Yorker, a woman, a writer.

DeBlieu deliberately combines the personal and the documentary impulses in *Wind*, much as Terry Tempest Williams does in *Refuge*, her parallel tale of her family's struggle with cancer and a flooding wildlife refuge, moving back and forth between the private and public arenas.

Capote's *In Cold Blood* is a reportorial narrative that is based not just on conventional research but on imagination, intuition, speculation, and, to some degree, on omitting his personal connection. It mimics the novel, and that's what he called it: a nonfiction novel.

And while Fussell's *Wartime* makes a powerful argument for his thesis, the evidence is often stories—anecdotes of combat GIs, personal memoirs, twice-told apocryphal tales. In *The Guns of August*, Barbara Tuchman makes a compelling argument about the nature of the folly that led to World War I not only with documentary evidence but with an accurate sense of story—knowing what to emphasize, what to leave out, and casting events as a tragic drama: Generals and statesmen, characters with fatal flaws, especially pride, make rash choices toward questionable goals and trigger horrific consequences.

Quammen's *The Song of the Dodo* is a classic documentary about how life evolved on this planet and is now going extinct in far too many locales. It also makes a fairly explicit extended argument about how to repair at least some of the ecological damage we've caused and how to stop from doing more. And it does both through delicious adventure stories about scientists and explorers.

Technical Writing

Subjects that inspire big books are usually complex. As we've seen, respecting the complexity of the subject is key to the writer's approach. But we encounter a paradox: how to express complex technical material in a way that not only lets the lay reader understand it but that completely captivates him.

Quammen has to explain the mechanisms of evolution and extinction—two difficult biological concepts. FitzGerald has to navigate the politics of multiple regimes on two continents. DeBlieu has to demonstrate in words how a wind tunnel or a hang glider works.

Technical subjects are not limited to science. All the following are technical subjects:
- How to sail a square-rigged ship (Melville).
- How a climbing expedition is organized and led (Krakauer).
- How a swordfishing boat sets its gear (Junger).
- How news magazines cover a story (Fallows).
- How the Supreme Court decides a case (Woodward and Armstrong).
- How police interrogate a witness (Johnson).

Unless your reader is an expert in the profession or discipline of your subject, to that reader it's a technical subject. This goes for sports, cooking, politics, the law, medicine, the stock market, gardening, psychology, religion, anything. So take the time and thought to teach the reader what he needs to know about the subject.

Part of the genius of successful writers is McCourt's: the ability to forget what they know and relearn it with their readers looking over their shoulders. Good teachers know this: If they can remember back to the time before they knew what they now know, they can re-create their own sense of discovery in the classroom. They can cast the material in terms that make sense to a novice. They remember to define all their terms. They repeat the lessons using different metaphors. Technical writing expresses the teaching function of a book; it gets inside the mechanisms of the subject at hand.

If you are not an expert on the subject, so much the better. Go to people who are the experts, and listen to what they say. Watch them demonstrate what they do. Read their reports, their biographies, their memoirs. Ask them to draw diagrams, pictures. Ask them dumb questions, and then repeat their answers back to them in your own words until you are sure you understand exactly what they mean and can express it in words they will vouch for as accurate.

Last week, in the course of researching an article that seems to be ballooning into a book, I spent a day on the Cape Fear River with a team of very articulate biologists monitoring water quality. We covered fifty-odd miles of river, tested the water at seven locations with exotic electronic equipment, and talked. I have no aptitude for science, but by the end of the day—having previously studied many technical articles and conducted several hours of interviews on other days—I could more or less clearly explain how sediment in a river is connected to pollution, how riverine wetlands function during a flood, how locks and dams thwart endangered anadromous (spawning) short-nosed sturgeon, and the strange parasitic life cycle of a local freshwater mussel called the green floater and why it has been supplanted by the Asian clam, and why that matters.

The next day at dusk I rode down river on a tugboat, then climbed up the moving hull of a 950-foot container ship on a rope jacob's ladder. On the bridge, I watched a docking pilot slide the 52,000-ton vessel sideways into her berth, then later listened to him debrief the apprentice pilot over coffee in the tugboat galley, maneuvering his handheld VHF radio like a toy ship on the galley table. He himself gave me the metaphor to describe what he was doing, which required some fifty commands, reversed engines, rudder, bow thrusters, and the use of two tugboats: "It's kind of like driving on ice, and you have to make your car go sideways into the parking space."

Technical writing can be rich, entertaining, and metaphorical. Above all, it has to be right.

Exercises

1. List three subjects or events that might make a first-rate nonfiction book. For each one:
   - Identify the central character(s).
   - Decide *who* will tell the story: You as participant? An effaced narrator? The collective versions of others as reported by you?
   - Figure out what is at stake (who wins or loses, and how big) for the characters.
   - Give a good reason why it will matter to the reader.

2. Within the subject above, choose a sustained complex action that is technically challenging—arranging the flowers for a society wedding, performing coronary bypass surgery, painting a portrait, defusing a bomb, choreographing a Broadway musical—and describe the action in such a way that you achieve three things:
   - The literal action is vivid. The reader *sees* it clearly and can follow the stages of the action without confusion.
   - The portrayal is so clear and well organized that a reader with the appropriate talent and tools could—using your passage as a guide—actually perform the action you describe.
   - You capture some inherent tension within the literal action.

3. Write an op-ed piece on an issue close to your heart—but write it as convincingly as you can *from a point of view with which you disagree.*

Issues of Ethics and Art

How far can the truth be "bent" in the service of a "larger good"? Does it make a difference whether you call your truth "fiction" or "nonfiction"? How much privacy is owed to real-life people? What are the writer's responsibilities—to his reader, to the people he writes about, to his craft? What subjects are off-limits?

Sebastian Junger, in his best-seller *The Perfect Storm*, portrays a real-life sailboat skipper named Ray Leonard as ineffectual, frozen by fear, cocooned in his bunk sucking on a bottle of whisky while his two female crew members heroically arrange for his rescue in the midst of a raging gale. This portrayal well serves one of Junger's key themes: that there is no predicting how any individual will react in the face of overwhelming natural catastrophe, including the storm-of-the-century encountered at sea. Sometimes the novice, the frail or inexperienced person, will conduct herself with bravery and daring, while the strong authority figure may cower, paralyzed by terror.

The problem is that, according to Herb Payson's April 1998 article in *Sail* magazine, Junger never interviewed Leonard to hear his side of the story—instead relying on the tale as told by one of the female crew, Karen Stimpson, and a Coast Guardsman who came on the scene only at the end of the drama, in time for the rescue. Junger told Ellen Barry of *The Boston Phoenix* in an interview, "Ray Leonard is understandably upset by the book, but everything Karen Stimpson said was corroborated by the Coast Guard. Everything and more. . . ."

Junger went on to say that he knew even worse things about Leonard that he chose not to include in the book. His purpose was not to make a villain out of Leonard but to capture the harrowing experience of being in the storm.

But other critics were quick to take Junger to task. Warren St. John tracked down some of Junger's sources, interviewed them, and in a front-page story in *The New York Observer* attacked the book as "A Fish Story Awash in Errors."

Even Junger admits he made some errors. In the Barry interview, he said, "When I first found out there was anything wrong, I was so upset. I wished I had never written the book. . . . There were twelve things, and a lot of them were things where someone would tell me something and I wouldn't check it—he sounded authoritative and I didn't have time to check it."

So is Junger's version inaccurate? Is it a gross distortion, or is it entirely true in every detail except those dozen slips, or does it fall somewhere in between? If the writer makes small errors—spelling a key person's name wrong, mistaking one location for another, inaccurately describing a piece of gear—the reader gets a little nervous, at least the reader who recognizes the error. We wonder, what else did he get wrong that I don't recognize?

We're likely to forgive the small errors, but a nagging voice says we just can't trust the book the way we want to trust it.

There's an element of surprise in Junger's reaction to criticism in the Barry interview—surprise that *The Perfect Storm* became a big book: "It wasn't supposed to be a big book—not a Book in capital letters, you know. . . . I was sure I was condemned to write a journalistically interesting book that just wouldn't fly." Shades of William Faulkner's famous and perhaps apocryphal remark about his gritty novel *Sanctuary*: If I'd known it was going to be a bestseller, I'd have written it better.

Respecting the Material, the Reader, the Craft

So when you embark on *your* Big Book, respect the material. Treat it as the most important project you will ever undertake. Don't cut corners. Don't assume you can get away with anything. Take the time to check "facts" someone else—even an expert—tells you. Don't cheat. You will always regret it later. Always. No exceptions. Make that last inconvenient visit to the archive. Make that last redundant phone call to the source you really don't enjoy talking to. Go over the chronology of events one last time.

Because, as meticulous and conscientious as you are, it is impossible to write a long fact-based narrative and *not* get something wrong. Your notes are not always as legible as they might be, especially if you scribbled them in the back of a moving car at night, or in a state of jet lag or sleep deprivation. Your tapes are not always bell clear: Someone slams a door at a key moment in the interview and a crucial word goes missing, or a generator comes on somewhere in the building—a noise you barely noticed during the interview but the sensitive electronic microphone amplified it and ruined minutes of conversation. Or you just forgot to write something down. Or you misremembered something you were sure you'd never forget. Or your source was wrong. Or you had the document and lost it.

Or, like Junger, you were in a hurry. Being in a hurry is the source of much of the evil that writers do, and it's built into the experience of writing for deadline. Sometimes, if you're lucky, you can correct the manuscript for a later edition. If there is a later edition. Gregory Hemingway quotes his father in *Papa: A Personal Memoir*:

> "And almost all reporters are inaccurate. Have you ever noticed when you read about something in the papers you truly know about that ninety percent of it is inaccurate? A lot of mistakes have to do with early deadlines, of course, the need to get something down in a hurry for the afternoon or morning editions. Often there's just no time to check the accuracy of your sources. I know—I started out as a reporter on the *Kansas City Star*. But some of it comes from the reporter's conceit, and the contempt for a reader's intelligence that only a truly conceited reporter can have. And a lot comes from laziness, or, to be more accurate, from fatigue."

So make sure that if you make mistakes, they are exactly that— honest *mistakes*. We live in an era when few people in public life seem to understand the difference between *doing wrong* and *making a mistake.* A congressman takes a payoff and calls it a mistake, but it's not: It's doing wrong. The difference lies in *choice*: The congressman had a choice whether to take a bribe. He took the money. That was wrong.

On the other hand, when a writer conscientiously checks the facts but an error slips through, that was not a matter of choice. The writer *chose* to do the work to get it right, but life being what it is and people being imperfect, the error happened anyway.

So the proper attitude is to do the best you can to get it right—to choose to respect the material, the people about whom you are writing, and your reader. That's what you have control over. Those three elements weigh on the writer. The writer lives a public life: His or her words shape the culture, define the issues in elections, express our collective values and sense of justice, create the shared community memory by which we live.

Jon Krakauer is painfully aware of his responsibility to living people—as well as to the dead friends he left on Mt. Everest. There were many, many fine reasons not to go, but attempting to climb Everest is an intrinsically irrational act—a triumph of desire over sensibility. Any person who would seriously consider it is almost by definition beyond the sway of reasoned argument.

"The plain truth is that I knew better but went to Everest anyway and in doing so I was party to the death of good people, which is something that is apt to remain on my conscience for a very long time."

In the introduction to *Into Thin Air*, which began as a magazine piece, he admits, "Within days after the *Outside* article went to press, I discovered that a few of the details I'd reported were in error. Most were minor inaccuracies of the sort that inevitably creep into works of deadline journalism. But one of my blunders was in no sense minor and had a devastating impact on the friends and family of one of the victims."

He does his best to remedy that inaccuracy—the account of how and where one of the climbers was killed—in the book-length version. He respects the dead climber and his loved ones enough to want to make an accurate record of his final ordeal; he respects his reader enough to admit he made a mistake and try to remedy it, rather than hiding behind a facade of omniscience; and he respects the craft enough to earn his effects truthfully.

His forthrightness in admitting fault actually makes the reader trust him more: Here's a writer who could have gotten away with something that only a handful of people would ever have known about, yet he chooses to come clean with the reader. We would trust our house keys to this man.

And it actually reminds us of our responsibilities as readers: In this book and in others, we can't afford to take everything at face value. We need to bring to bear our own judgment, our own common sense, our own healthy skepticism, our own moral compass.

Equally, he reminds us that at best writing nonfiction is a difficult and imperfect craft—in this case exacerbated by hypoxia, fear, fatigue, and all the stresses of the climb—but that this author's attitude is basically to tell the truth, even when it makes him look bad.

Fiction and the Truth

Does a novelist have the same ethical obligations as a nonfiction writer?

Clearly not—he is working inside an invented world. Casting real people and events as fiction is rarely done wholesale. Usually the writer draws composite characters, gives them made-up names, puts them in invented situations. So even if she is writing about her own love affair or parents or high school friends, there is likely to be a protective coloration. The writer herself is camouflaged in the persona of the narrator—we never assume that even a first-person fictional narrator is the author.

And the roman à clef—the novel in which real, usually prominent people are thinly disguised, inviting the reader to figure out which character is which real person—is no longer as fashionable as it was when Hemingway portrayed Harold Loeb as the whining bore Robert Cohn in *The Sun Also Rises*. Libel suits have dampened the impulse. The exceptions, novels such as *Primary Colors*, tend to focus on public figures with limited recourse in libel court.

But that doesn't mean that the novelist has *no* ethical obligations.

The kind of novel we're talking about here—the one that addresses big ideas, public subjects, and universal themes—is based in reality. There's no getting around it. And reality carries with it certain obligations to the actual truth.

If you're writing about the Civil War, as Michael Shaara does in *The Killer Angels*, you can't just make it up. The reader expects the historical novelist to take certain liberties—casting dialogue in a more dramatic or lively fashion, compressing events to leave out the dull periods when not much happens, creating some composite fictional characters to stitch the action together more coherently. That's all part of the fictional contract.

Yet the reader also expects to get good history. He trusts that you have researched your subject, that you know what you're talking about. The reader craves authenticity. In today's culture, readers are more likely to learn history from historical novels—especially those made into films—than books of scholarly history. In a sense, the civic culture depends on novelists being conscientious in re-creating the past.

A.B. Guthrie Jr., author of *The Big Sky*, among many other historical novels about America, writes in "The Historical Novel," "I believe all of us become better citizens, better and richer human beings, through a famliarity with the dreams and deeds of the men and women who went before us in this adventure that we call the United States of America."

It matters that you get it right. Thus the historical novelist will do just as much close research as the nonfiction writer.

In his signature essay "On the Writing of History," Wallace Stegner argues the novelist's value to the appreciation of history. He writes of *The Preacher and the Slave*, his novel about the life and death of Joe Hill, a legendary martyr of the International Workers of the World (IWW) or "Wobbly" movement:

> As necessary, I invented characters, scenes, motivations, dialogue, and though Hill's execution gave me an inescapable ending, I bent the approach to that conclusion as seemed to me needful. But the bending that seemed needful was also

imposed on me, in a way, for I had spent four or five years collecting documentary and other evidence on both Joe Hill and the IWW, had hunted down seven or eight people who had known the elusive Joe Hill in life, had studied the trial transcript and many newspaper files, had talked with the family of the two men Hill was accused of murdering, and with the sheriff who conducted the execution by firing squad, with the Wobbly editor who arranged Hill's public funeral in Chicago, and with balladeers who had written Joe Hill songs. I had attended IWW martyr meetings. I had gotten the warden of the Utah State Penitentiary to walk me through a mock execution so that I would know imaginatively how a condemned and blindfolded man might feel in the very soles of his feet his progress toward death down iron stairs, across paved courtyard, into cindered alley to the chair with the bullet-battered backstop.

The truth of the history—and the excitement in the narrative—comes from *knowing*. Not just knowing the broad outlines of the IWW movement, or the folk legend Hill became after his death, but knowing the exact words spoken at trial, the reminiscences of old friends and enemies, the feel of the iron stairs and cinders on the soles of the condemned man's feet.

As Stegner points out, it's not dramatizing the narrative that makes false history false: "Falseness derives from inadequate or inaccurate information, faulty research, neglected resources, bias, bad judgment, misleading implications, and these afflict the expository among us about as often as they afflict the narrative."

False history does damage. It gives us a distorted view of who we are, where we came from, how well or badly we've honored our founding principles. It creates the wrong stories to live by.

But what of the contemporary novel? Consider: By the time you have finished writing a novel, the subject is already two or three years old. If you're writing about a public event—the Clinton election campaign depicted in *Primary Colors*, say—that event is already becoming history. In that important sense, every novel about public matters is

213

a historical novel, shaping our comprehension of our past even as we are living through it. And inside the novel there is a past—the back stories of the main characters—receding even farther into history. You're creating a record, whether intentionally or not. So pay attention to the "bending that seems needful"—the ways in which you are manipulating reality to make a better story. Is it a bending toward truth, or merely toward the sensational?

Fiction always begins with the question, What if? It can venture into any territory, contain the most fantastical and allegorical inventions, employ ghosts and talking animals and magic and anything else the writer needs to carry the story. Kurt Vonnegut uses fanciful space aliens to help tell the story of the firebombing of Dresden during World War II in *Slaughterhouse-Five*. Yet the book is authentic.

Somehow even the most whimsical fiction always has its feet firmly planted on the ground—the ground being the writer's accurate knowledge of the world. George Orwell's *Animal Farm* stars a pig, a horse, and assorted barnyard animals, yet it uncannily depicts Soviet-style bureaucracy, with all its cruel inequities. If in his allegorical barnyard all the animals worked selflessly for the common good, we would test his utopian vision against our experience in the world and find it false, mere propaganda meant to deceive us. Orwell may be no historian, but he's certainly a gifted anthropologist.

I always feel grounded in the actual business of the world in any really good novel—whether it's Cormac McCarthy writing about the desert West of hardscrabble cowboys and Mexican border towns, Jane Smiley writing about the Midwestern family farm, or Don DeLillo writing about a toxic incident threatening a suburban family. You get the sense these writers have looked behind the curtain of clichés and found the true gen. They're not just going to perpetuate melodramatic fallacies. Their characters move beyond stereotype and do justice to the full range of human possibility. To me that's as much an ethical concern as an artistic one. Their characters face the same ambiguities we face. Their choices are hard and rarely absolute. The consequences are never clear in advance, yet there are always important consequences. Their virtues are clouded by their dark sides. Their villainy is confounded by their altruism.

As in life, there are no totally happy endings. Yet among the damage there is always, somehow, rectitude. A gleam of hope, of belief, of dignity.

Off-Limits

The question I posed to my nonfiction writing class was simple: Is there any subject you would not write about?

They were a talented bunch, spirited and overflowing with curiosity. They had already written wonderful pieces about firefighters in Pennsylvania, a ballerina with a prosthetic leg, a bounty hunter, a contortionist, the exotic dancers at a topless men's club, the Columbine High School massacre, the rave phenomenon, the *Pfiesteria* epidemic, an expatriate princess from Ghana, child abuse, and an unsolved murder, among many other wide-ranging subjects. I expected a rousing no.

Instead, almost all of them in turn announced at least one thing he or she wouldn't write about. Some of the answers were predictable: Several students put family members, especially parents, off-limits, at least while they were still living. Others went further: They wouldn't write about friends, victims, terminally ill cancer patients. A few vowed never to write about themselves. Only a couple of them insisted they would write about anything that interested them, no holds barred.

The particulars didn't interest me as much as the reasons: One way or another, they were mostly concerned about the rights of other people, friends, family, and strangers—the right to privacy, to not suffer public embarrassment, to retain their dignity. We talked at some length about the fact that it would often be the vulnerable, the victimized, the heartfelt experience with a loved one or close friend that would ignite passion for a subject, that indeed writing about such people and subjects might be doing them—and their readers—a great service.

I know that as they go on in their writing they are likely to change their minds many times, but their response was heartening. They were reacting in a sensible, humane way: They valued friendship or family loyalty or simple kindness above a good story. They were recognizing that it was a question worth asking—better now than several months into a project when they find themselves instinctively avoiding certain subjects or presenting them with kid gloves.

Dismiss this attitude as sentimental if you want—an aggressive journalist almost surely would—but it bespeaks a decency that is essential to a writer trying to write with any depth about the human soul.

The danger of course is obvious: that a writer may elect simply to avoid writing about difficult subjects, subjects that make him or her uncomfortable or troubled. That the writer will risk offending no one and thereby lose the edge of candor and truthfulness that always marks the best books. And often it's the subject that troubles you the most that is driving your passion. But I have faith that sooner or later these students will tackle all those subjects, in part because they will not blunder into them accidentally or lightly. They will think long and hard before taking them on. But they will take them on.

Can any subject truly be off-limits to a writer?

The long answer is that every writer will balk at certain subjects at different stages of his or her career and for different reasons. Philip Lee Williams writes, in *Crossing Wildcat Ridge: A Memoir of Nature and Healing,* about preparing for open heart surgery to replace a congenitally defective heart valve. As he is leaving his doctor's office after being told in chilling detail about the impending procedure, during which his heart will be stopped, he passes by the doctor's secretary:

> "You're the novelist, aren't you?" she says pleasantly.
> "I guess I am," I say.
> "Well, you can write a book about this."
> "I doubt that," I say, and I mean it.

At that moment, he cannot face contemplating the danger and (hopefully) the painful recovery to come. And yet eventually, after enough time has passed, he does write a book—a beautiful and moving book about facing his life at a moment of potentially fatal crisis, falling back on his family and his homeplace to heal.

Ron Hansen's novel *Hitler's Niece* chronicles the strange and fatal "love" affair between Hitler and Angelika Raubal, the much younger daughter of his half-sister. Critics have taken issue not just with the style and craft of the novel but with its very subject matter—Hitler as lover, however strange, is somehow out of bounds to them. Hansen says, "There's this suspicion that I'm humanizing Hitler, that I'm becoming far too sympathetic to him." What he's doing, of course, is trying to get inside the monster, just as Joyce Johnson tried to fathom Joel Steinberg—not to justify monstrosity but to understand it.

Some reviewers have taken the tack that this material simply shouldn't be written about, whatever Hansen's narrative stance. "Some people would rather you spend your time writing about the Holocaust, but not what caused it," Hansen explains. "But I think it's an important story to tell. Had FDR had an affair of this kind and his niece found dead in her apartment, people would have been writing about it."

He's right, and the result is a deeply troubling and utterly absorbing novel that matters. According to *Booklist*, "Hansen's insightful, brilliantly interpretive, and frightening novel does more to illuminate the welter of evil that fueled Hitler than a dozen biographies."

Note the word "frightening."

The short answer is no. No subject is off limits. To any writer. Ever.

The Writer's Power

My students were recognizing an important basic fact about writing, one we rarely speak of but that readers know well: The writer has tremendous power.

It does not seem that way when we are writing, wrestling with facts, scenes, ideas, and sentences, but in turning ephemeral experience and knowledge into hard words on the page, we create a record that becomes its own kind of truth to the reader—sometimes the definitive truth—even when it is grossly in error.

To portray a sailboat skipper as a cowardly drunk—accurately or not—forever seals that man's reputation in amber.

A common retort from some writers to people they have savaged in print: "If you don't like what I've written, write your own book."

Fair enough, if you're talking about a celebrity, a president, a best-selling author. But there's usually something disingenuous and unfair in the challenge of a rebuttal. We're writers. They're most often not. We have access to the tools of our craft, to publishing venues, ultimately to an audience. They're just people living their lives—sometimes very private lives—according to their best lights, which indeed may be the lights of criminals and frauds and villains, or might just be the lights of ordinary flawed human beings like ourselves who never expected to show up in anybody's book. Ray Leonard, for example, is not a professional writer—and even were he to become one, he would not likely have access to Junger's audience. So in a very real sense his reputation lies forever in Junger's hands.

While Junger's depiction of Ray Leonard is now the subject of debate on Web sites and in the pages of critics' reviews, his role in the drama has already been defined and will not change unless a more compelling version also becomes a best-seller—highly unlikely.

This is not to imply any inaccuracy or animosity on Junger's part. I believe he set out to write the most accurate book he could write. Plenty of Gloucester fishermen applauded the book as the truest account of their lives they'd ever read. I just wish he had interviewed Ray Leonard, and by now I'd bet he does, too.

It's only to say that the act of writing a private person's name and character into print is serious business with consequences that can't be taken back. Treat it seriously. Ask yourself, By what right do I make this person's private business public? On what evidence do I predicate his or her character?

And ask the most important question of all: What if I'm wrong?

The Durable First Account

The first record usually has the most sticking power—it's the controlling version, the one to which all subsequent versions must react. Newer versions can't ignore what everybody already knows to be "true"; somehow they must address it, account for it, if necessary revise or debunk it.

The first "author" to write the account of the racial massacre that occurred in Wilmington, North Carolina, on November 10, 1898, was an ex-Confederate colonel named Alfred Moore Waddell. Only a few weeks after the event, he published his account in *Collier's* magazine, in which he labeled the event a "race riot"—a label that stuck. He recounted how mobs of Negroes had threatened the city with mayhem, how he had led the fight to restore civic order and subsequently been installed as mayor, casting himself in a heroic role as savior of the city.

In fact, as I came to learn in researching the material for a novel, Waddell personally led the *white* mob that, unprovoked, burned down the black newspaper, *The Daily Record*, then went on a rampage through black neighborhoods. All as part of a planned coup d'etat of the elected city government, made up of a "Fusionist" party of mainly black Republicans and white Populists. For months, secret white Democratic businessmen's groups had been stockpiling weapons—including at least one machine gun—recruiting vigilantes, setting up an elaborate system of communications. They had even appointed block captains, whose job it was to evacuate white women and children to the armory and the adjacent (and well-fortified) First Baptist Church when the shooting started. They had hired Pinkerton detectives to report on the whereabouts and actions of prominent black leaders and white sympathizers.

A "riot" sounds like a spontaneous eruption of violence. A "race riot" inevitably carries the connotation that it is the blacks who are rioting, Neither was true in this case. Whites did all the killing and burning, and it was extremely well planned. And one of the ultimate goals of the white supremacists' leaders was to install their party men in the state legislature, where they could then legislate Negro voting rights out of existence. This they did: A savvy white supremacist lawyer named George Rountree composed the so-called Grandfather Clause, which effectively barred blacks from voting in North Carolina—and across parts of the South, where it was copied by other legislatures—until the Voting Rights Act of 1964.

So the event had huge implications. It can be argued that it helped to actually create the Jim Crow South and make necessary a decades-long civil rights movement to win back basic freedoms blacks in the South had already enjoyed by the 1890s—not the history we learned in school.

Nevertheless, for nearly a hundred years after the massacre, the public version of the event was based on Waddell's account, widely copied and rehearsed in other accounts. His version was so durable that when my novel *Cape Fear Rising* was published, a lot of critics accused me of fabricating events out of whole cloth for the sake of drama. But when it came to the public events of those terrible days, that's the one thing I tried my best not to do. I stuck to the record as meticulously as I possibly could, given the contradictions and gaps in that record.

At last historians are revisiting the so-called riot and Waddell's self-serving version is slowly losing credence, though it dies hard.

That's one way of looking at what writers do when we tackle large public subjects: We are entering our version in the marketplace of ideas, where it will compete with other narratives of the same subject. The reader will choose which story to live by.

Ours has a chance of driving out the false and lurid stories only if it is the best, truest story.

The Art of Character

Naval aviators have a saying: "You don't rise to the occasion—you default to the level of your training."

Writing is about *character*, and character is formed by *training*—practicing your craft to a fine point where instinct replaces conscious thought and art slips in, unnoticed.

Training requires *discipline*—the discipline to sit at your desk day after day, to think hard and precisely, to carefully and seamlessly integrate research into story, the discipline to rewrite a passage as many times as it takes to get it right.

Discipline comes from *will*—the force of personality that will not let you despair or quit, even and especially when things are darkest and most difficult.

And will ultimately derives from *passion*: the fierce, sustained desire to write a book that matters about a subject that has captured your heart and seized your imagination.

Nothing short of that passion will sustain you over the long haul of months and years that it will take to write that book. You may be writing for glory, but it is belief in the ongoing work at hand and joy in the act of putting words onto the page that will get you through the long days at the keyboard.

Not every day will bring joy. Some days will be a cold slog through swampy mire, a chore of perseverance in strange country.

It's a Big Book. It's going to take you a long time and require every ounce of energy you possess. It will test your faith in your judgment, in the world, in yourself. There will be times when you'll want to throw up your hands and quit. Lots of them. Probably it will never be published, you'll tell yourself. Probably if it is published, no one will ever want to read it.

You will remember Herman Melville, writing to Richard Henry Dana about the agonizing progress of writing *Moby Dick*: "It will be a strange sort of book, tho', I fear; blubber is blubber you know; tho' you may get oil out of it, the poetry runs as hard as sap from a frozen maple tree. . . ."

But there will be other days, days when the mists will part for a moment and you'll catch the glint of the high place you're trying to reach. The excitement you'll feel will be in direct proportion to the ambition of what you're trying to achieve. You will keep your head down and keep writing the pages and practicing your craft, learning what you need to know, what you never needed to know before.

If the book's ambition is worthy, even if you achieve it imperfectly, it will ennoble you. It will enlarge you as a writer and a person. You will in fact rise to the occasion—because even on your worst days, you will default to a very high level of training.

Make no mistake: Who you are and how you approach your work will find their way into the writing. The book will bear the stamp of your character as plainly and indelibly as a watermark.

If you persevere, if you call on your best craft and take your pride from the work in progress, you may remember how Melville finished his letter to Dana: "Yet I mean to give the truth of the thing, spite of this."

And you will finish your book. You will get a little taste of glory.

Exercises

1. Name one subject that is off-limits to you as a writer and *why*? Would it hurt a living family member? Is it too private? Would it be too personally painful? Is it too disgusting for some reason? Can you imagine that in the future you might change your mind? Why or why not?

2. Consider a public event about which you are inclined to write. If you cast it as nonfiction, how would your approach differ from if you cast it as fiction?

3. Select a memoir that you admire, such as *Angela's Ashes* by Frank McCourt or *The Kiss* by Kathryn Harrison. What ethical issues did the author face? How did he or she resolve them? How would you have resolved them differently?

4. Identify an ethical issue in a book you admire. How does the author's apparent decision about how to handle it enhance or detract from the art of the book?

About the Author

Philip Gerard directs the Professional and Creative Writing Program at the University of North Carolina at Wilmington. He has published fiction and nonfiction in numerous magazines, including *New England Review/Bread Loaf Quarterly* and *The World & I*. He has scripted shows for *Globe Watch*, an international affairs program, for PBS-affiliate WUNC-TV, Chapel Hill, North Carolina, and some of his weekly radio essays have been broadcast on National Public Radio's *All Things Considered*. Gerard is the author of *Creative Nonfiction* (Story Press, 1996); a memoir, *Brilliant Passage* (Mystic, 1989); three novels, including *Desert Kill* (William Morrow, 1994).

Index